Rock Landscapes
The Pulham Legacy
Rock Gardens, Grottoes, Ferneries, Follies, Fountains and Garden Ornaments

Rock Landscapes
The Pulham Legacy
Rock Gardens, Grottoes, Ferneries, Follies, Fountains and Garden Ornaments

Claude Hitching

With featured photography by
Jenny Lilly

GARDEN · ART · PRESS

ISBN 978-1-87067-376-1

British Library CIP Data
A catalogue record for this book
is available from the British Library

Printed in China
for the Antique Collectors' Club Ltd., Woodbridge, Suffolk IP12 4SD

Dedication

This book is dedicated to the memory of my grandfather, Frederick Hitching, who worked
as a 'Rock Builder' for James Pulham and Son between the late 1880s and early 1930s.
I hope he would be pleased with what I have managed to piece together.
Claude Hitching

CONTENTS

FOREWORD

Mavis Batey

Claude Hitching must be congratulated for a book that gives the Pulhams a place in garden history. He takes us on a journey through a remarkable number of gardens they created in Victorian and Edwardian England, beautifully illustrated every step of the way. The story involves four generations of the Pulham family – all of them named James – who adapted their special inherited art of stone modelling to the many gardening fashions through which they lived, from picturesque rock gardens to formal, Italianate, Japanese and Edwardian 'gardencraft'.

Where natural stone was not readily available, they coated heaps of rubble with cement, and modelled the surface to simulate the texture and colour of natural stone – this proprietary material becoming known as Pulhamite. The craftsmen who did this work were known as 'rock builders', and Claude's dedication to this story springs from the fact that no fewer than five of his ancestors worked for the Pulham firm in that capacity.

The second James Pulham also set up his own manufactory in Broxbourne, Hertfordshire, in which he produced an extensive range of ornamental garden ware including urns, vases, balustrades, sundials and fountains in terracotta – and sometimes also in Pulhamite. He exhibited selections of his wares at the Great Exhibition of 1851 – Prince Albert's rallying point for the Victorian age, uniting 'industry and art'.

The firm had more space and opportunities at the 1862 International Exhibition, sponsored by the Royal Society of Arts, Manufacture and Trade, which was held beside the Royal Horticultural Society's garden in South Kensington. A Pulham fountain was chosen to play at the entrance of the horticultural section, and was seen by six million visitors, so the Pulhams had truly arrived in the flourishing world of horticulture.

During the 1840s, when they first became involved, there were two kinds of rock landscape gardening already in existence. Not surprisingly one was where there was already a rocky landscape to be uncovered, and Redleaf – well written up in the *Gardener's Magazine* in July 1839 – was one such example. This garden was situated on a sandstone outcrop of the Sussex Weald, with overhangs buried under deposits of sand and humus, and many others followed in the Groombridge area. The Duke of Devonshire and his head gardener, Joseph Paxton, did not have such rock formations immediately to hand at Chatsworth, but, as money was no object in their case, Paxton resorted to acquiring boulders from the Peak District – some weighing 50 tons. In his 1845 guide, the Duke compared Paxton's 'bulky removals' to the achievements of the Stonehenge builders.

This is where the Pulhams stepped in to assist frustrated would-be rock gardeners by offering their less expensive – and one might now argue more eco-friendly – method of 'rock building'. As James 2 explained in a promotional booklet published *c*.1877:

> 'Where no real stone or rock exists, or if it is too expensive to get it to the place, it may be artificially formed – with burrs, rough bricks or concrete for the core – which is then covered with cement to imitate the colour, form and texture of the real rock most consistent with the geology of the district.'

Claude Hitching guides us through the steady evolution of their business: from the stone-modelling expertise of James 1 during the early 1800s; through the introduction, development, and progressive expansion of the landscaping projects undertaken by James 2 and 3 (who each earned their firm a Royal Warrant for their landscaping work at Sandringham and Buckingham Palace); to the decline and final demise of the firm *c*.1940, when it was managed by James 4. Claude's grandfather was actually the foreman who supervised the construction of the rock garden at Buckingham Palace and other sites.

Another of their more significant commissions in terms of

advancement was finding favour with the Royal Horticultural Society when they acquired Wisley in 1903 for the development of show gardens. Amongst all the other horticultural delights, they wanted to show 'an example of what a rock garden ought to be from both educational and picturesque points of view', and commissioned James Pulham and Son to do it.

Two new Victorian horticultural crazes had played into the Pulhams' hands: ferneries and alpine gardening, both of which needed rock work for effect and cultivation. Handbooks on ferns sparked off 'fern–strolls' to collect specimens that were pressed for decorative motifs, or given to the gardener to grow in grotto-like areas. In 1877 the Pulhams featured ferneries in their promotional booklet entitled *Picturesque Ferneries and Rock-Garden Scenery*. Nature walks had replaced picturesque carriage tours in Britain, and walking tours were even undertaken in the Swiss mountain scenery.

Alpine plants had been grown in pots for some time, but in 1870 – when William Robinson wrote his *Alpine Plants for English Gardens* – it became desirable to grow them naturally, as seen in the mountains. Once again the Pulhams sought ways to accommodate a new craze by making boulders with sheltering pockets and crevices for alpine plants. The bejewelled effect nestling delicately in the rockery blended well with the Ruskinian love of the minutiae of nature as seen in Pre-Raphaelite art.

At the opposite end of the scale to Alpine plants was the passion for rhododendrons, azaleas, and other exotic plants brought back from the East by professional plant hunters – most of whom were sponsored by the RHS. Sir Edmund Loder was one such rhododendron enthusiast, who raised the famous hybrid *Rhododendron loderi* in his rock garden at Leonardslee – one of Pulham's most charming examples of rock garden landscaping. Sir Edmund was into exotic fauna as well as flora, and James 2 provided him with an enclosure for mountain sheep, and a cave for use as wallaby breeding pens. Pulhams also created monkey and polar bear habitats for the London Zoo in Regent's Park, and craggy perches for pelicans in St James's Park.

New municipal parks – where gentleman's landscaping was now being offered for refreshment of the poor from industrial cities – would also benefit from Pulham's works. Three of the first of these parks were in Preston, in Lancashire, where the firm built 'rocks' for bridges and a rocky tunnel. Another new public park feature was the drinking fountain, where the visitors could cup their hands under the spout for a drink – something that their Lords and Ladies would never have done!

Battersea Park – opened by Queen Victoria in 1858 – is another important example. By 1870, thanks to the Pulhams, many people in Battersea saw a rocky waterfall for the first time in their lives. This is one of the more important Pulham sites today, and is included by English Heritage in its Register of Parks and Gardens of Special Historic Interest, as well as in its new database of Pulham sites. The establishment of this database indicates the importance that English Heritage places on the restoration and maintenance of these features, a number of which have already been restored with the help of the Heritage Lottery Fund. Claude Hitching has actually made a positive contribution to some of these projects as a result of his research by being able to vouch for the provenance of the features involved.

When I first became fascinated with his discoveries – and it seemed that everybody who was anybody in Victorian days would have consulted the Pulhams – I began to wonder if the Victorian owner of the stately home in Buckinghamshire where I worked for five years during the war might have been one of them. I knew nothing of garden history during my days at Bletchley Park, but, sure enough, when I consulted the *Gardeners' Chronicle*, I found that the wealthy financier, Sir Herbert Leon, had indeed been among their number, so I was very glad to be able to give Claude another entry for his gazetteer. I am sure that he would be delighted if anyone else could find a new site to add to his remarkable story of the Pulham Legacy.

Mavis Batey
Vice-President of – and a former President of –
The Garden History Society

INTRODUCTION

Background

Having retired, I thought it would be a good idea to research my family tree in order to create a record that I could hand down to my sons and future generations. The first person I decided to investigate was my grandfather, Frederick Hitching, who used to work as a 'rock builder' for the firm of James Pulham and Son - the eminent Victorian and Edwardian landscape gardeners who specialised in the construction of picturesque rock gardens, ferneries, follies and grottoes, etc. They also manufactured a wide range of highly prized terracotta garden ornaments, such as fountains, vases, urns, seats and balustrading.

I soon discovered that two of Frederick's brothers – Arthur and John - also worked for Pulhams as rock builders, as did their father, William, and their uncle George. This was something I didn't know, so I decided to delve further. The firm was based in Broxbourne, Hertfordshire, and I visited the local museum to see if I could find any archive documents that would give me some sort of insight into their history.

Neil Robbins, the Heritage and Education Officer of the Borough of Broxbourne, and Curator of the Lowewood Museum, was very interested in my enquiry. He told me that James Pulham and Son were one of the most important and interesting local firms during the 19th and early 20th centuries, but that, sadly, all their records had been destroyed when they went out of business at the beginning of the Second World War *c*.1939. 'In fact,' he said: 'I have been looking for someone to research this firm with a view to writing a book about them – and do you know something? I think I've just found him!'

This seemed to be an intriguing challenge – especially since it would also give me an interesting insight into the sort of work that my ancestors did – so I agreed to accept it. It proved to be the start of a truly fascinating journey that has enabled me to piece together the history of this firm over more than one hundred years and four generations.

I visited my first Pulham garden in 2000. During the course of my travels, I have been granted access to many places that I would otherwise never have had an opportunity to visit – from the incredible Norman folly at Benington, through the Pulhams' early church building and restoration projects to a glorious colonnade at the V&A Museum in London. From the beautifully serene and 'picturesque' woodland scenes of country house rock gardens to the majesty and theatrical grandeur of the rock gardens at Madresfield Court and Waddesdon Manor, and from the rock gardens in the Royal Gardens at Sandringham and Buckingham Palace, to the open parkland landscape of Dunorlan Park in Tunbridge Wells, with its newly restored 25-ft high fountain for which James 2 was awarded a medal at the 1862 International Exhibition.

From the pure subterranean fantasy of the gardens at Dewstow in Wales, Friar Park in Henley-on-Thames, and Merrow Grange in Surrey to the formal dignity of those at Warren House in Kingston upon Thames, Heatherden Hall in Buckinghamshire, and the pristine perfection of the gardens at Danesfield House, Medmenham, Buckinghamshire. From the grand rockwork features at the seaside resorts of Blackpool, Lytham St Annes, Ramsgate and Folkestone to the peaceful tranquillity of the wonderful Japanese Watergardens adjacent to Warren House. The Pulhams created them all.

About the Book

Many of the firm's most prestigious parks and gardens are discussed in this book, and the descriptions and pictures are of the sites as I saw them during my visits – many of which were some years ago now, which means that they may no longer exist exactly as they were then. I know that some have changed hands in the meantime, and some have been restored, which is wonderful. On the other hand, a few may have suffered from a lack of the care that they had previously enjoyed, but it would be impossible to keep a book like this completely up to date in all respects.

Over the ten years or so during which I worked on this project, I must have 'finished' it at least three or four times – only to find myself diverted into another avenue of investigation. That was mainly thanks to the website I set up at www.pulham.org.uk, which has brought me hundreds of emails, letters and phone calls from people all over the country – as well as from overseas – offering me information or clues that I felt obliged to pursue.

By the time I finally decided to draw a line under this project, I had accumulated many megabytes of computer data and picture files, as well as a couple of shelves of hard copy documents. Some of it is background information from members of the Pulham family, but I have also accumulated information about more than 100 of the firm's gardens and architectural features that I have visited. The only trouble was that, by the time I had written up my notes, it all added up to more than 700 pages, 140,000 words and 500 pictures and illustrations! However fascinating it might be to me – and possibly also to the serious garden history enthusiast – it was obviously far too much for any publisher to consider as a commercial proposition.

This book consequently represents a sort of digest of Pulhams' most significant projects around the U.K. In order to avoid jumping straight in at the deep end, however, the first two chapters are devoted to providing some very brief background details about the Pulham family, and how they gradually became involved in the creation of such fascinating landscaping features as rock gardens, ferneries, follies, grottoes and fountains, and the third chapter is concerned with the manufactory in which they produced their range of extremely high quality terracotta garden ornaments. From that point on, it is gardens all the way.

More than forty sites are discussed here, although, in a sense, this is only the tip of the iceberg, because many more have had to be omitted. This is a pity, because they all have interesting stories to tell – in fact, I can already hear the protests from people associated with some of those sites, wondering how on earth it could have been decided to leave them out! There is also the probability that no-one else will undertake this research in the future, and, unless that information is made generally available in some form, access to it will remain denied to the serious gardening student or historian.

But fear not, because these 'additional' sites are listed as 'Also Noted' at the ends of the appropriate chapters in this book, and plans are in hand to provide their stories in a supplementary digital format - such as on CD or as an eBook – under the provisional title of *The Lives and Work of James Pulham and Son*.

I also have copies of the firm's *Garden Catalogue, Garden Ornament Catalogue*, and *Alpine Plants* Catalogue, and the text of James 2's promotional booklet entitled *Picturesque Ferneries and Rock Garden Scenery*, published *c*.1877, so these may also be produced as part of a *Pulham Archive* volume. All details will be announced at the appropriate time on the Pulham website.

Thankfully, most of the Pulham gardens reviewed in this book still survive, and some of them are being maintained in remarkably good order. In view of their importance, the reader deserves the best possible pictures of them, and this is an area in which I have been particularly fortunate, because my research has brought me into contact with two members of the Professional Garden Photographers Association. One of them, Charles Hawes – five of whose photographs appear in this book – was kind enough to introduce me to Jenny Lilly, who happens to be very interested in grottoes and the work of James Pulham. Her beautiful photographs have illustrated many garden magazines – she has a website at www.jennylillyphotography.co.uk – and I was thrilled when she offered to take some pictures especially for this book. I feel sure that they will do much to enhance the reader's enjoyment of it.

Family Connections

My great-grandfather, William Hitching, was born in 1840 in the charming Essex village of Great Bardfield, which, until that time, had been the home of the Hitching family for well over one hundred years. He moved to live with his aunt in the North Hertfordshire village of Wallington *c*.1860, and married Ann Newling in 1864. They must have moved to Hoddesdon soon after their wedding, because that is where their sons, Arthur, Frederick – my grandfather – and John were born. It seems that William's brother, George, moved with them.

This is just about the time when James 2 expanded his business in Broxbourne to become James Pulham and Son, but whether William moved in response to an advert for additional workers in the local newspapers, or whether he had met James 2 during the course of a recent church restoration project is not known. Whatever the reason, it is inevitable that some of the later sections of this book will include some personal anecdotal notes that reflect the origins and course of my research, but I hope that this may serve to enhance, rather than detract from its interest.

On a Personal Note

There are obviously a few people who deserve my very special thanks for their help and support during the course of this project, and the first of these is my lovely wife, Patricia, who has endured much social deprivation with great patience and fortitude over the last several years. I am also grateful to our son, Bob, who helped by setting up my initial website, and to Mavis Batey – a Vice President and past President of The Garden History Society – who has graciously contributed the foreword to this book.

Two more people I have to select for special mention are my brother-in-law, Derek Myson, and my friend of long-standing, Bernard Linsell, who also took a number of the photographs included in this book. I am unable to drive a car, due to being partially sighted, which means that I have needed to involve someone else to take me around on my garden visits. Some of these have involved overnight stays, and I could not have been more fortunate in my choice of chauffeurs. We have had some great times together.

And then there are Elenora Johnson, Brenda Lewis and Kate Harwood. Ellie is an incredibly knowledgeable garden enthusiast, and has a huge personal library of gardening books. She is also very interested in the work of James Pulham, so her help, guidance, meticulous attention to detail, patience and untiring support has been invaluable to me throughout the extensive editing of this book. She has also been one of my top 'scouts', finding and bringing to my attention the wonderful Pulham gardens at Danesfield (see Chapter 28), and Stoke Poges (Chapter 42).

Brenda is an extremely active, and well-known member of the Surrey Gardens Trust, and has written and edited a number of books and articles. She proved to be a very strict taskmaster during the early stages of editing my notes, and her advice on such matters as style and targeted approach has been invaluable. Kate was, until recently, the Administrator of the Association of Gardens Trusts, and has also given me much appreciated and knowledgeable support.

In fact, I have met many wonderful people whose help and support is greatly appreciated. These include the owners of houses and estates I visited, gardeners, local authority officials, librarians, people at organisations such as English Heritage,[1] the Garden History Society and the National Trust, and many others who have taken the trouble to email or write to me with 'information'. They are listed at the end of the book, and my grateful thanks and appreciation goes out to all of them.

Stoke Poges Memorial Gardens, Buckinghamshire, see page 274

Direct Descendants of William Pulham

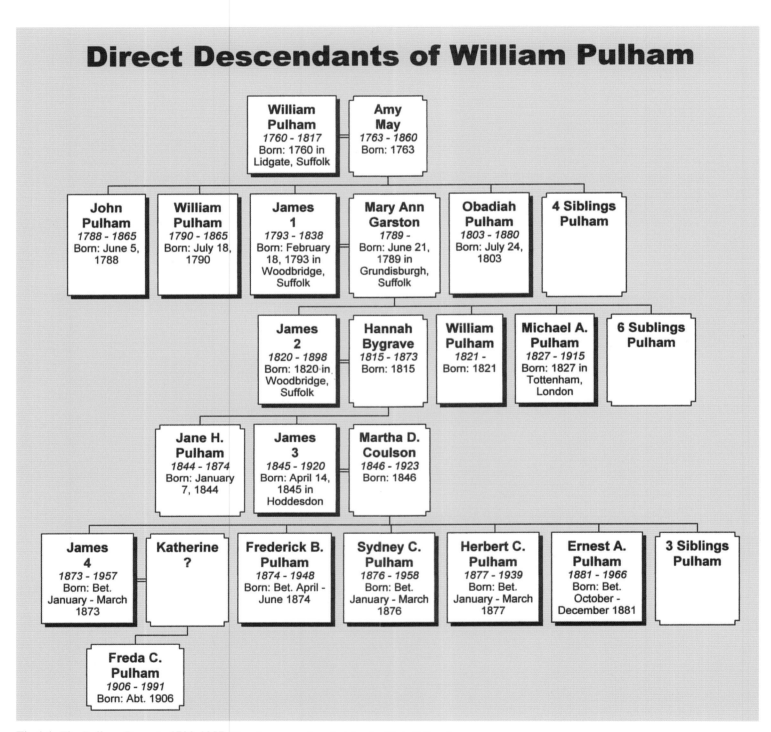

Fig 1.1 *The Pulham Dynasty 1793-1957* (Based on research undertaken by Chris Pulham)
(*I am indebted to Chris Pulham, a member of the 'non-James' branch of the Pulham family, for
researching this information, and giving permission for its reproduction here.*)

14

- 1 -

HOW IT ALL BEGAN

1793-1838

Some people may well ask, 'Who was James Pulham?' but those who know their garden history probably know the answer already. As has been noted in the Introduction to this book, James Pulham and Son were one of the most renowned firms of landscape gardeners of the 19th and early 20th centuries. In fact, it may be more accurate to describe them as 'landscape artists', rather than 'landscape gardeners', because that is the impression one gets when viewing some of their work that still survives. They are mostly remembered today for their creation of picturesque rock gardens, although this only formed part of their activities, because they were also happy to satisfy the demand for the more formal gardens that became fashionable around the turn of the century.

They constructed their rock gardens from both natural and artificial stone, and they took the greatest possible care to ensure that their creations blended, almost imperceptibly, into their surroundings. The harmonious mix of rocks, water, trees and plants was generally so masterful that it is often difficult to imagine how it could have been created by hand. That is not the whole story, however, because they didn't start landscaping gardens at all until the 1840s, so, rather than rushing ahead too quickly, one should really start by dealing with the first question: 'Who was James Pulham?'

As the Introduction also explains, there were actually no fewer than four of them! Four generations of Pulhams, with one son of each successive generation called James, so, for the purpose of this book, each one will be referred to in the general text by his generational suffix – i.e., James 1, James 2, James 3 and James 4, although their full names will be used in section headings etc. Each James continued the business of his father – a business that began with stone modelling and ornamental decorations and embellishments for buildings. It progressed from here to the building and restoration of churches, and then diversified into the construction of rock gardens, ferneries, follies, grottoes, and other landscaping features using their own 'artificial rock'. Ever conscious of changing fashions, they gradually expanded into the creation of grand, formal gardens, complete with balustraded terraces and the like. With this in mind, it is generally not too difficult to identify which 'James' was responsible for any particular feature.

In order to put things into perspective, the Pulham Family Tree is included here as **Fig 1.1**. This only includes the individuals in the 'James' branch of the tree who have some relevance to this story.

James Pulham 1 (1793-1838)

James 1 was the third son of a shoemaker, William Pulham, and his wife Amy, and was born in Woodbridge, Suffolk, in 1793. In those days, Woodbridge was a thriving port and garrison town and an important trading centre, and it was a profitable period for the local tradesmen and shopkeepers. By the turn of the 19th century, the town's principal builder was John Lockwood, who, in 1802, with work increasing, felt it necessary to take a partner. He decided to offer the position to his nephew, William Lockwood 1, and it was not long before he and John traded in partnership as J & W Lockwood.

Many years later, at the age of 80, William's son, William 2, compiled a set of *Reminiscences of Woodbridge in Olden Times*, based on a series of articles that he had written over the years for the local Woodbridge paper. In the Preface to these *Reminiscences*, he wrote:

> 'The original intention of the Newspaper articles from which the following pages were taken was to write an account of James and Obadiah Pulham's work, as an example of local self-taught men, who raised themselves by industrious ability from the position of ordinary plasterers to that of artists.'

He knew the Pulhams well, and recalls that it was his uncle, John Lockwood, who first gave James 1 and his younger brother, Obadiah, employment as apprentices in his building firm. He was well placed to recount the story of their work experiences, and he also recalls that his father, William 1, was particularly interested in the current fashion for ornamental stonework, and developed his own 'Lockwood's Portland Stone Cement' to use for this purpose, because he found its natural stone colour to be far preferable to the brown Roman cement that had invariably been used hitherto.[2]

The Early Signs of Talent

William 2's *Reminiscences* go on to say:

'My father, William Lockwood – [William 1] – took very considerable pains to foster and encourage these young men, and he was able, by means of his position as a master-builder, to introduce them to superior work. Recognising their talent, he employed every means to bring them forward, by setting them to work on the embellishment of his own buildings, and such other artistic work that his good taste led him to place in his own grounds.

'The elder of the two Pulhams, James by name, was the [third] eldest of a numerous family, born of poor parents, near the West end of the Thoro'fare, in that part of Woodbridge since called Cumberland Street. Neither he nor any of his brothers or sisters received through the medium of their parents any school education, but James was one of those children who innately begin to think for themselves. Although he was very early set to work at the very menial office of juvenile assistant to the bricklayers and plasterers as hawk-boy, it was not long before he found means to attend an evening school, and so picked up the rudiments of his afterwards self-accumulated knowledge.

'He was employed by John Lockwood, the uncle, and made apprentice some time before his nephew – my father, William 1 – came to join him. When the latter came into communication with James, he at once saw what sort of character he was, and immediately put him forward in the business, and frequently gave him difficult work to execute. He always succeeded in accomplishing this, with credit to himself and satisfaction to his employers, and, as soon as his term of apprenticeship was out, from having made good use of his evening school accomplishments, combined with his natural skill, he so far excelled his fellow workmen that he was made foreman over them all, then exceeding more than 30 in number.

Figs 1.2a and b *Examples of figures above doors and windows around the streets of Woodbridge today a) Keystone above a door   b) Lion's head on door portico* (Photo: Simon Swann)

'It was in the plastering department of the business that James Pulham first began to show his particular taste and skill – more especially in the modelling shop. The requirements in the decorative part of the business consisted in modelling enrichments for cornices, architraves, pilasters, and other parts, both of the interior and exterior of buildings.

'Figure-heads – or gargoyles – and bas-relief faces were frequently introduced as key-stones for arches and stops for the end of groins, etc. [as illustrated in Fig 1.2] in order to protect the building from evil spirits, and the modeller produced them by making an original in pipe-clay, from which he took castings in plaster of Paris. For this purpose he required an original drawing from which to copy.'

The practice of placing stone figureheads and bas-reliefs in the keystone – i.e. the central stone in the frame above or around a doorway, or above windows – became quite common during the 1770s, especially in London. This was almost certainly as a result of the London 1774 Building Act, which banned wooden porches and other decorations because of their potential fire hazards.

The London firm that benefited most from this Act was the Coade Factory,[3] which produced a large number of keystones and decorations that can still be seen around London today. In fact, it is possible that some of those one sees may actually be Pulhams' work, but it is not always easy to distinguish between the two. The pictures reproduced in **Fig 1.2** were taken around Woodbridge, however, and there is little doubt that these are genuine Pulham articles.

'The Castle'

There was a fashion in those days among people 'of certain means' to live in houses that gave the impression of great age, tradition and character. New houses had to be built in the style of ages past, to make them look as if they were really old – and a fake ruin would often be added for good measure! William 1 was no exception, and, when one of his friends offered to design him 'a respectable mansion' that he could build on a piece of land he had just bought in the town, he was quick to take up the offer.

The design was for a three-storeyed house, battlemented at the top, and with a tower at one corner with loophole windows. It soon became known as 'The Castle', an old photograph of which is shown in **Fig 1.3**. In producing the design, however, his friend undoubtedly had an ulterior motive in mind, which was to promote a new type of cement for which he and his uncle had recently been appointed agents. It was called 'Roman' cement, because it was said to equal – and for many purposes to be superior to – the famous mortar or cement used by the Romans.

Fig 1.3 *'The Castle' in Woodbridge, reproduced by permission of the Woodbridge Museum*

When set, it was said to be perfectly waterproof, and was specially adapted for water work, and for use on the outside of buildings – even for roofs. He therefore designed a flat roof for 'The Castle' so that it could be coated with this cement to demonstrate these qualities. All the mouldings round the windows and battlements were to be made of it, and then washed over with a stone colouring so as to represent Portland, or other kinds of building stone. In fact, it was effectively built from artificial stone, and William 2 goes on to say:

'It is easily seen on inspection that there is a good deal of intricate work about "The Castle" in the mouldings round the windows, and in many other parts. Now this was just the sort of work that Pulham was adapted for, and he was therefore the principal operator, and the supervisor of the Moulding and Ornamental Department – modelling, with his own hands, those two rough guardians of the northwest and southwest corners that have now stood exposure to all weathers for more than 80 years.

'Whilst the building of "The Castle" was going on, the proprietor, who was a man of some taste, engaged himself in laying out a suitable garden for its accompaniment. Towards the North end,

he planted a shrubbery of choice evergreens and other trees that afforded a suitable screen, and two nice shady approaches to "the wonderful grotto" – the entire construction of which was left to talented James Pulham.'

He goes on to describe many of the decorations and figures and to extol the artistic talents of James 1; and he explains that this was the project that inspired his father to research the possibility of creating his own new, light coloured Portland Stone Cement:

'The introduction by my father of the new Portland Stone Cement created a further development of the business, and – having a very considerable amount of ambition and energy – he was soon pushing his business into the Metropolis. . .

'He had already erected a lime kiln, and built a tower windmill for the manufacture of the Roman Cement – of which he had found a large sale in the neighbourhood, besides a constant demand in London for almost any quantity – and now he could also make the Portland Stone Cement at home. So the Woodbridge [builders'] business became almost entirely a Cement trade.'

Figs 1.4a-e *The sign of the 'Black Bull' of Holborn*
1.4a (left) *Original situation in Holborn* (Illustrated London News)
1.4b-e (above) *Current situation in Hammersmith with details inset*
(Pictures by John Woodcock)

The Move to London

William Lockwood expanded his business to London in 1824 – to 22 Elder Street, Spitalfields – and took James 1 and Obadiah with him to supervise the modelling work:

'During this time, the two Pulham brothers were kept employed in the ornamental work, such as Porticos, Colonnades, Entablatures, Pediments, and other similar decorative features of the Classic Styles, which were then so much in vogue – the gothic style not having yet been much introduced into new buildings . . .

'Work on many business houses, banks, and offices in the City and the West End was then carried out, and, as the cement could be worked out in any form, many royal arms and insignia of public bodies, signs for hotels, and all manner of architectural and other devices were made. Amongst those that remain to this day there is the sign of the "Black Bull" in Holborn, nearly life size, which was modelled by Obadiah Pulham, who was especially clever at animals – his brother James being more employed on figure subjects, etc.'

Hardly any evidence seems to be available as to where these items may be found – or even if they still exist – but one interesting exception is the 'Black Bull Tavern', that used to be at 121 Holborn, on the corner of Leather Lane, near Chancery Lane and Holborn Viaduct.

'In the days when access to the City of London was not possible after sundown, the Black Bull and many others, situated outside the boundary, catered for those late comers who could not enter the gates. . . . The Black Bull was the terminus and starting place for coaches, and its courtyard, like most of the others, was large and surrounded by galleries. . . But it had a more distinctive and prominent sign than the rest of them in the district, which, perhaps, made it more conspicuous. This was the very fine specimen of a black bull, with gilt horns and hoofs, and a golden band round its body. Its perfection of workmanship stamped it as that of some renowned artist.'[4]

'The old "Black Bull", after many alterations, was rebuilt in a very commonplace style in 1825, and in later years it became a merely sordid public house, with an unlovely pile of peculiarly grim "model" dwellings in the courtyard. In spite of these later changes, the great plaster effigy of the Black Bull itself, with a golden girdle about its middle, remained on his bracket over the first floor windows until the house was pulled down, May 18th, 1904.'[5]

It is thought that Charles Dickens also referred to this inn in *Martin*

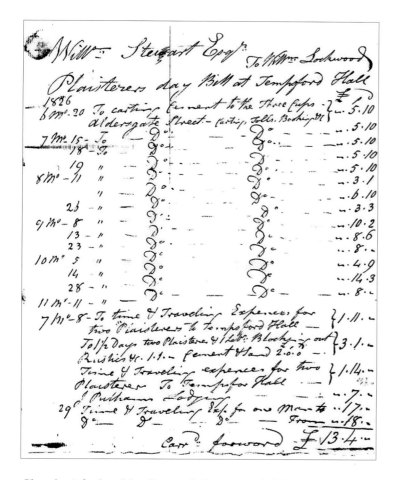

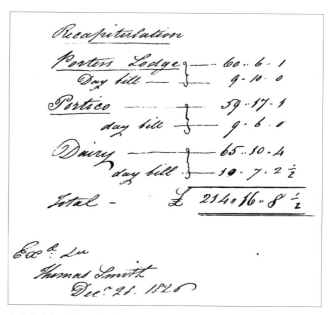

Fig 1.5 (left) *Sheet 1 of the Plaisterers' Day Bill at Tempsford Hall* (Reproduced by permission of the Bedford Records Office)

Fig 1.6 (above) *Thomas Smith's approval of the final bill* (Reproduced by permission of the Bedford Records Office)

Chuzzlewit,[6] when Mrs Gump tried to persuade Mr Mould that she was 'The soberest person going, and the best of blessings in a sick room' when it came to night-nursing a gent who had been 'took ill' at the Bull in Holborn.

Fig 1.4a is a picture of the statue in its original situation above the first floor window of the Black Bull in Holborn, taken from an old issue of the *Illustrated London News*. This picture seems to have been taken shortly before the tavern was demolished in 1904 to make way for the expansion of Messrs Gamage's popular department store, but the effigy of the bull was saved by the M.P. for Hammersmith, Sir William Bull.

Despite the fact that it was 5ft long and weighed 4½ tons – an incredible weight to be supported on a 'window ledge' – he organised its removal to King Street, Hammersmith, where it stood guard outside the offices of Bull and Bull, his firm of solicitors. When these premises were also demolished, the bull was transported once again – this time just a few hundred yards along King Street to adorn the front of the Ravenscourt Arms, near Vencourt Place, where it has stood ever since. **Fig 1.4b** is a picture of the bull today, together with close-up images of its head and the two plaques that are fixed to its 8-ft high plinth.[7]

This branch of the business continued to expand, and, in 1826,

William 1 decided to move to larger premises in Tottenham.

> 'Finding this branch of his business required more personal attention than he could give whilst living in Woodbridge, he determined to remove (with his family) to the neighbourhood of his work, and he selected premises at Tottenham, about six miles out on the Great North Road, where he turned a large greenhouse next the street into a Show Room for the different artificial Stone wares made out of the new Cement.'

William 1 spent a lot of his time visiting his various works-in-progress in and around London and the Home Counties, and one of his projects was Tempsford Hall, in Bedfordshire, where Obadiah Pulham was carrying out some ornamental cement work, including a coat of arms at the entrance lodge. In his *Reminiscences*, William 2 noted that:

> 'Obadiah's work was very good – the best example of his work I have seen.'

Very little of this work still survives, but Bedford Records Office were able to provide some fascinating bills of account relating to the work done for William Stuart on the portico, dairy and lodge at Tempsford Hall. Two pages from these are reproduced in **Figs 1.5 and 1.6**.

Figs 1.7a-c *'Smith's Folly' in Hertford*

This project was completed in December 1826, and signed off by Thomas Smith – the eminent architect based in Hertford, Hertfordshire, who held the esteemed post of County Surveyor of both Hertfordshire and Bedfordshire, and specialised in the design and construction of churches.[8]

William 1's workload gradually decreased during the worsening economic situation of the mid-1820s, but, fortunately, Thomas Smith had been so impressed with Obadiah's work at Tempsford that, in 1827 – just a few months after the completion of that project – he offered him a job in Hertford. Obadiah accepted, and left James 1 in sole charge of the London branch of the Lockwood business.

William 2 rather lost touch with the Pulham brothers around this time, because he decided to stay in Woodbridge to set up the Castle Brewery, which continued for many years. This obviously had some implications for his father's business, and William 1 decided to leave Tottenham to return to Woodbridge himself in 1835, effectively resulting in the break up of the London branch of the Lockwood business.

James 1 continued working under his own name, and directories of the 1830s show him as living in Moselle Place, Tottenham. One of his main contacts was obviously Thomas Smith, who was able to employ him on a number of projects, on which he was thus able to once again work alongside his brother, Obadiah. Among the first such projects are thought to be St James' Church, Silsoe, in Bedfordshire (1828-31), the Hertford County Hospital (1832-33), and possibly the Clock House in Hoddesdon, Hertfordshire, in 1836.

Thomas Smith was very enthusiastic about follies, and even had one built in his own back garden in Hertford, in the shape of a Norman tower and gateway. There is no clear record of when it was built – probably *c*.1834 – or by whom, but he could not have found better builders than Obadiah and James 1, who had played such a significant part in the construction of 'The Castle' at Woodbridge. **Fig 1.7** shows a reproduction of an early drawing of Smith's Folly, alongside pictures of the back of the gateway – with its steps – and the side of the tower as it is today. Smith's original garden has now been split up into sections, with the result that the folly is no longer directly associated with the house.

Fig 1.8 *Reproduced from* Picturesque Ferneries and Rock Garden Scenery *by James Pulham (2) c.1877*

Fig 1.9 *The fake Norman gateway at Benington Lordship*

Benington Lordship, Hertfordshire

There is no such doubt at all about who was responsible for building the folly at Benington Lordship, just a few miles up the road from Hertford, however. The Manor House – or 'The Lordship', to use the traditional Hertfordshire term – stands on the site of an old Norman castle, surrounded by a dry moat. The castle was built by Roger de Valoignes in 1138, but only lasted for about forty years, because Henry II ordered its demolition in 1177. All that now remain are the moat, and the ruins of parts of the ramparts and the old keep.

The present Lordship was built *c.*1700, and was bought by George Proctor in 1826. He was so taken with the place that he decided to recapture some of its previous mediaeval character by building a folly on part of the site of the old castle. The centrepiece was a large neo-Norman entrance gatehouse, linked to the house by a corridor and two rooms. On the other side, a fake 'ruined' curtain wall runs around part of the moat, leading to a summer house, thus forming a small courtyard at the side of the house. The apartment extension is on the right, and the 'ruined' wall leading to the summer house is on the left.

Some recent research[9] has led to the conclusion that Thomas Smith was the architect for this project, and James 1 is known to have been the builder, since it is mentioned in his promotional booklet,

Picturesque Ferneries and Rock Garden Scenery,[10] to which a number of references will be made throughout this book. Specifically in respect of Benington, he writes:

'There is a fine example of various parts of a Norman castle, forming a courtyard to a gentleman's house at Benington, including an apartment for smoking room, corridor, large dining hall; gateway, with high towers each side; a staircase, with enclosing buttressed walls, etc, all built of flint, with artificial stone dressings, mouldings, windows etc, executed by us in 1835-36-37 and 1838, as a ruin, supposed to be real, and of which a photograph may be seen.'

It may indeed. **Fig 1.8** shows what the view was like as one approached the Gatehouse all those years ago, and **Fig 1.9** shows what it was like more than 170 years later. The fake ecclesiastic-style wall with its interlaced arcading on the front of the Apartment Extension can be clearly seen on the right of the Gatehouse in the early photograph, although it is today largely obscured by a mature tree.

The gatehouse towers are dressed in flint, and are linked by a Norman arch, with a storeroom above. The facing of the arch is dressed with cement, modelled by brushing, combing and lining to appear like ashlar, which is a thin, hewn, dressed stone used for facing masonry walls.

Figs 1.10a-c *Terracotta frieze and faces on the courtyard side of the Benington Gatehouse*

Fig 1.11 *The Apartment Extension and Gatehouse from the courtyard*
(Photo by Harry Bott)

On the courtyard side of the Gatehouse, there is a terracotta frieze above the archway, and a pair of gargoyle faces at either side – shown here in **Figs 1.10a, b and c**. These are just like the ones in Woodbridge – typical 'Pulham faces' that continued to be a significant feature in the Pulhams' later work.

Fig 1.11 is a picture of the Gatehouse and side of the house, taken from the opposite side of the courtyard. The 'large dining hall' described by James 2 in his booklet was actually left unfinished, but has since been incorporated into the main house. The 'smoking room' to which he referred is now used as the farm office. Like the twin towers of the Gatehouse, the walls of the Apartment are faced with flint, and the remains of some 'Pulham faces' can just be seen at the ends of the window hood moulds – a sure sign that 'Obadiah was here'!

Fig 1.12 *The curtain wall and summer house* (Photos by Harry Bott)

Fig 1.13 *The side of the summer house, and sample cement rendering* (Photos by Harry Bott)

Figs 1.14a and b *The winged horses at Benington Lordship and Thunder Hall, respectively*

On the right-hand side of the Gatehouse, the 'ruined' flint-faced curtain wall traces the edge of the moat around in a quarter-circle to the Norman-style summer house, shown in **Fig 1.12**. Go closer, however, and look around the side, and one can see that this, too, is a folly. As can be seen in **Fig 1.13**, it is, in reality, nothing much more than an ordinary outbuilding with an ornate front. The inset picture to **Fig 1.13** shows a small section of the brickwork, overlain with some of the cement that formed the basis of the ornamentation. The work done at Benington is a prime example of the lengths to which some people would go in those days to satisfy their dreams of grandeur, and to impress their friends, when social status was probably much more dependent on ancestry and the possession of ancient country houses and estates than it is today. The Pulhams were just the right men to bring those dreams to life, and one cannot help but be impressed by the tremendous amount of extremely skilled work that they put into this particular project.

The final building I looked at was the stables, which were probably built by George Proctor. They were not included as part of Pulham's list of constructions, but there seems little doubt that they were involved with their decoration. Hanging on the walls are a couple of winged-horse sculptures – there were originally six of them – that, once again, are almost certainly the work of Obadiah.

Both horses now show signs of damage, although one is still in fairly good condition. It is pictured here in **Fig 1.14a**, alongside another (recent replica) that hangs at Thunder Hall, the home of George Proctor's brother, just a few miles away, in Ware, Hertfordshire.

Figs 1.15a-c *The 'Pulham Faces' on the columns and window frames at Thunder Hall*

Thomas Smith extended the house in 1841, and Obadiah is known to have been involved. One only has to look at all the faces that surround the windows and doorways for confirmation of that, and some examples of his Thunder Hall decorations are shown in **Figs 1.15a-c**.

The Untimely Death of James Pulham 1

According to the testimony of William Lockwood 2, it is evident that James I was an extremely gifted and intelligent self-educated man, and it comes as quite a shock to learn that he died an untimely and sudden death in March 1838 – just a few weeks after the completion of his work at Benington – in Northumberland House, Stoke Newington.

This simple and stark statement masks what must have been a very sad story. A J Francis reports in his book[11] that he died 'as the result of an accident', and that none of his family was with him when he died, but John Corfield uncovered some further details, and recorded them in an item published in the magazine of the Hertford and Ware Local History Society.[12] He refers to the death of James 1 as '*his finally successful suicide*', which implies that he must have made some earlier 'unsuccessful' attempts to end his life.

Corfield found a diary kept by a man called James Rowley, who was an Edmonton bookbinder of the period. He refers to two quotes from this diary, reproduced in **Fig 1.16**. The first entry, dated 21st March, 1838, reads:

'Cut his throat in a fit of insanity (in a field of Mr Holbrook's near Tottenham Church), Mr Pulham, Plasterer, but being fortunately seen, he was conveyed home, and from there to the Madhouse, Green Lanes, with faint hopes of recovery.'

In a further entry, dated 10th April, 1838, Mr Rowley records:

'Died, the before-mentioned Mr Pulham, by tearing open the wound on his way to the Madhouse he had inflicted on himself the day before.'

James Rowley goes on to say:

'He was one of the cleverest and best-informed workmen I ever knew. If his line of life had led him in the direction of engineering, he would have become a second Brindley or Telford.'

This gives the impression that Mr Rowley was a close acquaintance

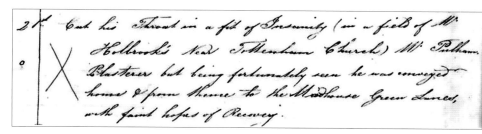

Figs 1.16a and b *Two entries from the Diary of James Rowley*
1.16a *(top) The entry for 21st March 1838*
1.16b *(bottom) The entry for 10th April 1838*

of James 1, but the words he uses are so close to those written by William Lockwood 2 in his *Reminiscences* (see below) that one cannot help but wonder if that could have been the inspiration for them. Be that as it may, it is interesting to note that the 'Holbrook's field' referred to in James Rowley's diary was next to All Hallowes Church in Tottenham, not far from Moselle Place, where James 1 lived. So maybe he was engaged in some restoration work at this church when he finally decided to go into the adjoining field to take his own life.

Whatever the detailed circumstances of this tragic story, James 1 was survived by his widow, Mary Ann, and their four children, including James 2 and Michael Angelo. James 2, the eldest, was born in 1820, and Michael Angelo was born in 1827. The family remained in Moselle Place until about 1841, where they were still shown as residents in the 1841 Census.

James 2 consequently inherited his father's business at the tender age of eighteen. Unlike his father, he was fortunate in having been given the advantages of a good education by his parents. He also inherited many of his father's talents, being described in those early years as 'adept in the use of cement'. His story will be taken up in the next chapter.

A Man of Character

It is quite obvious that William 2 had a great respect and admiration for James 1, because his *Reminiscences* also included the following comments:

'There is another special branch of James Pulham's character that ought always to go with him, and not on any account be lost sight of, for whosoever possesses the like has the most elevating notions of creation and of the Creator that man well can have. He was a great student of Astronomy, and of the Natural Laws in general. Every thing that came under his notice, he studied "the why and

the wherefore" of, and in that way stored his mind with many Truths that others let pass without noticing. He made a very unique little globe sundial from his knowledge of Astronomy, that he called Pulham's "Universal Solar Horologium".

'This pretty much ends the story, so far as my knowledge of him went – of one of the cleverest and best informed workmen I ever knew – as an uneducated or only self-taught man, there was hardly a subject but what he could give you some information upon, and he was never at a loss for an expedient in difficult cases of business or work. If his line of life had led him in the direction of engineering, he would have become a second Brindley or a Telford.

'James Pulham was a student of natural philosophy, and it was his great and keen observation of the way in which nature performs her wonderful works that advanced his mind in so much practical knowledge. A great man – a Fellow of the Royal Society, whose life I have just been reading – says in one of his lectures to his fellow members:

''We see that, in the works of nature, there is ample scope for the exercise of our rational faculties, and, limited as those faculties are, they are strengthened by use, and worthily employed when we endeavour to acquaint ourselves with as much of the wonders of creation as the great Author has permitted us to comprehend. As we proceed, new discoveries reward our search, and the sources of intellectual enjoyment pour an increasing stream of satisfaction upon the delighted mind etc.''

'It was by example, as well as by such precepts as these, that James Pulham gave me such a high opinion of his intellectual character.'

Also Noted:
1828-31 – St James' Church, Silsoe, Bedfordshire

THE SECOND GENERATION

1838-1845

James 2 takes over his Father's Business

It is difficult to imagine the trauma felt by a young man of eighteen as a result of the news of his father's sudden death in very tragic circumstances, but that is what James 2 (1820-98) had to endure in March 1838. He obviously got through it very well, however, since he took over his father's business, and continued to live at the family home in Moselle Place, Tottenham – at least until the time of the 1841 Census – with his mother, younger brother and two sisters.

It is not clear exactly how he ran the business during his early days, although it seems likely that he continued to develop his skills alongside the experienced craftsmen who had previously been employed by his father. As mentioned in the previous chapter, he was also lucky that his uncle, Obadiah, was then working for the firm of Thomas Smith, who, by this time, had been appointed County Surveyor for Hertfordshire. It is known that Smith employed James 2 on a number of his building and restoration projects over the next few years,[13] and Thunder Hall, in Ware, Hertfordshire – described in the previous chapter – may well have been one of them.

Some 'Pulham Faces' in London

Reference has already been made to the fashion of putting bas-relief faces and figureheads above doors and around windows during the early 19th century, and it is known that James 1 and Obadiah were responsible for some of them – especially at Woodbridge, Suffolk, where they were brought up and apprenticed as stone modellers with the firm of J & W Lockwood.

There are a number of figureheads around the doors and windows in London, but it it difficult to identify their creator. If one assumes that they were modelled at the time of construction, however, there were a number of houses built in the vicinity of Moselle Place during the 1830s, so it is quite possible that those pictured in **Fig 2.1** could have been done by either James 1 or James 2. It seems extremely unlikely that Thomas Smith was involved here.

The top two faces in **Fig 2.1** are located in Islington, and the bottom ones are in Manchester Street, near Baker Street, W1, and Clyde Road, Tottenham. The first three all show a remarkable resemblance

to the ones in Woodbridge and Ware (Fig 1.15), while the fourth has now become quite worn. It is also rather different in style to the others, but is included here partly because of its location in Tottenham, and partly because it is very similar to some others that are mentioned in later chapters.

The Sun Inn, Amwell Street, Hoddesdon

James 2 moved to Hoddesdon, in Hertfordshire – about fifteen miles north of London, and three miles south of Ware – with his family *c*.1841, and took up residence in Amwell Street at a house that later became the Sun Inn, but which no longer exists.[14] He continued in business from there, and probably brought a number of his best workmen with him from Tottenham. This would have made them more locally available to Thomas Smith, and also to other contacts in the area that had been made by his father and Obadiah some years previously, while working for William Lockwood 1.

1842-43: Rawdon House/Hoddesdon House, Hoddesdon, Hertfordshire

One such person was John Warner, who owned a number of properties in and around Hoddesdon. John was head of the family firm, John Warner and Sons, Metal Founders in the City of London – a firm that specialised in the manufacture of pumps, plumbers' brass work, steam fittings, copper baths and various coppersmiths' ware. They also made handbells, and later diversified into the casting of church bells – one of their prime commissions in later years being to cast the original 'Big Ben Chimes' for the Great Hall of Westminster in 1856. Unfortunately, the bell cracked whilst on exhibition prior to being mounted, and the replacement was cast at the Whitechapel Bell Foundry.

John Warner bought Rawdon House on Hoddesdon High Street in 1840[15] – a red brick Jacobean house built by Marmaduke Rawdon in 1622, and known at various times in its history as Hoddesdon House, Hoddesdon Great House and Rawdon House. Soon after its purchase, he decided to 'beautify it', commissioning James 2 – not Thomas Smith, in this case – to undertake the work. An article in the *East Herts Archaeological Society Transactions*[16] noted that the brick walling was:

a) Duncan Terrace, Islington

b) Highbury Terrace, Islington

c) Manchester Street W1

d) Clyde Road, Tottenham

Figs 2.1a-d *Some Pulham Faces in London* (Photographs by Diana Clements)

'... covered with plaster (probably much of it in the year 1842) by the late James Pulham.'

Later in the same article, the writer describes the interior of the house, and especially the carved figures on the *'grand old oak staircase'* as:

'... grotesque, and the walls are panelled to the height of the rail; but although this has often been regarded as oak, much of it is plaster, and was modelled by the late Mr James Pulham of Broxbourne, during the years 1842-43.'

It is likely that John Warner only bought Rawdon House as a speculative purchase, because, having commissioned all these embellishments to it, he decided to move into a new house on another piece of land that he owned, called 'Woodlands', which was just a few yards to the south, on the opposite side of the High Street. Rawdon House was eventually purchased – in 1875, or thereabouts – by Henry Ricardo, who promptly had all the external stucco to the front of the house removed, and carried out a number of other alterations. The house was later used as a priory for many years, and is now a commercial property. Apart from the staircase – and probably the impressive plastered ceilings and the fireplace in the hall – little now remains of the decorations that were once a major feature of the house.

Fig 2.2 *The entrance hall of Hoddesdon House, as it was in 1891. Note the 'old oak' staircase, ornamental fireplace and ceiling mouldings.* (Photograph reproduced by permission of English Heritage NMR)

Fig 2.2 shows what the entrance hall looked like in 1891, and one can be forgiven for thinking that the striking central staircase was indeed constructed in beautifully carved oak. But a careful look at **Fig 2.3** – a photograph of the staircase as it is today – will show that the *'Queen's Beasts'* newel posts and staircase panels are all stone carvings, but now painted white and gold.

Figs 2.4a and b show a couple of staircase panels, and **Fig 2.4c and d** show parts of two of the plaster ceilings. One cannot be certain that these ceilings were actually the work of the Pulham craftsmen, or whether Henry Ricardo engaged someone else to replace the originals, but I have seen very similar work elsewhere at sites on which the Pulhams are known to have done the garden landscaping – some of which is illustrated later in this book – so I regard it as a strong possibility that these are likely to be the work of James 2. Similarly, the meticulously detailed – but recently painted – coat of arms shown in **Fig 2.4e** is very similar to those found on other Pulham sites.

1842-62: 'Woodlands', Hoddesdon, Hertfordshire

The grounds of John Warner's house at 'Woodlands' extended over about eleven acres, and ran down to a stream called Spitalbrook, near which John's father, William, built two pairs of gothic cottages during the 1830s, ostensibly to act as lodges for the house he never built. It was left to John to build 'Woodlands' later, however, in a position higher up the hill relative to the cottages.

Unfortunately for Warner, a new gasworks was built near 'Woodlands' soon after he started to live there, so, in 1842, he commissioned James 2 to help him construct some artificial cliffs and a cave in the gardens to hide the view – in just the same way that the rockwork in Battersea Park was later designed to block the view of Clapham Junction from the lake. They also built an orangery, an indoor swimming pool – or 'bath house' – and an artificial lake – dammed from the Spitalbrook stream – which had

Fig 2.3 *Staircase at Rawdon House with stone 'Queen's Beasts' figures on newel posts*

a 40-ft fountain showering a statue of Neptune, *'situated in a niche of rustic masonry at its base'*.

This was James 2's first attempt at building garden rockeries in artificial stone – later to be described as 'Pulhamite' – and he certainly got off to an impressive start! A journalist from the *Gardeners' Chronicle* visited the garden a few months after its completion, and it was he who wrote the *'niche of rustic masonry'* description quoted above. He goes on to assure his readers:

'To all appearances, it consists of huge pieces of granite. It appears to have weathered a thousand winters, and its manufacture, as well as the artistical disposition of the mass, reflects great credit upon the ingenuity and taste of Mr Pulham. This is a most beautiful spectacle from all parts of the grounds.'

a and b *Two staircase panels*

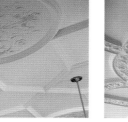
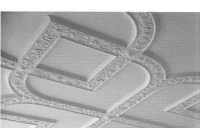

c and d *Two plaster ceilings*

Figs 2.4a-e *Plasterwork at Rawdon House as it is today*

e *Coat of Arms above the front door*

Fig 2.5 *The 'table stone' in the lake at 'Woodlands'* c.*1860*

Fig 2.6 (below) *The 'Neptune Fountain' at 'Woodlands,'* *in Hoddesdon c.1860*

Fig 2.7 (right) *The ruined folly at 'Woodlands'*

He particularly liked a table stone (Fig 2.5):

> '. . . contrived and arranged for the water to meander over in its egress from the lake, and the eschewing of the monstrous practice of mixing three or four kinds of stone, for where in nature did one encounter more than one type of stone in the same location?'

The rose garden specialist and writer of the period, William Paul, also wrote a lengthy description of the 'Woodlands' gardens,

> '. . . with its lakes and watercourses, spanned by rustic bridges, and magnificent Neptune statue in the middle lake.'

These features no longer remain, but, fortunately, some consolation can be gained from the fact that there are still some old photographs that show what the house and gardens looked like around this time – all reproduced by permission of Lowewood Museum. Fig 2.5 shows the 'table stone' in the lake, and Fig 2.6 is a picture of the main fountain, showing Neptune in his *'niche of rustic masonry'*, and the water splashing into the artificial lake. Could either of the two figures on the rustic bridge

Fig 2.8 *The 'gothic folly' cottages at Spitalbrook*

on the right be John Warner or James 2? We shall probably never know.

John married twice, and had thirteen children in all, so there were many grandchildren, one of whom was Metford Warner, who had this to say about the Neptune Fountain:[17]

'. . . we pressed through the holly hedge to the meadow beyond and passed under the great oak tree which was there when my grandfather came into the property. It was here that the narrow canal opened out into a small lake with an inlet on which had been erected a massive structure of Pulham-made rocks and an almost life-size figure of Neptune with his trident [Fig 2.6].

'From behind the trident sprang a fountain of water some 60 feet in height; the water finding its natural level from the springs in the hillside plantation. It was a beautiful sight on a summer's day to see the fence-protected lawn which sloped down from the path, almost to the water's edge, covered with gaily plumaged ducks of all kinds basking and preening themselves on the sunny bank while the brink of the lake was rippled with the water which came splashing and dripping over the long trails of greenery which had grown luxuriantly over 'Neptune' surrounded by overhanging trees.'

Fig 2.7 is a picture of the ruined folly built in a corner of the grounds. In this case, there is a positive clue to the identity of the man on the bridge, since a note on the back of the photograph refers to a 'Henry Hull Warner – The Ruins'.

The following details of the gothic cottages near the Spitalbrook stream come from a letter written in 1973 by a Mr C H Curtis:[18]

'. . . these cottages are described as "a mock mediaeval fancy", composed of two pairs of cottages united by an ornate gothic screen, which throws a lofty pointed arch across the drive, and extrudes a romantic skyline of turrets, pinnacles and castellations in brown cement.'

The carriageway between the two pairs of 'gothic folly' cottages was used as a convenient access to a house to the west of the 'Woodlands' estate called 'Sheredes' – sometimes known as 'Braithwaite's Castle' after its owner. One can see what the cottages looked like from an old photograph, reproduced in **Fig 2.8**,[19] and this is of particular interest to me, because my grandfather's elder brother, Arthur – another Pulham 'rock-builder' in our family – lived in the front cottage on the left of the arch.

Sadly, these buildings have since been demolished to make way for more modern developments – 'Woodlands' itself is now a police station – but there can be little doubt that this façade was included as part of the Pulhams' work on the gardens as a whole. One only has to look at the mock towers at each corner, with their arrow slits; the castellated roofline, and the shape of the windows and central arch. This same description could also have been applied to 'The Castle' (Fig 1.3) at Woodbridge, where the Pulhams learned their craft.

Most of the old gardens at 'Woodlands' now belong to the owner of a house called 'Little Woodlands' – converted from the stable block of the old house – and it is fascinating to walk round, trying to envisage what they used to be like from the various notes available. The stream and the lake still survive in good condition, and the fountain still works, although Neptune has now retired hurt and is lying on his back – in pieces – in the shrubbery. The old Orchid House also remains, and there are still goldfish swimming here – just as there were in Metford Warner's days – with the central pool still surrounded by the original 'massive rocks', as can be seen from **Fig 2.9**.

Although neither man is likely to have realised it at the time, it seems quite clear that John Warner made a very significant decision when he introduced the young James 2 to his first garden landscaping assignment, because these were almost certainly the first fountain, and the first piece of artificial garden rockwork ever made by James 2. It was a project that obviously provided him – and two Pulham generations to come – with the inspiration to diversify into a new career.

1845: 'On Cements, Artificial Stone, and Plastic Compositions'

Even though he was still in his early twenties, James 2 was already becoming an authority on the qualities and use of cement for both building and decorative purposes. In 1845, he contributed an extensive and knowledgeable article to *The Builder* magazine,[20] in which he described various types of artificial stone and cement, including Roman cement; Atkinson's or Mulgrave cement; Pulham's Portland Stone Cement (presumably similar to Lockwood's Portland Stone Cement); Metallic cement; Mastic or Oil cement; Keene's cement; Portland cement; John's Patent Stucco Paint Cement; Blue Lias Lime cement, and several others. There is no need to reproduce this article here, but this is what he had to say about his own Pulham's Portland Stone Cement, and about interior plastering generally:

> **'Pulham's Portland Stone Cement**, or artificial stone, is so called from its near resemblance to Portland stone in colour, hardness and durability – its natural colour is that of Portland stone, and therefore it requires no artificial colouring. It has stood the test of twenty-four years' use, and remains perfect. It has deceived the trade – the imitation is so complete.

'It is excellent for both exterior and interior purposes of stucco and mouldings, and for fountains, vases, and even floors etc, and is capable of being trowelled to a very smooth face, like marble, and hardens by the influence of atmosphere. Simple water washing is sufficient to clean it when dirty, and it does not vegetate as much as stone. It is an excellent finishing for Roman cement, and its use has been allowed by the Church Building Commissioners for the exterior of a new church at **West Hyde, in Hertfordshire.**

'Much might be done in restoring our ancient edifices and dilapidated stonework generally in buildings, for, where a stone is only decayed on the face, an inch thick of cement would answer the purpose, instead of cutting out the stone. And, where a stone is too much decayed, it may be cut out and replaced with bricks laid in cement, and covered to imitate the stone in any colour.

'Many of our beautiful structures are going to destruction in consequence of the great expense of restoring with stone, and it may be done to advantage at one-third or fourth the expense of stone, and answer every purpose. Much that has been done in restoring with cement has failed, owing to the incautious manner in which it has been used – nothing requires more care – especially on clunch and limestone, of which many churches are built.

'Interior Plastering Generally. In writing about cements etc, I cannot forbear saying a little in reply to an article in *The Builder* by a correspondent "J.W.", who calls an ornamented ceiling a "palpable falsity", and says that it contains noxious vapours – not knowing, I suppose, that there are simple means of ventilation. I should be glad to know in what respect it is palpable falsity, and, if it is, why has so much been done in that way in almost every house that is built, noble and simple. Most of this could not be accomplished with other materials than plastic composition of some sort.

'I certainly admire wood carvings etc in their place, and where expense is no object, but, even then, why increase the materials for fire? I should be glad to see some of his (as he says) "more honest and ingeniously and equally elaborated" timber soffits by the side of an ordinary plaster enrichment, such as is used in good buildings.

'What can be dishonest in a plaster ceiling? It is not intended generally to deceive, or to appear to be any thing other than what it is, although mouldings and ceilings may be – and are – grained to imitate oak in the old English or Tudor style, as for beams, ribs etc. Can any other material be made so available, and answer the purpose so well as plastic compositions, and at so trifling a cost? . . . Plaster endures after timber has failed, as is a well-known fact, proved in many of our ancient mansions, when plastering was very inferior, and materials such as we now have were unknown.

I am, Sir, etc., James Pulham, Hoddesdon.'

Fig 2.9 *Inside the Orchid House at 'Little Woodlands', the back wall of which formed 'a background to a pool enlivened with goldfish, and blocked in right and left by massive rocks'.*

Apart from the technical aspects of this article – in which James 2 refers to which cements should be used under what circumstances – his comments about the use of plaster rather than wood for certain interior decorative work may well explain his approach to the work he did on the staircase at Rawdon House.

This was not James 2's only contribution to the Letters columns of *The Builder*. In another letter,[21] he advocated the use of terracotta as a legitimate decorative material, and gave several examples of where it had been used very successfully – one such place being the Church of St Mary Redcliffe, in Bristol. In another, he refers to his work in scagliola – imitation marble made from coloured gypsum plaster:

> 'I have now in hand a first rate staircase and a hall, the scagliola work of which consists of a great number of columns, pilasters, and pedestals in imitation of various marbles, with white mouldings and imitations of statuary caps, bases, cornices etc, most of which are being done in Hoddesdon and will be conveyed to **Kilnwick Percy** in Yorkshire.'

Fig 2.10 *The Church of St Thomas of Canterbury, West Hyde* (Photo by Ellie Johnson)

Figs 2.11a and b *Moulding around a side door and windows at St Thomas's, West Hyde* (Picture by Ellie Johnson)

Fig 2.12 *The interior of the Church of St Thomas of Canterbury, West Hyde*

Figs 2.13a and b *Two angel figures on the internal beams of St Thomas of Canterbury* (Pictures by Kate Banister)

1844-45: The Church of St Thomas of Canterbury, West Hyde, Hertfordshire

Thomas Smith designed the Church of St Thomas of Canterbury, in West Hyde, Hertfordshire, in 1843, and the external walls are built of knapped flint and red brick, with rendering and trimmings made from Roman Cement, finished with Pulham's Portland Stone Cement. It was completed in 1845, and is one of the churches referred to by James 2 in his letter to *The Builder*. It really is quite a remarkable building, in which the spectacular knapped flint work on the external walls is reckoned to be the best in Hertfordshire. **Fig 2.10** is a general view, while **Fig 2.11** shows details of the flint facing and cement mouldings around a door and windows – moulding which must still be as crisp and pristine as it was 160 years ago. If one looks closely at **Fig 2.10**, it is also possible to make out a series of 'Pulham faces' just below the rim of the bell tower – there are no fewer than 16 in all.

Inside, it is a lovely church, with an appropriately sublime, restful atmosphere – a feeling that comes through from the picture in **Fig 2.12** – and one of its more intriguing features is the angel figure-head at the end of each of the hammer beams in the roof of the nave. As can be seen in **Fig 2.13**, some are 'waist-up', and some are of full-bodied angels standing on clouds – each one holding a different shield, or emblem. I am not sure what they all depict, although the one in the left-hand picture is probably meant to be holding the shield of St Thomas of Canterbury, since this could be a cut-down version of the coat of arms of the City of Canterbury, which incorporates three choughs in its design.

At first sight, it would be easy to assume that these angels are modelled in wood, but this is not the case. Just like the staircase newels at Rawdon House, they are in fact made of stone. The Parish Church Council took upon themselves the task of cleaning and redecorating the interior of the church in 2002, and I was informed by one of the members who actually climbed up the scaffolding to clean and repaint the heads that there is no doubt about this. Having read James 2's article in *The Builder*, one can appreciate how this came about.

Figs 2.14a-d *North Door of St Mary Redcliffe, Bristol* (Photo by John Pickard)

1845: St Mary Redcliffe, Bristol, Avon

Another church restoration project to which James 2 referred in his letters to *The Builder* was the Church of St Mary Redcliffe, in Bristol.[22] This time, it was in connection with the use of terracotta in decorative adornments, and what a truly magnificent church this is – having once been referred to by Queen Elizabeth I, while on a visit to Bristol in 1547, as 'the goodliest, fairest, and most famous parish church in England!'

The original building was begun in 1280, so it was hardly surprising that a number of restorations were commissioned over the intervening years. One such period was between 1842 and 1872, during which time quite a lot of work had to be done on and around the Great North Doorway, and this fits nicely with the date *c*.1845,

when James 2 wrote his letter to *The Builder*. The restoration was done under the direction of the architect, George Goodwin, and James Wilson – a verger at the church during the 1990s – discovered a set of plaster models of the North Doorway that would almost certainly have been Pulham's work. These models were made from casts of the doorway, taken after the work was completed, so that future restorers could see exactly what this restoration of the original was like.

The main picture in **Fig 2.14** is a general view of the North Porch, with niches for figures intended to illustrate how the prosperity of the town – and its Kings and Queens, some of whom are modelled in the niches around the tower – had been built upon the labours of 'the common man', who is depicted by the corbel figures struggling to support them on their stooped shoulders.

THE GRAND STAIRCASE, KILNWICK PERCY,
the seat of Captain Whitworth, M.F.H.

—*Photo by E. C. Smart, Market Weighton.*

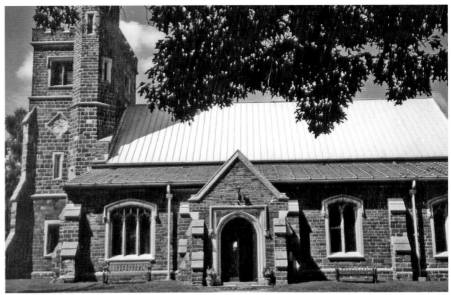

Fig 2.15 (left) *The Grand Hall and staircase at Kilnwick Percy* (Photo reproduced by kind permission of the Madhyamaka Buddhist Centre)

Fig 2.16 (below) *The scagliola pillars in the hall at Kilnwick Percy today*

Fig 2.17 (above) *Front of St Mary's Church, Clophill, 2001*

One can get a good idea of what was involved in this work from an old painting of the North Doorway that dates from 1813. This is reproduced in the top picture on the right of Fig 2.14, which shows the terrible state into which the stonework surrounding the doorway had been allowed to deteriorate. The lower section shows two detailed photographs of the extremely intricate gothic tracery around the doorway as it is today. These pictures of the top of the arch and the right-hand border provide a very clear idea of the skills and craftsmanship that were demanded for this particular piece of restoration.

1848: Kilnwick Percy, Pocklington, Yorkshire

The third specific reference to 'work in hand' made by James 2 in his 'Letters to the Editor' related to the *'first rate staircase and hall'* being produced in scagliola at the works in Hoddesdon for transport to Kilnwick Percy, in Yorkshire. John Corfield notes that Thomas Smith designed and built a vicarage at Kilnwick Percy in 1848,[23] so this was presumably part of the same project, and also means that Obadiah and James 2 would have worked together on it.

Kilnwick Percy Hall was an elegant Georgian mansion, set in forty acres of ground near Pocklington, at the foot of the Yorkshire Wolds. It was the home of Capt. Arthur Duncombe, who purchased the house in 1843 after moving from Stagenhoe Park in Hertfordshire, which is likely to explain how he knew of Thomas Smith, and also, perhaps, of James 2. **Fig 2.15** is an old photograph of the main hall and staircase as it was after it had been given its 'Pulham makeover', and does at least give some idea of the magnificent work that was involved. No clue is given as to the date of this photograph, but it must have been after Capt. Duncombe sold the Hall to a Captain Whitworth, Master of Fox Hounds.

Sadly, the Hall was badly damaged by a fire in the latter years of the 19th century. One half of the original wrought-iron staircase was destroyed, and the remaining half was reinstated in the surviving part of the house, so there is hardly anything remaining now of the imposing view shown in Fig 2.15.

Figs 2.18a and b *The 'Pulham Faces' and 'terracotta copings' at St Mary's, Clophill*

Figs 2.19a-c *The terracotta hood mould round the door*

Two magnificent 'marble' pillars still stand in the hall, however, and these are shown in **Fig 2.16**, so these must presumably be two of the columns – with their white capitals referred to in James 2's 'Letter to the Editor'.

1849: St Mary's Church, Clophill, Bedfordshire

In his biography of Thomas Smith, John Corfield records that one of the first projects on which Obadiah Pulham was engaged after entering Smith's employment in 1827 was the building of St James' Church, in Silsoe, on the fringe of Wrest Park, Bedfordshire, the seat of the Earl de Gray. The Earl later commissioned Smith to design and build a new church at Clophill – a charming little village, not far from Silsoe.[24] It was completed in 1849, and it is known that James 2 was involved here alongside his uncle, Obadiah, because the church is described by Sir Nikolaus Pevsner (1903-83)[25] – the German art historian who moved to England and became a

renowned authority on English architecture – as:

> '…an archeologically convincing job in the Tudor perpendicular style … a very neat edifice … comfortable to worship in. The terracotta copings used at the church were those by James Pulham – he was much admired by Thomas Smith.'

It could almost have been built from the same plans as St James', because each has a double row of castellations along the side aisles to the nave, and each has a rectangular-shaped tower that extends across the entire width of the church. The photograph in **Fig 2.17** was taken in 2001, soon after the roof had been completely replaced. But something else of interest becomes apparent as one draws closer. Each of the side windows has a hood mould, just like the ones around the windows at Benington Lordship, Thunder Hall and St Thomas's at West Hyde – and are shown here in **Fig 2.18**. There is also a pair of faces in very good condition on either side of the doorway, as can be seen from **Fig 2.19**.

Fig 2.20 *An early artist's impression of Ware Cemetery Chapel, built in 1854* (Photo reproduced by permission of Hertfordshire County Records Office)

Fig 2.21 *Ware Cemetery Chapel as it is today – now converted into two flats*

1855: Ware Cemetery Chapel, Hertfordshire

As Thomas Smith's reputation spread, he obtained several projects around Europe, but his next project in Hertfordshire, with which James 2 is known to have been involved, was the Cemetery Chapel in Ware. Smith was commissioned to design and build this in 1854, and the specification called for two chapels – one for Anglicans, and one for 'other denominations'. He solved this problem by designing the building in the shape of a 'T', with one chapel in the 'vertical' arm, and the other in the 'horizontal' arm. **Fig 2.20** shows a litho of

the chapel at that time, and **Fig 2.21** shows it as it is today.

John Corfield records that the Chapel was:

'. . built of brick, with a thick coarse rendering applied to the surface of the brickwork. The rendering was then ruled horizontally and vertically, and filled with a dark material to give the impression of joints, but this only serves to make it look artificial. Some "stone" elsewhere, as in the window and door openings, is, in reality, pre-cast artificial stone made by Pulhams.'

Figs 2.22a and b *Side of Ware Cemetery Chapel today, showing 'Pulham Head' hood-moulds at the door and window stops. Inset is a close-up of a head to the right of the doorway*

Fig 2.23 *Base of pillars to the right of the East doorway, embossed with 'Pulham' name*

Figs 2.24a and b *Figures in the roof of the Ware Cemetery Chapel*

The '*thick, coarse rendering, with the dark, ruled infills'* to simulate an 'old stone', or ashlar finish can be clearly seen in the picture of the East Doorway in **Fig 2.22**, and the terracotta hood moulds around the doors and windows – complete with their 'Pulham Faces' (see inset) – are again very reminiscent of the other Smith churches, such as the one at West Hyde. And then there is the extremely rare – if not unique – 'Pulham' name embossed on the door pillars (**Fig 2.23**), so it is quite evident that, in this case at least, James 2 wanted to ensure that everyone knew who had built it.

The chapel was taken out of use in 1983 because it was considered to be structurally unsafe. The Ware Council gardening squad moved in, and used it for some time as a store for their lawnmowers and other equipment, but they were only too happy to open it up for me during my visit in 2001. I was very intrigued to see if there were any 'Pulham figures' inside – either on or supporting the ceiling beams – as there are in the Church of St Thomas of Canterbury at West Hyde (Fig 2.12), and I was not disappointed. The left-hand picture in **Fig 2.24** was taken during my visit, and reveals all.

The two ex-chapels have since been converted into very pleasant split-level flats, and I returned for another look in 2004, while they were up for sale. I was delighted to see that the angels are still reading their bibles – in fact, they have been very nicely brought back to life. By going up to the first floor, I was able to get up very close and personal to one of them, and the right-hand figure in Fig 2.24 shows just how detailed and intricate they are.

1855-57: St Augustine's Church, Broxbourne, Hertfordshire

The Church of St Augustine, in Broxbourne, is only a few yards from Pulham's manufactory, which will be discussed in the next chapter.

Figs 2.25a and b *The front of St Augustine's Church in Broxbourne, with an angel head on either side of hooded front door*

It dates back to AD 680 [26], although a number of changes and additions have obviously been made to it over the centuries. By the early years of the 19th century, both the interior and the exterior were in urgent need of repair and restoration, and it was decided to commence the restoration of the external walls in 1855,[27] although I have personally seen no evidence that Thomas Smith was involved here.

Fig 2.25 is a view of the main west entrance to the church today, and it can be seen that the stonework is flint faced – as is also the front boundary wall, which dates from this time, and is now a listed structure. How similar this is to the knapped flint facing to the walls at St Thomas of Canterbury's Church in West Hyde, shown in Fig 2.10. There are also 'faces' on either side of the door, but it is evident from the one inset in this picture that it is a later 'replacement' of the original.

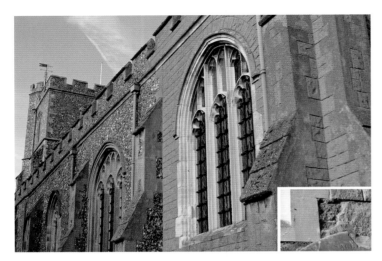

Fig 2.26 *The restored external 'ashlar-coated' wall to the South Chapel, showing the old flint-faced wall of the main church to the left. The inset picture to the right shows a small segment of the cement coating broken away to reveal the plain brickwork beneath*

Fig 2.27 *'Villa Ste Ursule', Cannes, c.1880* (Picture provided by Sven Vik, Cannes)

Accounts records exist that relate to payments made to Pulhams for restoration work around the church, and the more obvious area on which they were involved can be seen on the east face of the church. The central chancel wall is still faced in flint, but the chapel walls on either side are faced in a familiar-looking 'ashlar' finish. A close inspection of the southeast corner – **Fig 2.26** – shows that this restoration only extended to the west end of the South Chapel, beyond which the original flint facing remains. Just near the bottom corner of the east window, however, a piece of the new facing has broken away to reveal ordinary brickwork beneath, as can be seen on the inset picture. The 'ashlar' surface is actually sculpted from a one-inch coating of cement, which is identical to many other examples of Pulham's work that have already been discussed.

1852-70: The Travels of Obadiah

Several references have been made during these first two chapters to the work of Obadiah Pulham – the younger brother of James 1, and uncle of James 2 – so I can hardly conclude this chapter in the family history without recording some further details of this remarkable man.

Based on my research, I get the impression that Obadiah Pulham was a very religious man, as well as being an extremely talented stone modeller. William Lockwood 2 records (in Chapter 1) that he had:

'. . . the greatest appreciation of Obadiah's artistic abilities. . . [although] . . . he never evinced anything like the general knowledge that his brother possessed, for, while one was more especially an artist, the other [James 1] was an astronomer, a philosopher, an engineer, a chemist, and a general student of science, and was never at a loss for knowledge of any topic of the day.'[28]

As noted in Chapter 1, William 1 expanded his business to London *c*.1824, and put James 1 and Obadiah in charge of that end of the operation. Work declined during the economic depression of the mid-1820s, and he accepted the offer of a job with Thomas Smith in Hertford, leaving his brother to continue the Lockwood business on his own. He is likely to have moved to London when Smith opened an office in Bloomsbury Square *c*.1830, and he married Elizabeth Sellwood at St Mary's Church, Whitechapel, in March 1832.

They are known to have lived in John Street – presumably the John Street in Whitechapel – during the late 1830s, and they had four children – William, Elizabeth, Mary and Lucy. William and Elizabeth were twins, and all four children were born between 1834 and 1836. Obadiah's wife sadly died in 1841, and his housekeeper, Sophia Martin, cared for the children while he was away at work – as he was at the time of the 1841 Census, where I happened to find him as lodging in Crib Street, Ware, during the building of Thunder Hall. He married Sophia in April 1845 – also at St Mary's, Whitechapel – but there were no children from that marriage. The 1851 Census showed them as living in the Mile End district of London, so this could also have been in John Street.

His job with Thomas Smith involved a considerable amount of travel, because, according to James 2's letter to *The Builder* in 1848, he spent:

'. . . [some time in] France to do some work, as his specimens were superior to the French artists.'

In his biography of Thomas Smith,[29] John Corfield records that Obadiah worked for Smith in France, Italy and Germany between *c.*1852 and 1870. The first European project that he mentions was a villa in Cannes, which was just beginning to become popular as the playground of royalty, the aristocracy and other wealthy people from England and elsewhere who liked to relax and enjoy themselves in quiet, secluded foreign lands. Smith's patron in Cannes was Sir Thomas Robinson Woolfield – a sort of titled land speculator who arrived in Cannes in 1838, and was astute enough to recognise the potential popularity of the area.

Corfield only mentions one of Woolfield's properties by name – the 'Villa Ste Ursule' – which Smith designed and built between 1852-56. It was a typically flamboyant confection of gothic castellated towers and turrets and, thanks to pure chance and the magic of the internet, I have been able to locate an old photograph that is reproduced here in **Fig 2.27**. The building is still standing, but has been considerably expanded and redeveloped over the years, and now forms part of the Villa Vallombrosa.

Smith also built another villa for Woolfield between 1857-59 – the 'Villa Victoria' – and a small Anglican church close by for the local community at Woolfield's own expense. He then designed and built the Church of the Holy Trinity in Nice in 1859, and Obadiah was again the Clerk of Works. Smith designed it as a traditional British mediaeval structure, with a central nave, a chapel, and two side aisles. The work was finished in 1862, and the *Hertford Mercury* reported that:[30]

'The structure is of the true British type in its mediaeval

Fig 2.28 *Church of the Holy Trinity, Nice* (Picture lent by Father Ken Letts, Anglican Chaplain of the Church of the Holy Trinity in Nice)

development. Internally, the roofs are vaulted, with enriched moulded ribs with bosses at the intersections, and richly-carved capitals – the whole providing, both internally and externally, "an exceedingly imposing effect".'

The church still stands today, and the Anglican Chaplain, Ken Letts, kindly sent me a copy of an old picture that is reproduced here in **Fig 2.28**. He also sent me some current photographs in which I noted that there was a rather familiar adornment at the bottom of all the window hoods – a compilation of which is shown in **Fig 2.29**.

Figs 2.29a-l *A selection of 'Pulham faces' on the Church of the Holy Trinity, Nice. The first six are on the south side, and the others on the north side.* (Photos by Ken Letts, Anglican Chaplain of the Church of the Holy Trinity in Nice)

Fig 2.30 *Building Committee of the Church of the Holy Trinity, Nice, 1863*
Standing (left to right) *Dr Hennen, Charles Unwin (Treasurer), Obadiah Pulham (Builder), Rev'd W. Percival Ward*
(Hon Secretary)
Sitting (left to right) *Benjamin Hutt (Treasurer), Rev'd Boileau Eliot, W.D. Hull (Chairman), Rev'd Charles Childers*
(Chaplain), Peter Browne (Archive photo provided by Father Ken Letts, Anglican Chaplin of the Church of the Holy Trinity in Nice)

Another fascinating archive photograph sent to me by Ken is of the Building Committee at Nice – shown in **Fig 2.30** – with Obadiah standing at the back. These pictures have obviously made a valuable contribution to my research.

Thomas Smith's next important project in Europe – for which Obadiah was again the Clerk of Works – was the Anglican Church in Naples, Italy (1862-65), and St. Catherine's Church in Stuttgart, Germany (1865-66). The latter was badly damaged by the Allied bombers during the war, but was later rebuilt – nearly as the original – and is still used as a church in the former Catholic Parish of Stuttgart. There is, however, a beautiful engraving of the interior of the Anglican Church in Naples that was published in *The Builder* on 24 Oct 1863. One can even see the 'Pulham Faces' around the walls, and it is reproduced here as **Fig 2.31**.

Nothing more is known of Obadiah's whereabouts until his return to Woodbridge, which William Lockwood 2 reports in his *Reminiscences* as being *c*.1871. However, I have been contacted by at least five members of the Pulham family – one of whom lives in Australia – and they have all been extremely helpful. Chris Pulham comes from another branch of the family to the one in which I am primarily interested, but has researched a tremendous amount of genealogical data, and has been able to provide a lot of the dates and family links that I have used throughout this book.

He tells me that Obadiah lived with 'Elizabeth' during his final years in Woodbridge, so this presumably refers to his eldest daughter. His residence was listed in the 1871 Census as Castle Street – although Elizabeth was not listed as a co-resident at that time – and he died in 1880, at the age of 76.

Fig 2.31 *Interior of the Anglican Church in Naples, taken from* The Builder *dated Oct 24, 1863*

Obadiah the Apprentice

Some time after discovering this, I received another message – this time from Ian Denney, whose family is descended from Obadiah himself. One of Ian's relations actually had a copy of Obadiah's Apprenticeship Indenture, framed and hanging on their wall! It is reproduced here as **Fig 2.32**.

It is a fascinating document, although it is very difficult to read at the reduction required here. I have therefore copied it, and inserted one or two pieces of current punctuation and formatting to help make it more readable:

THIS INDENTURE WITNESSETH . . .

. . . that **Obadiah Pulham**, son of **Amy Pulham** of Woodbridge in the County of Suffolk, Widow, of the age of seventeen years or thereabouts, of his own free will and desire and by and with the assent and approbation of his Mother, doth put himself **Apprentice** to **William Lockwood** of Woodbridge, aforesaid **Plasterer**.

To learn his art, and with him after the Manner of an Apprentice to serve from the twenty-ninth day of August hereof until the full end and term of five years from thence next following to be fully compleat and ended.

DURING which Term the said Apprentice
- his Master faithfully shall serve,
- his secrets keep,
- his lawful command everywhere gladly do,
- he shall do no Damage to his said Master nor see to be done of others, but to his Power shall let or forthwith give Warning to his said Master of the same,
- he shall not waste the Goods of his said Master nor lend them unlawfully to any.
- He shall not commit Fornication nor contract Matrimony within the said Term.
- He shall not play at Cards, Dice Tables or any other unlawful Games whereby his said Master may have any loss.

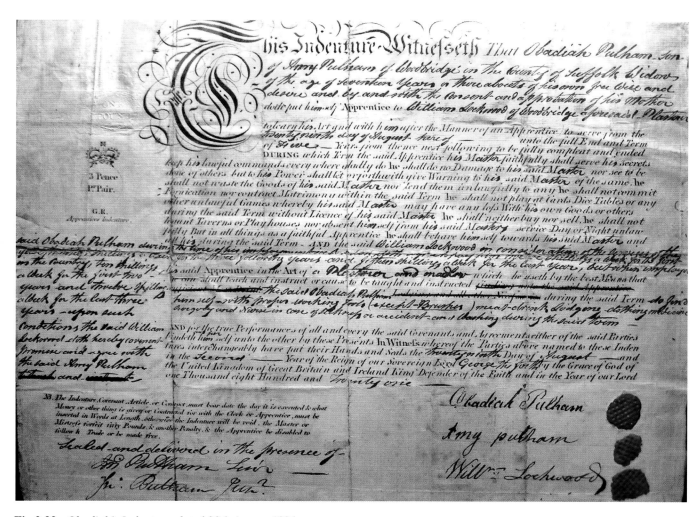

Fig 2.32 *Obadiah's Indenture, dated 29th August 1821*

Fig 2.33 Mount Vesuvius, *painted by Obadiah Pulham 1862-65* (Reproduced by permission of Ian Denney)

- With his Goods or others during the said Term without Licence of his said Master, he shall neither buy nor sell.
- He shall not visit Taverns or Playhouses nor absent himself from his said Master's service day or night unlawfully.
- But in all things as a faithful Apprentice he shall behave himself towards his said Master and all his during the said Term.

AND the said **William Lockwood** in consideration of the Services of the said **Obadiah Pulham** during the time of his employment doth pay him five shillings a week for the first year and the three following years, and fifteen shillings a week for the last year, but when employed in the country, ten shillings a week for the first two years, and twelve shillings a week for the last three years upon such conditions the said **William Lockwood** doth hereby covenant, promise and agree with the said **Amy Pulham**. This said Apprentice in the Art of a Plasterer and Modeller which he useth by the best means that he can shall teach and instruct or cause to be taught and instructed the said Obadiah Pulham during the said Term to find himself with proper working tools (except brushes), meals, drink, lodging, clothing, medicine, surgery and nurse in case of sicking up or accident and of choking during the said Term.

AND for the true Performances of all and every the said Covenants and Agreements either of the said Parties bindeth himself unto the other by these Presents. **In Witness** whereof the Parties above named to these Indentures interchangeably have put their Hands and Seals the 29th day of August [1821], and in the second year of the reign of our Sovereign George the Fourth by the Grace of God of the United Kingdom of Great Britain and Ireland, King Defender of the Faith, and in the Year of our Lord One Thousand Eight Hundred and Twenty One.

Signed: Obadiah Pulham: Amy Pulham: William Lockwood. Sealed and Delivered in the Presence of: J [*John*?] Pulham: J [*James*?] Pulham.

One doesn't have to be a student of history to realise that there was no minimum wage legislation in those days.

It is also interesting to note that this document was proposed by his mother, because William, his father, died four years previously, in 1817. Both of the witnesses appear to be J Pulham, but it is assumed that one could be John – his oldest brother – and the other was probably James 1, who had been working for William Lockwood for a few years, and had probably served out his own apprenticeship by this time.

Obadiah the Artist

Ian Denney then produced evidence of another side of Obadiah's character of which I had previously been unaware, although, on reflection, it came as no surprise. It seems that he was also an artist of some merit, because Ian's family have two oil paintings signed by him. One is of Mount Vesuvius, which was presumably painted during his time in Naples between 1862-65. This is shown here as **Fig 2.33**.

And finally – in **Fig 2.34** – is a photograph of the man himself. He looks quite an elderly man in this picture, so it can be assumed that it was probably taken in Woodbridge sometime during his retirement years in the 1870s. What a bonus these pictures are, because they help to provide an entirely new dimension to the character of the artist and craftsman who has been the subject of the latter sections of this chapter.

Also Noted:
1841 – Church of The Holy Trinity, Wareside, Hertfordshire
1845 – Bayfordbury, near Hertford, Hertfordshire

Fig 2.34 *Obadiah Pulham, 1870s* (Reproduced by permission of Ian Denney)

THE BROXBOURNE MANUFACTORY

1845-1939

1845: A Major Diversification

Work was picking up nicely for James 2 during the mid-1840s, and his premises in Amwell Street, Hoddesdon, in Hertfordshire, would almost certainly have begun to feel rather inadequate. Perhaps his initial ventures into landscaping prompted him to realise that he was more interested in that line of activity than he was in the construction and restoration of buildings, or perhaps he spotted a potential gap in the market that would enable him to expand his business into other areas.

Whatever his true motivation, he decided in 1845 – when he was still only 25 years of age – to acquire a much larger portion of land in Station Road, near Broxbourne Station. He built a mock-Elizabethan house for himself and his family, and an adjacent 'manufactory' – consisting of a grinding mill, kilns and workshops – in which to manufacture his own extensive range of ornamental architectural objects, such as vases, urns, bosses, groins, brackets, sundials, fountains and balustrades from his own 'artificial stone' materials.

This was not exactly a revolutionary idea, since artificial stone ornamentation had already been around for quite some time – the most famous English producer having been Eleanor Coade.[31] She started her artificial stone manufactory in Lambeth in 1769, and continued until her death in 1821, at the age of 88.

According to John Davis, in his book *Antique Garden Ornament*,[32] there were three great terracotta specialists producing artificial stone ornaments by the end of the 19th century. One was James Marriott Blashfield, who operated mainly throughout the second half of the century; another was Henry M Blanchard, who worked off and on throughout the century, and the third was James 2. Unfortunately, one's ability to identify the maker of some individual products is not helped by the fact that all three manufacturers imitated some of each other's designs to the smallest detail, with the result that their unsigned work – and the great majority of it *was* unsigned – is often indistinguishable.

James 2 held one advantage over the others, however, because he was able to produce two distinct ranges of product. One of these was based on his own 'Pulhamite' cement, and the other on clay-based terracotta, which he produced in both a buff colour – a little darker than that used by both Coade and Blashfield – and in a rich pale red. John Davis

suggests that the production process for the cement-based products probably involved a sectional mould, lined with a flexible substance, such as gelatine, and held rigid with plaster. When the formula had dried, the mould could be removed, followed by the gelatine. Having watched my grandfather at work when I was very young, I feel sure that this was somewhere close to the truth.

All of which raises another issue: the use of the word 'Pulhamite' in this context. Most people these days tend to use this name to identify the special cement with which the Pulhams rendered the artificial 'rocks' in their rock gardens, so it would seem quite logical to assume that they would use this same name to describe the material from which they made their cement-based ornaments. For some strange reason, however, this was not always the case, because, in their *Garden Ornament Catalogue*,[33] published *c*.1925, they go out of their way to draw the reader's attention to the materials used in the composition of their products. It reads:

> 'The productions herein illustrated are made of 'Pulhamite' stone, which is considered the best material for all designed stonework in connection with the garden for the following reasons:
>
> • 'Pulhamite Stone is more durable than natural stone. Cement is **not** used in its composition. It is, moreover, much lighter in substance, making more elegant productions than any other so-called artificial stone. This is an important point, as the sides of a Pulhamite vase give more space for soil. It is the colour of light stone, and, if desired, can be made antique colour.
>
> • 'There is nothing deleterious to plant life in it. In fact, owing to the nature of the material, the opposite may be said in its favour.'

This assertion that cement is not used in the production of these ornaments can only mean that the Pulhamite 'Stone' used to manufacture some of their garden ornaments was quite different from their Pulhamite 'Cement' used in their rock gardens etc. As will be noted later in this Chapter, this is not difficult to believe, although I have to say that the vast majority of Pulham ornaments that I have seen are made from clay-based terracotta, which is much more durable than the 'stone'.

Figs 3.1a and b *Pulham wares illustrated in the* Art Journal *in 1859 in an article under the title of* '*The Terracotta Works of James Pulham, Broxbourne*'
a) Hebe Fountain
b) Two vases and a fountain

This suggestion is supported by John Davis, who points out in his book that:

'. . . their cement-based stone did not prove as durable as the terracotta, although it is an adequate weather-resistant compound. It suffered from being cracked and pitted – both of these being features that frequently occur with this type of artificial stone.'

It also has to be said that, by the time their catalogue was published, the firm were not constructing very many Pulhamite rock gardens – the use of natural rock was very much more in vogue by then – so the introduction of the term 'Pulhamite **Stone**' to describe their garden ornaments was understandable. For the purpose of this book, however, I propose to avoid this confusion by ignoring the application of this trade name to their ornaments, and restrict it solely to the cement-based coating of their artificial rocks.

1851 and 1862: The Great Exhibitions

There is some evidence that things did not go as well as James 2 would have hoped during the first few years at the Manufactory, because an entry on page 448 of the 1849 issue of *The Jurist* states that the bankruptcy of '*James Pulham, Broxbourne, Hertfordshire, Plasterer*' would be granted, unless an appeal were duly entered.[34] I have no further evidence of this, but it is apparent that he soon recovered from whatever difficulties he had, because, in 1851 – less than five years after they commenced production – his firm exhibited examples of both their cement and terracotta wares at the Great Exhibition at Crystal Palace. He also decided to exhibit at the International Exhibition of 1862, and, this time, the *Art Journal*

produced a special catalogue in celebration of the event, and included the following comments about the examples from the Pulham Manufactory – one of which will be discussed in some detail later in this Chapter.

'Mr Pulham, of Broxbourne, is a large exhibitor of works in Terracotta, not only for architectural purposes, but for those of gardens, conservatories, and general ornamentation of grounds. They are of excellent design, carefully and skilfully modelled, and so "baked" as to be uninfluenced prejudicially by the weather.'

The catalogue also describes James 2 as a 'Designer and Manufacturer', which clearly implies that he was responsible for at least some of the designs featured at the Exhibition.[35] Unlike Blashfield, however, he was not awarded a medal on that occasion, but was commended for his '*architectural decorations in terracotta, and for a sound and durable material*'.

On page 2 of its Exhibition Catalogue, the *Art Journal* also illustrated an engraving of:

'. . . the Hebe Fountain – an elaborate and skilfully-executed example of terracotta, manufactured by Mr Pulham, of Broxbourne.'

This is reproduced in **Fig 3.1a**, and John Davis notes that this fountain:

'. . . stood over 15 feet in height, and was derived from a marble fountain by Niccolo Tribolo (1485-1550), which is now in the Villa Petraia, outside Florence.'

Soon after the Exhibition, James 2 supplied this fountain to Henry Reed, who owned the Dunorlan Estate on the outskirts of Tunbridge Wells, Kent, where it remains today. Further reference to this will be made in Chapter 4.

1859: 'A Visit to Mr Pulham's Manufactory'

By the time of the 1862 Exhibition, the *Art Journal* was no stranger to the Broxbourne manufactory and its terracotta garden ornaments. Three years earlier, in 1859, it drew its readers' attention to the skills of the Pulham craftsmen by publishing a long article under the title of *The Terracotta Works of James Pulham, Broxbourne.*[36] This provided a fascinating insight into the materials and processes used in the production of these items – for which there is no space here – and Fig 3.1b is one of several illustrations that were also included. It comments that:

'The pages we have devoted to this subject contain engravings – (*one of which is reproduced as Fig 3.1b*) – of a number of Mr Pulham's productions; and we have selected those examples which, for the most part, more particularly illustrate the terracottas of the highest order as '*works of Art*'.'

The 1925 Garden Ornament Catalogue

Pulhams published a small promotional booklet entitled *A Pulham Garden* sometime during the 1920s, and two editions of their *Catalogue of Garden Ornaments* – one *c.*1925, and the other a little later. The two are almost identical, and references throughout this book will relate to the *c.*1925 edition. It includes illustrations from their range of Vases, Terminals, Pedestals, Sundials, Seats, Fountains, Balustrades, Figures etc, and also explains that the firm were:

'Specialists in the design and construction of rock and water gardens, lily pools, pergolas etc.'

No information is given about the dates on which any of the product designs were introduced, although it is known that the vases date from the earliest days. Some of the items, however – like the balustrading, seats and pots etc – have only been found in gardens that are known to date from the 1880s and later. Neither is it possible to prove that, just because a picture of an item does not appear in the *c.*1925 Catalogue, it is not a Pulham product, because it may have been discontinued or excluded from that edition. It is also known that a number of bespoke designs were produced for specific clients, and they may even have produced detailed copies of ornaments that originated from one of the other manufacturers.

Vases and Tazzas

In all, forty-three vases and tazzas – a shallow, saucer-like container – are illustrated in the Catalogue, although this may not have been

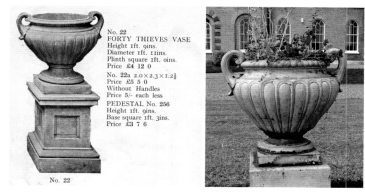

a and b *The Forty Thieves Vase*

c and d *The Westonbirt Vase*

e and f *The Temple Gardens Tazza*

Figs 3.2a-f *Three examples of Pulham Vases and Tazzas*

the total range. Three of them are illustrated in **Fig 3.2** alongside pictures of samples that I have seen for myself. These are among the more popular shapes, but the firm produced a number of variations on their basic designs and themes, and pedestals and vases were often interchanged.

A lot of the firm's products were named after the locations for which they were designed, such as the Otford Vase, the Westonbirt Vase (pictured in Figs 3.2c and d), and the Newport Tazza, for example. Others were given 'descriptive' names, like the Forty Thieves Vase (Figs 3.2a and b) or the Wreath Vase. The Catalogue illustrations reproduced in Fig 3.2 also show the dimension and the 1925 prices of the items.

a) Broxbourne

b) Alexandra Front

c) Alexandra Back

d) Paris Vase

Figs 3.3a-d *The 'Broxbourne / Alexandra / Paris Vase'* (Photographs **b and c** are reproduced by permission of Chilstone Garden Ornaments)

Not all of Pulhams' vases were 'patio-type' containers that generally stood on fairly plain pedestals, or along the terminals of a balustrade. As one can see from the vase in **Fig 3.3d**, some were designed to act as ornamental feature pieces, with very intricate designs – this one is more than 7ft tall on its pedestal – and they were sometimes placed on equally ornate pedestals.

The 'Broxbourne / Alexandra / Paris Vase'

One of the first pictures I saw of one of these vases was of the so-called 'Broxbourne Vase' – the name of which I assumed had been taken from its place of manufacture. I found a copy in a collection of archive papers, and the caption noted that it was possibly exhibited at the Great Exhibition of 1851. The engraving is reproduced in Fig 3.3a.

As far as I knew, nothing had ever been written about its possible whereabouts since that picture was published. The 1925 *Pulham Garden Ornament Catalogue* contained no exact illustration of this vase, although one or two came very close to it. I therefore assumed

that it was probably one of the first vases ever made in the manufactory, and that there were no known surviving examples of it.

My attention was then drawn to an illustration in a catalogue produced by Chilstone Garden Ornaments – a firm who have perfected the process of reproducing historical garden furniture and ornaments from reconstituted sandstone moulded in glass fibre moulds, and who are consequently one of the 21st Century equivalents of the Pulham manufactory. The illustration was of their 'Alexandra Urn' (Fig 3.3b), and the only difference between this and the 'Broxbourne Vase' was that the two cherubs shown sitting on top of the ammonite 'handles' of the 'Broxbourne Vase' were missing from the 'Alexandra Urn'.

I then noticed that the Chilstone catalogue had a second photograph of the urn – this time taken of the reverse side (Fig 3.3c). Checking through the Pulham catalogue again, I found exactly what I was looking for – only, this time, it was called the 'Paris Vase' (Fig 3.3d). It transpired that Chilstone had been sent a sample of this vase by Preston District Council, and asked to replicate it. It was apparently one of a collection that had resided in a local park, and the council wanted to replace some that had been damaged or destroyed over the years. Chilstone always thought that the original was a Pulham item, but had no idea of its proper name, so someone decided to call it the 'Alexandra Urn'. There was no real reason for them to suspect that the cherubs were missing, since the breaks on the ammonites of the sample they received were quite clean.

My conclusion is therefore that this vase was originally made for display at the International Exhibition of 1862, and then installed later in Miller Park, where their copies now stand.

The 'Exhibition Vase' and the 'Grape Vine Vase'

I have been lucky enough to see one of the vases illustrated in the *Art Journal* article of 1859. It was almost the same as the centre vase in Fig 3.1b, and is pictured here as **Fig 3.4a**. The handles are a little different to those on the 'Grape Vine Vase' illustrated in the *Pulham Garden Ornament Catalogue* – **Fig 3.4b**.

The two pedestals are quite different, but it is interesting to note that the names given to the pedestals were comparatively mundane compared with those given to the vases – the one shown here with the 'Grape Vine Vase' being 'Pedestal No. 274', for example.

One of the things to notice about my photograph of the 'Grape Vine Vase' is that it was taken indoors, and one might well ask why an ornament that was produced for display in a garden should end up inside like this. The answer is unfortunately only too simple – it proved to be too risky to keep it outside.

The current criminal tendencies of certain members of our society mean that no valuable garden ornaments are safe in the surroundings for

a) *Exhibition Vase*   b) *Grape Vine Vase*

Figs 3.4a and b *Two imposing Pulham Vases*

Figs 3.5a and b *The Paget Pot*

Figs 3.5c and d *The Luton Tub* (Photo by Ellie Johnson)

which they were intended. This particular example started out as being one of a set of four, but two of them were stolen, so the owner moved the remaining two indoors, where he could keep a constant eye on them – and who can blame him? When one considers the weight involved, it is difficult to imagine how items like this could ever be spirited away without the owner's knowledge, but I have even heard stories of helicopters being used for the 'collection' and transport of items like this being stolen to order. This is a sad reflection of the times in which we live, and means that I shall generally be unable to identify the locations of most of the ornaments mentioned in this book.

Tubs and Pots

The Pulham catalogue illustrates no fewer than 24 tubs and pots, although I have only ever seen two of them – the Paget Pot and the Luton Tub, shown here in Figs 3.5a-d. The Paget Pot stands nearly 22ins high, and has a top diameter of 26ins, while the Luton Tub stands 2ft 7ins high, and has a diameter of 3ft 6ins. They don't make flowerpots like this anymore!

Balustrades

Any self-respecting late-Victorian or Edwardian country house had to have a balustraded terrace with steps leading down to the formal gardens, and Pulhams had a wide range of patterns from which their patrons could choose. The Kingswood Balustrade is shown in **Fig 3.6**, and note the rusticated brickwork along the wall supporting the terrace – this will be ordinary brickwork rendered and modelled into the sort of 'ashlar' finish for which the firm was renowned. **Fig 3.7** shows the Heatherden Balustrade, with terminal vases along the top, and sphinx-like figures in the garden. Both of these pictures are taken from the 1925 *Garden Ornament Catalogue*.

Fig 3.6 *The Kingswood Balustrade*

Fig 3.7 *The Heatherden Balustrade*

Fig 3.8 *The Milton Balustrade with the Carrington Vase*

Fig 3.9 shows the catalogue illustration of the Milton Balustrade paired with an Otford Vase, while **Fig 3.8** shows an example I saw in 2001 – this time paired with a Carrington Vase.

Fountains

Pulham fountains came in all shapes and sizes. Some were quite small, simple fountains tailored for the domestic garden, and others were large and elaborate, made especially for municipal parks or large country estates, and these were generally made on an individual bespoke basis. As with the vases and pedestals discussed earlier, it was often very much of a 'mix and match' situation, in which any one of a number of pedestals could be matched with a range of different bowls and basins. **Fig 3.10**, for instance, shows an illustration from the catalogue of the Brighton Sundial, the pillar of which is very similar to – but not quite as ornamental as – the small domestic fountain shown alongside.

This one also combines both of the Pulham materials – i.e. the pedestal is terracotta, and the bowl is Pulhamite cement. This is probably fairly unusual in itself, but there is no doubt at all about which of the two materials is the more durable. The cement bowl is now quite coarse and pitted, whereas the terracotta pedestal is as smooth – and the detail as sharply defined – as it must have been on the day it was made. What's more, the fountain still works, and is used quite frequently during the summer months.

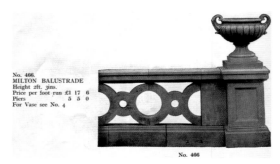

Fig 3.9 *Catalogue illustration of the Milton Balustrade and the Otford Vase*

Figs 3.10a and b *A domestic fountain, and a sundial from the* Pulham Garden Ornament Catalogue

Fig 3.11 (left) *A small domestic rockwork fountain believed to be by Pulham*

Fig 3.12 (below left) *A Pulham fountain at one of the major Exhibitions, for which the firm was awarded a Gold and Silver Medal* (Photo provided by Greg Kobett)

Fig 3.13 (below right) *The Ewell Fountain* (Reproduced from the *Pulham Garden Ornament Catalogue*, c.1925)

The pedestal of the fountain in **Fig 3.11** is made from tufa, and has pockets for planting, so that, when the fountain is playing, the water cascades through the fluted lip of the bowl, thus providing the plants with the moisture they need – a simple, but quite ingenious, attractive and unusual device. There are some other, larger ones like this that will be discussed in later chapters, in which the base is constructed from natural or artificial rocks.

Neither of these fountains is as grand or impressive as some of the exhibition samples upon which the firm built part of its early reputation – two or three of which are illustrated and discussed in some detail in later chapters. There are, however, two examples that are appropriate to this section. **Fig 3.12** is a picture of a fountain for which they won awards at one of the exhibitions – the actual date and location of which is not known, although the quality of the photograph suggests that it was probably one of the later ones – and **Fig 3.13** shows the Ewell Fountain, as illustrated in the *Garden Ornament Catalogue*.

Close inspection of these two photographs reveals a number of interesting similarities. The bottom basins are undoubtedly very different, but the central pedestal and top basins are almost certainly identical. The actual fountains above this basin are not the same, however: the Exhibition sample includes a putto, while the Ewell Fountain – the base of which is situated in the ground of Ewell Court House, near Epsom, Surrey – is comparatively plain.

Figs 3.14a-c *The Norbiton Seat (top); a seat similar to the Clipstone Seat, with a wooden seat and back (centre); an unnamed seat (bottom)*

Garden Seats

Another section of the catalogue is devoted to garden seats, of which the firm made a fairly extensive range. The top picture in **Fig 3.14** is an example of the Norbiton Seat, and the one in the centre is somewhat similar to the Clipstone Seat, in that it has a wooden seat and backrest, rather than stone. I have no idea what the massive seat in the bottom picture was called, but many of these were custom made. I am confident of its provenance, however, because it has all the style of a Pulham seat, and is situated on a site where there are many other Pulham items. Having tried them, I can confirm that these seats are all a lot more comfortable to sit on than they look!

Terminals

There are a number of examples of terminal ornaments in the catalogue, most of which are plain balls, pineapples or acorns. It has to be said, however, that the Coade factory also made terminals like these, and the ones in **Fig 3.15a** are similar to ones made by them. This building was erected after the closure of the Coade factory, however, and there is extensive evidence that Pulhams were active on this site at that time, so it is possible that they could have produced these ornaments to a Coade pattern. **Figs 3.15b and c** show examples from the *Pulham Garden Ornament Catalogue*.

Figs 3.15a-c *Pineapple and Ball Wall Terminals, similar to Coade's patterns, with comparisons from the Pulham* Garden Ornament Catalogue *inset*

The catalogue also illustrates a selection of other decorative vases and figures for the decoration of terminals. The Kingswood Terminal Vase is illustrated in **Fig 3.16**, and the Lindley Vase – not quite an exact copy, but very close – in **Fig 3.17**. **Fig 3.18** shows the Griffin Terminal, where the photograph is actually of a recent copy. This is incredibly faithful to the original illustrated in the *Garden Ornament Catalogue*, and there was originally a set of four of these on site, three of which got rather weatherworn over the years. As the fourth was in good condition, however, the owners had a cast taken, and another set replicated.

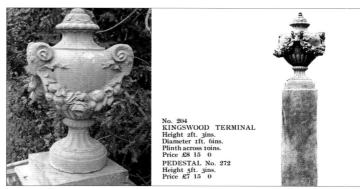

Fig 3.16 *The Kingswood Terminal Vase*

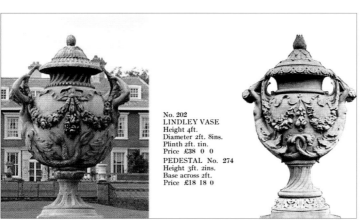

Fig 3.17 *The Lindley Terminal Vase*

Fig 3.18 *The Griffin Terminal*

No. 499
DIANA ROBING
Height 5ft. 2ins.
Price £32 0 0

No. 499

Figs 3.19a-d   *Four Pulhamite stone figures: Diana (a), Hebe (b), unidentified goddess (c), and Bortheus the Warrior (d)*

Figures

A fairly wide range of decorative statues and figures were also produced in the manufactory, ranging from 'nearly life size' statuettes to small garden ornaments standing less than 2 feet tall. Four of the larger ones are shown in **Figs 3.19a-d**, showing Diana (a) – noted as being 5ft 2ins high in the Garden Ornament Catalogue – Hebe (b); an unidentified goddess, (c) and Bortheus the Warrior (d). The photographed figures are all about 5ft high, which suggests that they are all possibly from a set. They are all made of very finely-grained Pulhamite Stone, which is still remarkably smooth, but does show a greater susceptibility to deterioration than the terracotta items.

Fig 3.7 shows the catalogue illustration of the Heatherden Balustrade, but there is also something else of interest in that photograph – the two sphinx-like figures in the foreground. They no longer stand in front of the balustrade, but I saw something during one of my site visits that looks as if it could have come out of the same mould. It is shown here in **Fig 3.20**.

Fig 3.20   *A Pulham Sphinx*

Fig 3.21 *Memorial to the Irish painter William Mulready, in Kensal Green Cemetery* (Photo by Anne Rowe)

Memorials and 'Special Commissions'

One of James 2's more unusual and artistic pieces was featured at the Exposition Universelle de Paris in 1867. It was not one of his own designs, having been commissioned by the Science and Art Department of the South Kensington Museum – now the Victoria and Albert Museum. The designer in this case was Geoffrey Sykes. It was a terracotta monument to the Irish painter William Mulready (**Fig 3.21**), and Sally Festing – in her article for the *Journal of The Garden History Society* entitled 'Great Credit Upon the Ingenuity and Taste of Mr Pulham',[37] describes it thus:

'. . . it had a pedestal, sketched with outlines of some of the artist's principal pictures, supporting his effigy. It obtained a silver medal, was highly commended, and spoken of as a *chef-d'oeuvre* in terracotta. The Science and Art Department of South Kensington Museum, who commissioned the piece, sent it to Paris [*for the Exposition*] before it found a home, where it now rests, in Kensal Green Cemetery [*in London*].'

Finally in this section are two items that I am sure came from the Pulham manufactory, although they are not illustrated in their *Garden Ornament Catalogue*. They are pictured in **Fig 3.22** – on

sites where the Pulhams were very prolific – and I have been told that they could either be well-heads or large Italian garden urns. I favour the latter, because there are other examples serving that function in the Kitchen Garden at Sandringham (Fig 8.9), and in an archive photo of the 'Round Garden' at Bawdsey (Fig 19.3).

Figs 3.22a and b *Well-heads or large Italian garden urns? Whatever they are, they are almost certainly by Pulham*

Fig 3.23 *The round-headed ground-floor colonnade on the façade of the Henry Cole Wing of the Victoria and Albert Museum in Exhibition Road, London*

1867-68: Ornamentation at the V & A Museum, London

As explained in the previous chapter, James 1 and Obadiah Pulham were responsible for a lot of ornamental stonework around London during the 1820s and '30s, although it is not known where, or even if, much of this can still be found, due to an almost complete lack of documentation. Thanks to the meticulous archives maintained by the Victoria and Albert Museum, however, there are records of some work done there by James 2 during 1868, so it is quite likely that this could have been – at least in part – in consequence of his work on the Mulready Memorial.

The work in question is on the Exhibition Road façade of the Science School – now known as the Henry Cole Wing. The main features here are a large quantity of terracotta ornamentation along the open, round-headed colonnade on the 'ground floor', and the open arcaded balcony along the top floor. In his authoritative book on the Museum, John Physick[38] explains:

'At the beginning of 1868, [Henry] Cole recorded that the capitals of five of the ground-floor columns were in position, and that the Schools [i.e. The Science School and the Royal College of Art situated behind it] were up to that level generally. These columns are identical to those on the Lecture Theatre front

of the Museum, designed by Geoffrey Sykes – the designer of the *Mulready Memorial* – and modelled by James Gamble.

'The top-floor gallery . . . is composed of twenty-one round-headed arches . . . made by A Wilson and Sons, and included Cole's motto.

'The decoration of the ground-floor windows, designed by Gamble using Sykes's sketches, was executed by J Pulham, while that of the basement, the remainder of the ground floor, first and second floors, the principal entablature and the pediments were the work of Blanchard.'

There were obviously quite a few master craftsmen involved here, and it is not too easy to sort out exactly who was responsible for each of the features. An abstract of correspondence from the V&A archives provides some further clues, however, and confirms John Physick's account that the work was done in 1867-68, following the completion of the Mulready Monument.

The term 'ground-floor' in those notes is rather misleading. It would be quite easy to walk right past it without noticing 'the windows', because they are actually almost at first floor level, but, once one glances upwards, everything is there for all to see and admire, as shown in **Fig 3.23**.

John Physick credits Pulham with the execution of *'the decoration of the ground-floor windows'*, which presumably includes the facing of the arches and the mosaic work beneath their ceilings, as well as the pillars themselves, although his reference to Blanchard's contribution slightly confuses things.

1865: A Change of Name

In 1865, just three years or so after the International Exhibition, James 2 decided to bring his son, James 3, into the business, from which point the firm became known as James Pulham and Son. James 3 was only twenty years of age at the time – just two years older than his father was when he took over the business following the untimely death of James 1.

This change of company name possibly coincided with the firm's decision to change the monogram with which it stamped its wares, although this didn't really seem to make a great deal of difference, because they seldom stamped them anyway. Of all the items I have seen so far, only a few carry a stamp.

Fig 3.24 carries pictures of all the stamps that I have so far seen. The first is from the 'Grape Vine Vase' – pictured in the left panel of Fig 3.4 – that could date from around the time of the 1851 Exhibition. John Davis suggests in his book, *Antique Garden Ornament*, that the oval stamp (top right) was possibly used between 1851 and 1865 – before the firm changed its name to 'Pulham and Son' – although I suspect that it was probably used for some time after that.

The centre stamp was actually found *underneath* a vase – which could very easily explain why so few have been seen. It must date

from later than 1895 – since that is the date when the firm opened a sales office in London – and finally, the bottom example was embossed on a pedestal, and must date from after 1902, when the firm moved its sales office to its Newman Street address.

Michael Angelo Pulham: 1827-1915

There is one more Pulham figure that merits special mention here, and that is the memorial above the graves of Michael Angelo Pulham – younger brother of James 2 – and his wife, Charlotte Annie. It stood in the Cheshunt Cemetery – some two miles south of the Broxbourne manufactory – for many years, until recently being transferred by the family to the Lowewood Museum, and is shown here in **Fig 3.25**. It dates from some years after the Mulready Memorial.

Fig 3.25 *Memorial to the family of Michael Angelo Pulham (1827-1915) in Cheshunt Cemetery*

Figs 3.24a-d *Four Pulham monograms, although very few products carry them*

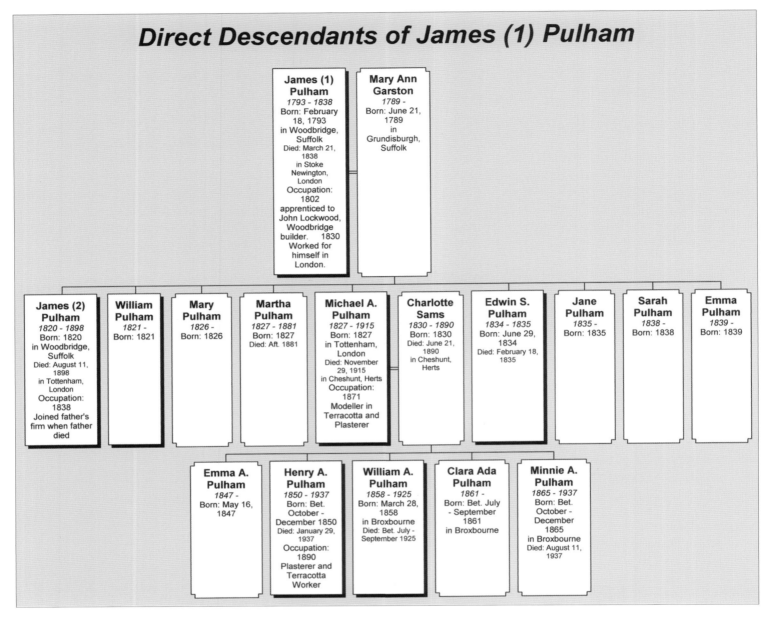

Direct Descendants of James (1) Pulham

James (1) Pulham
1793 - 1838
Born: February 18, 1793 in Woodbridge, Suffolk
Died: March 21, 1838 in Stoke Newington, London
Occupation: 1802 apprenticed to John Lockwood, Woodbridge builder. 1830 Worked for himself in London.

Mary Ann Garston
1789 -
Born: June 21, 1789 in Grundisburgh, Suffolk

James (2) Pulham
1820 - 1898
Born: 1820 in Woodbridge, Suffolk
Died: August 11, 1898 in Tottenham, London
Occupation: 1838 Joined father's firm when father died

William Pulham
1821 -
Born: 1821

Mary Pulham
1826 -
Born: 1826

Martha Pulham
1827 - 1881
Born: 1827
Died: Aft. 1881

Michael A. Pulham
1827 - 1915
Born: 1827 in Tottenham, London
Died: November 29, 1915 in Cheshunt, Herts
Occupation: 1871 Modeller in Terracotta and Plasterer

Charlotte Sams
1830 - 1890
Born: 1830
Died: June 21, 1890 in Cheshunt, Herts

Edwin S. Pulham
1834 - 1835
Born: June 29, 1834
Died: February 18, 1835

Jane Pulham
1835 -
Born: 1835

Sarah Pulham
1838 -
Born: 1838

Emma Pulham
1839 -
Born: 1839

Emma A. Pulham
1847 -
Born: May 16, 1847

Henry A. Pulham
1850 - 1937
Born: Bet. October - December 1850
Died: January 29, 1937
Occupation: 1890 Plasterer and Terracotta Worker

William A. Pulham
1858 - 1925
Born: March 28, 1858 in Broxbourne
Died: Bet. July - September 1925

Clara Ada Pulham
1861 -
Born: Bet. July - September 1861 in Broxbourne

Minnie A. Pulham
1865 - 1937
Born: Bet. October - December 1865 in Broxbourne
Died: August 11, 1937

Fig 3.26 *Family Tree of James 1 through to descendants of Michael Angelo*

Very little is known about Michael Angelo – in fact, the only information I have been able to find is that contained in the census reports of 1871 through to 1901. These describe him as a *'Modeller in Terracotta and Plasterer'*, which indicates that he was almost certainly involved in the design of at least some of the firm's decorative garden ornaments. Michael Angelo's son, Henry Angelo Pulham, was also a terracotta modeller at some time, and **Fig 3.26** shows the family tree of James 1, through to the descendants of Michael Angelo.

Figs 3.27a and b *Henry Angelo with his wife, Elizabeth; and Clara Pulham*

Figs 3.28a-d *The Michael Angelo Pots and figureheads*

The link between individual items in the firm's catalogue and their creator will probably never be known, and it is similarly not quite clear who designed this family memorial. It seems likely that Michael Angelo created it in memory of his wife, who died in 1890, when he was 63, and probably still at work. On the other hand, Henry Angelo may have designed it as a memorial to both his parents after Michael Angelo died in 1915. In either event, this memorial angel is – like all the other examples of Pulham's terracotta that I have seen – amazingly tactile, especially when one considers that it has stood the test of more than one hundred winters.

To my knowledge, no pictures are available of either James 2 or Michael Angelo, but a copy of an old photograph of Henry Angelo with his wife, Elizabeth, has come my way. It is shown here in **Fig 3.27**, alongside one of his younger sister, Clara Pulham.

There is a story behind these two pictures. Sometime during 2009, I was sent photographs of two pots that were claimed to be by Michael Angelo, and were due to be presented to the Lowewood Museum in Hoddesdon – the place that marks the start of my research journey. Pictures of these pots are reproduced here in **Figs 3.28a and b**, and I have to admit that, when I first saw them, I was rather doubtful about their provenance, because they were unlike any Pulham vases that I had seen. There was certainly nothing like them in the *Garden Ornament Catalogue*, and, for the want of a better name, I have called them 'The Lowewood Pots'.

The pots came to the museum via a Mr and Mrs Thomas, the current owners of the house in which Henry Angelo once lived. They received

them from a descendant of Henry Angelo who decided to return them to their original home, and Mrs Thomas kindly handed them on.

The pots stand about 10in. high, which is very small compared with the vases illustrated in the catalogue, but take another look at the right-hand photograph in Fig 3.27. The two pots standing on either side of Clara Pulham's door are exactly like the right-hand pot in Fig 3.28, so could this mean that Michael Angelo gave some samples of his work to each of his children? Another clue comes from the pair of small moulded figureheads now owned by Clara's granddaughter, shown in Figs 3.28c and d. These must be the originals from which Michael Angelo made the heads for the pedestal of the 'Exhibition' Vase shown in Fig 3.4a.

The Kew Fountain

There is another twist to this story. One of the Pulham items illustrated in the *Art Journal* 'International Exhibition Catalogue' of 1862 was called the 'Kew Fountain' (**Fig 3.29**). It was accompanied by the following comment:

'Mr Pulham exhibits a variety of Vases … His principal contribution, however, is a Fountain, which, in the Exhibition, plays perpetually near the entrance to the Horticultural Gardens. It is an agreeable object, not too large for any moderately-sized conservatory.'

Fig 3.29 *The Pulham Fountain that played at the entrance to the Horticultural Gardens at Kew for the International Exhibition of 1862* (Reproduced from the Art Journal Catalogue published to celebrate the event)

Fig 3.30 *The 'Kew Fountain' – now in residence at the Bellagio Casino Hotel in Las Vegas* (Photo by Susan Williams, Virtual Reference Section, Las Vegas Library)

In her *'Great Credit . . .'* article, Sally Festing describes this 'moderately sized' fountain as a 'comedy in eclecticism', but John Davis tries to take a more serious view in his book, *Antique Garden Ornament*. He describes it as:

> '. . . consisting of four columns, each surmounted by a shell, surrounding a larger column, surmounted by a copy of Verrocchio's famous bronze '*Pluto (or cherub) with a Dolphin*' in Florence.'

Before moving on to the story of the fountain, take a look at the ring of pots around the base. Here again, these are very similar to the ones in Fig 3.28 – perhaps not exactly the same, but fairly evidently by the same artist – which means that they must almost certainly have been designed before the 1862 Exhibition. Henry Angelo was only twelve years old at this time, which, in turn, must indicate that Michael Angelo must surely have been the designer of the 'Lowewood Pots'.

Now back to the 'Kew Fountain'. It had long been assumed that this fountain had been lost or destroyed, and I said as much in an article I wrote under the title of 'In Search of Pulham's Fountains',[39] published in 2003.

Imagine my surprise when I received a call from the director of a firm of craftsmen who specialise in the restoration of terracotta artefacts. He told me that he had seen my picture of this fountain, and claimed that he had personally restored it a few months previously. It apparently came to him in a very dilapidated and fragmented condition from somewhere in the Isle of Wight, but he restored – or remade – the pieces he had, and put them together as best he could, doing his best to 'recreate' the pieces that were missing altogether.

This was exciting news, and I was very keen to know where it was now. In the 'interests of client confidentiality' he was reluctant to give me the exact details, apart from saying that he 'thought it was now in America – possibly in a Casino'!

That set me thinking. The most obvious place in America that fitted these criteria seemed to be Las Vegas, so I sent a copy of the engraving to a couple of friends who I knew had visited there. One of them came back with the news that they thought they might have seen 'something like it' in the Bellagio Casino Hotel.

I discovered that the Las Vegas Library operated a Virtual Reference service, so I emailed them with the picture and the background story to see if they could help. It was a lucky strike, because an extremely helpful lady picked up my note, and immediately replied to say that she would be delighted to follow it up for me. True to her word, she came back sometime later with a whole batch of photographs that she had very kindly taken for me. One of them is reproduced here as **Fig 3.30**.

This is indeed encouraging – even though the fountain is no longer in England – but a close study of the details reveals one or two discrepancies with the original drawing. This can be accounted for quite easily by the fact that the restorers had never seen the picture that had happened to come my way, and consequently had no real idea of how the various parts were supposed to be fitted together, or what its final appearance should be.

Some pieces, like the putto at the top, were missing altogether, so they had to do their best to create something to fit, and they didn't get it quite right. The set of four putti that originally sat around the base were also interchanged with the set of shells around the tops of the four columns, but, apart from that, the fountain is at last functioning once again, albeit in a slightly different form, and in a location far removed from that for which it was first intended.

- 4 -

HIGHNAM COURT
GLOUCESTERSHIRE
1847-1862

In 1845 – three years after he created his first ever rock garden for John Warner at 'Woodlands', in Hoddesdon – James 2 was commissioned by William Robert Baker to build a rockery and rose garden at his imposing Georgian and Regency mansion at Bayfordbury, on the outskirts of Hertford. William Robert was the grandson of Sir William Baker – one of the wealthiest and most successful businessmen in England at that time – and the Baker family were renowned for their love of gardens, and were particularly devoted to arboriculture.

Bayfordbury is not one of the sites featured in this book, but James 2's work there was obviously well regarded, because a year or so after it was completed he was approached by Thomas Gambier Parry, William Baker's brother-in-law. Parry's son, Hubert Parry was later to become Sir Hubert Parry, nowadays remembered as the composer of 'Jerusalem'.

Like the Bakers of Bayfordbury, Gambier Parry bestowed much loving care on his garden, and maintained a large pinetum about a mile or so from the house. One can imagine him being invited by William Baker to check out the latest additions to his Bayfordbury plantation, and, while there, perhaps admiring the rockery that had just been constructed by 'that excellent young Mr Pulham from Broxbourne'. He was undoubtedly impressed and intrigued by what he saw, because he invited James 2 down to his home at Highnam Court, in Gloucestershire, to discuss what he might do for him there.

The gardens at Highnam Court were described in a *Country Life Illustrated* article [40] more than one hundred years ago as:

'. . . a green home of well-ordered beauty, in which light and shade and finely-contrasted colours create a very remarkable charm. The house stands well amid its surroundings; its front touched here and there with green, the growths of climbing plants and flowers in the terrace border, with its relieving standard roses, and the dark cedar of Lebanon filling the picture on the left. The advantage of situation is here very manifest, for the position is very good, and the surrounding country full of varied beauty – a forest land, moreover, with many hoary survivors of the greenwood day. There are thus at Highnam Court our English familiar trees in happy unison with many gathered from other climes.

'Through the walled garden, we see a beautiful avenue of Irish yews, which is also among the finest in the land. This garden might, indeed, be called a garden of conifers, though it is to be observed that these are most happily contrasted with deciduous trees, and with flowers, as in the trim beds in the south walk leading from the winter garden, each thus relieving and enforcing the particular beauty of the other.'

These gardens are the earliest surviving complete example of a Pulham rock garden, and, thanks to the care of their present devoted owner, are still in remarkably good order.

The centre section – between the upper and lower lakes – used to be a bog in the old days, and the idea was to connect them via a stream running through a series of small pools and cascades. According to James 2's records, [41] his original contract covered work that was done between 1847-49, and he was also invited to return for additional periods between 1851 and 1862, so it is not obvious exactly what work was done at which time. However, it seems safe to assume that the stream and cascades were part of the initial work in 1847-49. **Fig 4.1** is a charming scene of the gardens taken by an anonymous photographer – probably around the turn of the 20th Century.

Fig 4.1 *The Gardens at Highnam Court c.1900* (Photo © Country Life)

Thanks to Thomas Gambier Parry's great-grandson, Thomas Fenton – who still lived in the Old Rectory at Highnam at the time of my visit in 2000 – it is possible to get some further glimpses of what the gardens were like around that time. These pictures were taken some sixty years or so after the gardens were constructed, and provide a fascinating glimpse of how things had evolved over time. **Figs 4.2 and 4.3** show the pools, the stream, and the path that runs around the back of the garden.

In the early days, there used to be a rather irritating problem with duckweed in the watercourse. It appears that this problem was never properly solved, because, in an article in the *Journal of The Garden History Society* magazine, Sally Festing quotes from an unpublished journal written by Ernest Gambier Parry[42] – the son of Thomas – *c*.1902. He records that the rock garden was created:

'. . . partly out of a wood, partly a large pond, and partly out of orchard. The pond was drained, and water was fed through a brick-cemented trench – from a lake about half a mile away – into a course of Pulhamite and Yorkstone rocks and islands. It was wooded with native trees from the old Forest of Dean, and newly introduced species – all carefully positioned and nurtured into splendid growth in a very secluded area. Many thousands of tons of York stone were used to supplement the artificial material, all of which remains basically as it was built.'

At that time, there were probably about eight gardeners on the staff at Highnam Court, whereas today there are officially only 'one and a half,' although, 'now that he is officially retired', the present owner is also able to spend the majority of his own time out there. When he first acquired the property, the rock garden was seriously overgrown, but he has persevered with the restoration work, and the gardens are now back to their former glory. He commissioned a comprehensive restoration survey from a firm of specialist contractors, who commented on the fact that the gardens comprise:

Fig 4.4 *The sample wall section requested by Thomas Gambier Parry before he commissioned James 2 to build the wall of the Walled Garden at Highnam Court*

Fig 4.2 *The two top rock pools* c.*1900* (Photo reproduced by permission of Tom Fenton)

Fig 4.3 *The lower rock pool, looking upstream* c.*1900* (Photo reproduced by permission of Tom Fenton)

'. . a range of styles and construction methods that indicate the experimental nature of some of the work . . . [However,] the general structure is well conceived and generally structurally sound, as is most of Pulham's surviving work.'

It was later decided to build or replace the high wall around the Walled Garden, so it is possible that this was part of the additional work done between 1851 and 1862. This is definitely the work of James 2, although it is also clear that he was not invited down to Highnam with a *carte blanche* offer to come in and do just as he liked. Thomas Gambier Parry obviously had some very definite ideas of his own about the way certain things should be done, and he asked James 2 to prepare a sample of the finish and copings that he suggested would be appropriate for the main wall. **Fig 4.4** is a picture of the sample he produced, which still stands near the house, complete with a new statue that stands on top of it.

So what of the gardens today? **Fig 4.5** shows the run of the completed wall along the 'Ladies' Walk', which runs outside the south wall of the Walled Garden, and confirms that James 2's suggestions were approved – the main wall is of brick, with Pulhamite pillars, each faced with James 2's proposed 'dimpled' finish. Like the figure that now stands on the sample, the ones on the pedestals along this walk are also later replacements.

Fig 4.5 (opposite) *The 'Ladies Walk', with Pulhamite pillars, on the south side of the Walled Garden at Highnam Court* (Photo by Jenny Lilly)

Fig 4.6 *The 'Owl Cave' grotto, at the far end of the 'Ladies Walk'*

Figs 4.7a and b *The Pulhamite outcrop at Highnam Court*
a) (above) The huge rock outcrop comes into view (Photo by Jenny Lilly)
b) (below) Looking back at the supporting wall from the other side

Fig 4.8 *The lower grotto* (Photo by Jenny Lilly)

Just through the hooped archway, at the far end of the 'Ladies' Walk', is the 'Owl Cave' grotto, which, considering its age, must be one of the best preserved of all Pulham's grottoes, and is shown here in **Fig 4.6**. Follow the path around the corner, and one comes to a massive rock outcrop (**Fig 4.7a**), that would make any unsuspecting visitor wonder how on earth anyone managed to manipulate 'rocks' of that size into that position. Or could they possibly have been there all the time?

The answer to both these questions becomes clear when one looks at **Fig 4.7b**, which looks back at the huge 'outcrops', from the other side. It is clear that James 2 either built a wall – or perhaps utilised a section of the old Walled Garden wall that had partly collapsed – and built it up with rocks and his Pulhamite cement to create the impression of a completely natural phenomenon when viewed from the correct angle. This is undoubtedly the place where their very specialised craft of 'rock-building' was first put to a serious test, and – bearing in mind that it is still standing after more than 150 years – they obviously passed with flying colours.

Just opposite this, at the bottom of the bank of the stream that runs through the gorge, is the lower grotto – shown here in **Fig 4.8** – although this is not in quite such good order as the Owl Grotto. The path leads down to a Japanese-style bridge that spans the main

watercourse, although, at the time of our visit in 2010, this had been partly drained for maintenance. The rocky banks were still in good order, as can be seen in **Fig 4.9**, while **Fig 4.10** shows the large outcrop that would normally be one of the 'islands'. There are a few sections of exposed brickwork along the edges of the stream where the Pulhamite facing has come away from the brick core, but it is hardly surprising that the effects of frost, and the root expansion of overgrown vegetation should have had some effect over all those years.

Higher up the bank, on the right along the path beside the gorge, there is another area of land that was among the last to be cleared, and it is here that Pulhams might have constructed the first section of their rockwork in these gardens. There is also another grotto here, and there can be no denying that this rockwork is not quite of the same standard as in other parts of the garden. It is slightly 'rougher' – one might even recall the suggestion of 'experimental' in the restoration survey – and a section is shown here in **Fig 4.11**.

Fig 4.9 (opposite page) *Japanese bridge, upper pool and gulley* (Photo by Jenny Lilly)

Fig 4.10 (above) *Island in the partly-drained upper stream* (Photo by Jenny Lilly)

Fig 4.11 (left) *Rock-lined path and old rock garden at Highnam Court* (Photo by Jenny Lilly)

Returning to the house via the 'Ladies Walk', one comes to a charming rose tunnel (**Fig 4.12**) that leads around to a gate into the Walled Garden. **Fig 4.13** is a picture of the gateway on the far side – visible beyond the iron gates in Fig 4.12 – with (non-Pulham) urns on the piers, and a coat of arms above the gateway. In another part of the wall, there is a feature alcove, complete with a figure and surrounding vases (**Fig 4.14**) although none of these items could be ascribed to the manufactory in Broxbourne.

Before leaving Highnam, one could also reflect on another extract from the article in *Country Life Illustrated*, published on 1st April, 1899. The anonymous writer concludes his essay as follows:

'It is not easy to fix upon any one place as the most beautiful in these attractive pleasure grounds, though everyone must like that quiet, sequestered, and sunny spot known as the rockwork or winter garden, as is the spring leading to that pleasant retreat. Here the formal garden paths bring the visitor to a most lovely range of rockwork, with abundant vegetation, and remarkable ornamental trees. The scene has a very delightful, natural character, and the diversity of plant life in the place is really wonderful. Ferns and rock plants in luxuriant masses clothe the stone, while lofty and well-proportioned conifers of noble kinds rise like sentinels above. There are glorious groups of rhododendrons in one place, yews and various conifers in another, remarkable depths of colour, with happy contrast, being relieved by the tints of lighter foliage.

'Birch, Irish yew, and other trees give charming effects, the evergreen shrubs making bold groups, with many graceful bamboos adding their special attraction. The cool margin of the merry stream, moreover, provides hospitable places for the flourishing bog plants and water-loving flowers that have been planted by its side.

'The rich floral beauties of the garden are enforced by the contrasts afforded by the growth of shrubs and trees. To group and happily proportion the varied effects in a garden is the work of a master, and the Gloucester home we illustrate has been fortunate. How to mass colour and relieve shade, to seize the advantages of position, to enforce what is beautiful, and eliminate the harsh or ungraceful, to create wholly acceptable garden pictures – this is the highest art of the garden lover; and certainly such places as the gardens of Highnam Court are fruitful in examples, and full of suggestion . . . . full of interest, and with a picturesque-ness and character of their own. Highnam, in short, is a particularly good example of what a large country garden ought to be.'

This was written just over one hundred years ago, but there can be little doubt that, if the writer could return to review his work today, he would almost certainly have come to the same conclusion.

Fig 4.12 (top left) *Rose tunnel leading to the walled garden* (Photo by Jenny Lilly)

Fig 4.13 (above) *Gateway into the walled garden, with family coat of arms* (Photo by Jenny Lilly)

Fig 4.14 (right) *Alcove and figure in the walled garden.* (Photo by Jenny Lilly)

Note: *The vases and figure in Figs 4.13 and 4.14 are not Pulham items*

- 5 -

DUNORLAN PARK
TUNBRIDGE WELLS, KENT
1862-1864

Dunorlan Park, in Tunbridge Wells, Kent, was purchased by Henry Reed – a Tasmanian millionaire and evangelist – in the 1850s, with the intention of demolishing the existing house on the site, and building himself:

'. . . a most elegant and substantial mansion, erected . . . entirely of Normandy stone, in the Italian style of architecture, finished throughout in the most perfect manner, and in every way adapted for the comfort and enjoyment of a nobleman or gentleman of fortune.'[43]

In addition to building a new house, he had the surrounding area – previously divided into fields – landscaped and planted to form a park. It was designed by Robert Marnock – the *'gentleman's gardener'* with whom James 2 had recently worked at Berry Hill, in Taplow, Buckinghamshire. Presumably well satisfied with his work there, Marnock engaged him to construct an artificial lake at Dunorlan, with – according to James 2's promotional booklet published *c.*1877:[44]

'Waterfalls, Rocky Stream, Spring, Rocky Banks, Plateau for Summer House, Fountain etc.'

Fig 5.1 *The staircase in Dunorlan House,* c.*1930s* (Photo provided by Marion Williams)

Henry Reed sold the estate a few years later, and the 1871 sales brochure states that this landscaping work was done:

'. . . in a truly superlative manner. [The small lake was adapted to form] . . . a fine ornamental sheet of water of about six acres, with prettily shaped islands, and well stocked with fish . . . [and he created] . . . a luxuriant avenue of deodars and Douglas firs, leading from an elegant Grecian temple to a handsome stone basin and fountain.'

The house was taken over by the War Damage Commission in 1943, and this turned out to be an appropriate name in the circumstances, because legend has it that troops were billeted there during the early years, and are thought to have been responsible for destroying many statues and ornaments around the grounds by using them for target practice[45] – a rather extreme version of a story that has become all too familiar during my visits to a number of Pulham sites.

The grounds at Dunorlan were sold to the local Borough Council in 1946, and they opened about thirty acres of it as a public park, which became increasingly popular over the years. The War Damage Commission vacated the house in 1957, but it was in such a dilapidated condition by that time that the Council decided to demolish it, and sell the land for redevelopment. Dunorlan House – the house that had been described in the 1871 sales brochure as having been *'in every way adapted for the comfort and enjoyment of a nobleman or gentleman of fortune'* – was no more.

A booklet entitled *The Dunorlan Story*[46] – written by James Akehurst, a local historian – also contains a description of the interior of the house that makes very interesting reading. It is a quotation from the reminiscences of a Mrs Carminhow, who worked there during the residency of the War Damage Commission:

'It is an architectural monstrosity which represented everything one might expect from a man with too much money and too little taste. It was grandiose, with plaster covered with gilt wherever you looked. There was a grand staircase with two pillars of hollow red marble; this broad staircase led to the first floor and bedrooms – then converted into offices. The rooms on the ground floor were large and high, with ostentatious decoration in which gilt cherubs figured largely.'

This description is intriguing, because it conjures up a vision of just the sort of work with which the Pulhams are known to have been associated. The mid-1850s was the period during which they were engaged on the restoration of the North Porch at St Mary Redcliffe, Bristol, and – just a few years after – their rather similar work at Kilnwick Percy in Yorkshire, as discussed in Chapter 2. In fact, an old picture of the staircase at Dunorlan Park – **Fig 5.1** – shows a striking resemblance to the one at Kilnwick Percy, shown in Fig 2.15. The banisters here are wooden, rather than cast iron, but the pillars could well be Pulham's scagliola, and the vase on the newel post on the bend in the stairs also looks interesting.

There was also a most impressive balustraded terrace around the house, with lots of vases and the like, but the problem with James 2's booklet is that it only refers to the landscaping work he did for his 'satisfied clients'. It contains no details of building work or external or internal ornamentation, so one can only base these assumptions on visual evidence. Another point to consider here, however, is that if Henry Reed wanted elaborate plasterwork to decorate the inside of his house, why would he employ someone else to do it when one of the acknowledged masters of the craft was working immediately outside his very windows?

A Walk Around the Gardens in 1881

A Mr 'W.H.' described a walk around the gardens at Dunorlan in an article published in the *Gardeners' Chronicle* in 1881.[47] The gardens had by then matured, and, following Henry Reed's departure, the estate had become the home of Brenton Halliburton Collins.

'From the projecting portion of the terrace a fine view of the lake is obtained, and the slope descending to it, together with the English Yews and belts of trees upon the park side, which are very beautiful. The planting by the side of the lake has been very successfully accomplished.

At one point the lake might be a deep ravine bounded by trees, but, a little farther in the distance, the gentle ripple of water reveals the fact that it is a beautiful winding lake, faithfully representing the natural curve of a river, having Weeping Birch and Willows overhanging the water's edge. The peeps between the trees, leading to and across the lake, are also exceedingly pretty, especially as the view is so commanding, and the eye can range over miles of woodland scenery and a country rendered interesting by its natural charms, and many sights and objects of historical note. . . .

'From a rustic bridge, you look upon a splendid waterfall with a Lily pond and glen immediately beneath; the water, after travelling a distance of several yards, falls from 12 to 15 feet, and is intercepted by the ledge of projecting rocks, which gives a magnificent effect [**Fig 5.2**]. There is a serpentine watercourse

Fig 5.2 *The rustic bridge, waterfall and glen at Dunorlan Park* (from the 1871 sales brochure)

Fig 5.3 *View towards Dunorlan House across the Lily Pond with rustic summer house* (from the 1871 sales brochure)

from the Lily pond to the extremity of the grounds, which is bordered by weeping trees and hardy aquatic plants, and adorned with summerhouses in shaded situations [**Fig 5.3**].

'At the end of this walk, one of the finest sights in England is in store for the visitor, it is the Cedar avenue leading to the temple already alluded to in these remarks. The green-grass avenue slopes gently to the north-west, and is bordered by Cedars and Pinus Douglasii planted alternately. I believe the original idea was to have removed the Cedars, but both have grown so well, are so handsome in shape, and are such an ornament to the place that it would require an ingenious mind to conceive anything more magnificent. There are figures placed between the lines

Fig 5.4 *The Dunorlan Fountain, Cedar Avenue and 'Temple'* (from the 1871 sales brochure)

Fig 5.5 *The Dunorlan Fountain and Cedar Avenue in 2001 – very much as described by John Davis in 1991*

of trees and, near the bottom of the avenue, there is a fountain – the centre figure of which is 25 feet high. The height and proportion of the different figures are in strict harmony with the base of the fountain. There are four figures with trumpets – which, when there is a strong force of water, are very attractive – and eight dolphins, while there are two basins continually flowing over into the base of the fountain.'

He goes on to describe the 'temple' at the far end of the avenue as:

'. . . containing a figure of Helen Douglas – of Sir Walter Scott's '*Lady of the Lake*' – with her dog Lufra.'

The Dunorlan Fountain

The fountain is well worthy of special note, because its top section is the 'Hebe Fountain' referred to in Chapter 3. It was originally made by James 2 for display at the 1862 International Exhibition, and was illustrated in the *Art Journal Catalogue* published to celebrate the event – the engraving is reproduced as Fig 3.1a. After the Exhibition, it was installed at Dunorlan, and John Davis described it in his book *Antique Garden Ornament* [48] as follows:

'One of the firm's monumental garden ornaments was exhibited by Pulham at the 1862 exhibition. Standing over fifteen feet in height [i.e. the statue excluding its present base], it was derived from a marble fountain by Niccolo Tribolo (1485-1550) – now in the Villa Petraia, outside Florence – which is surmounted by a bronze statue by Giambologna of Florence Rising from the Waves. However, Pulham's form of this fountain has many variations. Giambologna's statue was replaced by a terracotta figure of Hebe [the Greek Goddess of Youth] after Canova, which Jewitt described as "a perfection in burning . . . very successful."'

'Other variations include the upper bowl, which, on Tribolo's fountain, is in the form of an inverted platter; the putti decorating the side of the main bowl on Pulham's fountain are kneeling as opposed to standing, whilst the upper base of this fountain is decorated with four duplicate Naiads, as opposed to the different water deities found on Tribolo's. Furthermore, Pulham accentuated and altered the bas-reliefs between the Naiads, as well as those on the column supporting the upper bowl, and he exchanged the hexagonal panelled base for one of a very curious style, almost of an engineering nature, with tremendously deep grooves.'

'By at least 1867, probably soon after the exhibition, the fountain had been supplied to Henry Reed's estate of Dunorlan, just outside Tunbridge Wells, where it remains today. Unfortunately it has suffered extensive damage. The border, which is made of Pulhamite stone (cement), used to be adorned with four identical kneeling Triton figures which spouted water into the pool, and were no doubt made of terracotta, but these have since disappeared. So far no extant examples of the figures have been traced, which is a pity as a model of a kneeling Triton figure (raised on a tazza bowl), together with a number of other items, was awarded a medal at the 1871 Paris Exhibition. As is also clearly visible in the picture, the statue of Hebe has disappeared, with the exception of her ankles. Furthermore, quite a number of pieces have broken off due, no doubt, to vandals; indeed the first time the fountain was examined by the author he found several throwing stones at it. . . '

Dunorlan Today

I first visited Dunorlan Park in 2001, and it was a very appropriate time to come, because plans were afoot to completely restore the park to its original glory with the help of a Heritage Lottery Grant. **Fig 5.5** shows the fountain and Cedar Avenue, taken at the time of that visit from the same spot as the 1871 sales brochure picture shown in **Fig 5.4** – the temple can just be seen through the trees at the top of the avenue.

The Council's Parks Department had made a magnificent contribution towards the development of a management plan aimed at the 're-establishment of the path system, car parks, water systems, rockeries and water features, and the re-creation and restoration of the Marnock and Pulham views as far as possible.' Parts of the plan were to replace the existing approach, entrance and car park, and to create an initial viewing area that would mimic the views that would have been seen from the terrace of Henry Reed's house.

Their efforts were not in vain, for their application for a Heritage Lottery Fund grant of £2.1m for this work was approved, to which the Town Council were required to add a further £0.7m. The approval process was not always smooth, and actually took no less than six years to complete, but, as my guide, Jeff Kempster, the Parks Manager, commented, 'it is better to arrive late than not to arrive at all'. The Friends of Dunorlan Park also worked hard to raise funds to enable them to make a contribution of £10,000 towards the restoration of the fountain, so this was a really collaborative venture by all interested parties.

Their vision was that visitors could arrive at the new initial viewing area, and take refreshments while they drank in the overall view of the estate. The plans included the reproduction of the original shoreline around the lake, and the screening of the roads in order to create the original impression that the estate extended far beyond its actual boundary – a device of which Marnock and James 2 would have whole-heartedly approved.

The work duly went ahead, and was almost completed by the end of 2004. The lake was emptied and relined; the raggedy cedar and fir avenue was felled and replaced by new Deodar Cedars; the fountain was taken down piece by piece, and restored and re-erected by specialist restorers; a massive underground tank designed to pump water into the fountain and the cascade was installed nearby – meaning year-round flow, even if the lake's water level is low – and the Grecian temple underwent an £80,000 restoration, including the specialist repainting of its interior.

At the Reopening Ceremony, Tunbridge Wells Borough Council's Head of Leisure Services, Nigel Bolton, was also delighted to be able to tell a reporter for the *Kent and Sussex Courier* [49] that the project had been 'kept on budget, and on time'. He added:

> 'We have tried to keep as many mature trees as possible, and ensure they are in good health. We have planted 260 new trees and 15,000 plants and shrubs: these would have been familiar to Victorian visitors . . . . It was always intended that the firs would be felled as soon as the cedars were of a reasonable size, but it never happened. So both grew, and many were lost or damaged. The cedars were sourced from Italy.'

One aspect of the park that really thrilled Mr Bolton was the 1860s Pulham rockery that, until the restoration, had been covered by rhododendrons – see **Fig 5.6**. There is a new boat store, and a new cedar-clad boat kiosk in place of the previous small boathouse. The car park layout was improved and resurfaced, and the cafe was completely refurbished. Managers also used the project as an opportunity to treat any injured geese, ducks and wildfowl, and the Greylag geese – which now number more than 100 – have gradually returned.

Mr Bolton concluded:

> 'There is a huge sense of achievement. We are enormously proud we completed this project, and brought it into such good conditions for future generations. We are looking forward to public reaction.'

Fig 5.6 *A rediscovered rockwork cliff face in the Park gardens*

Fig 5.7 *The restored cascade and Lily Pond in 2010*

I returned to Dunorlan Park in 2005 and 2010, and I was told that the public reaction had been overwhelming – a fact that was soon demonstrated to me by the very well patronised new café.

My tour began on the terrace, and I was amazed at how clean and fresh everything looked, compared with my initial visit. The process of clearing and replacing some of the old trees and shrubbery had opened up the vistas, and this made the whole park more intriguing, because it constantly tempted one to explore further.

The two features that I most wanted to see were the waterfall between the lake and the stream that feeds into the lower pool, and the newly refurbished fountain – and I was not disappointed. The waterfall has been stripped of its overgrowth; the rockwork is now clearly visible, and, normally, the water is flowing freely. (Sadly, my visit in 2010 coincided with a long period of drought, and the water was not 'flowing freely' when the picture in **Fig 5.7** was taken.)

However, the fountain was playing freely – as can be seen in **Fig 5.8** – and the Cedar Avenue has been completely replanted, so that the view in this picture now looks almost identical to the way it did in 1871 (Fig 5.4), apart from the fact that the 'four figures with trumpets'

around the basin, and the 'figures placed between the lines of trees' have not been replaced, in order to avoid the risk of vandalism. The fountain stands in the bowl of a natural amphitheatre, and Figs 5.4, 5.5 and 5.8 were all taken from the rim of the bank, looking straight up the Cedar Avenue, from a point where there used to be a summer house. A Mr Robson – in an article in an 1864 edition of the *Journal of Horticulture*[50] – describes the spot as follows:

> 'The ground rises on the opposite side of the basin (from the Avenue), and – the avenue ending there – a summerhouse, with another shrubbery, formed a very good termination. The summerhouse or grotto being slightly elevated, the rising ground with the two lines of fine trees looked remarkably well, while the mansion and sloping ground in front of it was also seen to great advantage.'

It is quite a steep climb to the temple at the top of the avenue, but there are plenty of alternative routes that one can take, along the paths that lead back towards the lake, and up through the old flower beds. **Fig 5.9** shows the temple as I approached it in 2005, and **Fig 5.10** looks back down the avenue to the fountain, and the spot behind it where the old rustic summer house once stood.

Fig 5.8 *The recently refurbished Hebe Fountain at Dunorlan Park in 2010 The 'four figures with trumpets' and 'figures placed between the line of trees' were not replaced for fear of vandalism. The original fountain is pictured in Fig 3.1a*

Fig 5.9 *The Grecian temple in 2005. The figure of 'The Dancing Girl' is just visible through the glass*

Fig 5.10 *The Dunorlan Fountain from the temple plateau*

Figs 5.11a and b *The Grecian Temple at Dunorlan Park*
a) (left) Temple and figure c.1940s
b) (above) Corner of rear wall

The Grecian Temple

This is an interesting building because, when viewed from below, it looks to be octagonal, whereas inside it is circular. Walk around it, however, and one discovers that the walls at the back are flat – as can be seen in **Fig 5.11b** – which reminded me somewhat of the summer house at Benington Lordship, shown in Fig 1.13. In fact, the more I looked at it, the more convinced I became that this was also built by James 2 – it is certainly situated at exactly the point where he and Robert Marnock would have placed a vantage point, because it has such a commanding view over the park and down the magnificent avenue of pines and Deodars to the fountain of which he was so proud. The Grecian style of the building also blends ideally with that of the fountain.

This made me wonder if the building may originally have been built as an open-sided summer house, rather than with enclosed sides, as it is today? The wooden paling across the central panel in the old photograph in **Fig 5.11a** certainly appears to support that view, and,

it was also confirmed by an older member of the gardening staff to whom I spoke in 2005, who said quite firmly that he remembered the open sides being closed in when he was a boy.

And what about the figure inside the temple? According to James Akehurst, in '*The Dunorlan Story*', it is suggested that Henry Reed originally built the temple to house a statue of his wife, Suzanna Reed, who died in 1860. However, the article by Mr 'W.H.' in the *Gardeners' Chronicle* of 1881, quoted earlier, refers to the statue as being that of Helen Douglas – from Sir Walter Scott's '*Lady of the Lake*' – with her dog Lufra, which indicates that this may have been installed after Henry Reed sold the property.

This must consequently be the figure that can be clearly seen in **Fig 5.11a**. It was replaced in 1951 by a statue of '*The Dancing Girl*', created by William Theed in 1885, which is just visible through the central glass panel in **Fig 5.9**, but, sadly, that statue was stolen in 2006, so now there is none!

Fig 5.13   *Pedestal for one of the old statues alongside the cedar avenue in Dunorlan Park*

Figs 5.12a and b   *Detail of the partly-cleaned ceiling inside the temple*

The inside of the temple is cylindrical, and the walls are very expertly plastered. A section of the Council's restoration report noted that the internal decoration indicated traces of an original decoration scheme that was remarkably similar to that of the interior of the main house, as described by Mrs Carminhow in the extract from *'The Dunorlan Story'* quoted above. The left-hand picture in **Fig 5.12** shows a small section of the wall taken during the initial stages of restoration, and, bearing in mind that James 2's team of craftsmen included specialist builders and plasterers, it is not stretching the realms of possibility too far to imagine that they may well have been responsible for the work inside here, as well as in the main house. Especially when one looks closely at the small detail shown in the right-hand picture – could the decorations have included a face at some time?

Finally, just outside the temple there is a pair of hollow bases on which once stood the garden figures that were originally spaced down the Cedar avenue. One of them is shown here in **Fig 5.13** – and doesn't that remind one of the pattern of the pillars of the garden wall at Highnam Court, shown in Figs 4.4 and 4.5?

All in all, there can be no doubt that the Tunbridge Wells Planning Team have succeeded in achieving their objective of recreating the original vision of Robert Marnock and James 2, in which all the main features of the gardens are designed to lure the visitor from one landmark to the next.

The picture of Dunorlan today could not be better summarised than it is in another quotation from James Akehurst's booklet:

'Here we have a park where there's a lake for boating, the big hill for running down and walking slowly up, secluded dells to explore, ducks to feed, lawns to picnic on, the waterfall, café, putting green and beautiful gardens. All these add up to a perfect afternoon with the children on a sunny summer's day. Dunorlan lies on the highest point in Tunbridge Wells, with a view to the south of fields and woods, most of which once belonged to the house. The park now covers an area of seventy acres. Belonging to the Borough Council, it was once the pleasure ground of the wealthy.'

What more encouragement would anyone need to spend a happy day looking around at this wonderful collection of Pulham features, all assembled in one place?

Also Noted:

1854	– *'Broomhills'*, Tunbridge Wells, Kent
1858	– Ponsbourne Park, Newgate Street, Hertfordshire
1859-60	– Fonthill Abbey, near Tisbury, Wiltshire
1859-62	– *'Berry Hill'*, Taplow, Buckinghamshire
1859	– Danesbury Park, near Welwyn, Hertfordshire
1862-67	– Welbeck Abbey, near Worksop, Nottinghamshire
1863-70	– *'The Hoo'*, Sydenham Hill Wood, S.E. London
1864-66	– The Preston Parks, Lancashire
1864-71	– *'Lockinge'*, near Wantage, Oxfordshire
1865-70	– Bromley Palace Gardens, Bromley, Kent
1865-92	– Poles Park, near Ware, Hertfordshire

- 6 -

BATTERSEA PARK

WANDSWORTH, LONDON

1865-1870

Fig 6.1 *The Waterfalls in Battersea* c.*1900* (Photograph by W T Goodhew)

The motivation behind the creation and development of Battersea Park during the 1840s was typical of the period. There used to be a tavern called The Red House in Battersea Fields, notorious for illegal drinking, racing and gambling, and it was decided to create a public park to:

> '. . . regulate and formalise behaviour; provide space and beauty
> for healthy exercise and pleasure; encourage moral conduct and
> a respect for – and pride in – Britain and the Empire.'[51]

A speculative builder named Thomas Cubitt envisaged the development of the park, with the surrounding land designated for

housing, and rough plans were drawn up by James Pennethorne – who had already contributed to the design of Regent's Park – in 1845. The Government passed an Act of Parliament the following year that enabled the Commissioners of Woods and Forests to lay out a Royal Park in Battersea.[52]

The site was originally flat and swampy, so 750,000 tons of material excavated from the Surrey Docks – supplied free of charge by Thomas Cubitt – was used to raise the level, and further material was used to create the general shaping of the ground. The profits made from the sale of the houses in Albert Bridge Road and Prince of Wales Drive helped to pay for the creation, in 1854, of the features in the park that they overlooked, such as the formal avenue, the serpentine carriage drive, the irregular lake, and its flower gardens and shrubberies.

The defining elements of the park – which still survive today – were designed and built by the first Park Superintendent, John Gibson, a pupil of Joseph Paxton. Paxton not only taught Gibson the fundamentals of design and planting, but also sent him on a plant-hunting mission to India. This inspired him to create the subtropical Garden in Battersea Park – one of its most dramatic features – and he was also responsible for:

> '. . . the elegant circulation patterns; the serpentine undulations of the lake, which create such a sense of anticipation in the visitor; the substantial mounds, planted with a range of trees and shrubs, separating the distinctive areas of the landscape, and the sequence of views across and through the park.'

Queen Victoria opened Battersea Park in 1858, but it was not until 1865 that James 2 was invited to construct:

> 'Waterfalls, Rocky stream, Cave for shady seat on the peninsula and in other parts of the Park.'[53]

He completed the work over two periods – the waterfalls and cave being constructed during his first visit in 1865-66, and the work *'in other parts of the park'* in 1870. Some three years later, the author of an article published in *The Garden* magazine was obviously much impressed by what he saw. He wrote:

> 'This is the first attempt at making a really picturesque rockwork that has been carried out in any London Park. Considered as such, its effect is very good indeed, and the imitation of natural rock very happy, as might be expected when we state that it was executed by Mr. Pulham, of Broxbourne, who has made most of the really effective rock-gardens in the country.
>
> '. . . the general effect of the whole, as seen from the other side of the lake, is very different and very satisfactory of its kind. As yet, the rocks are not sufficiently covered or garnished with vegetation to present the best effect, but already their appearance is highly satisfactory. This rock garden is not one prepared especially for rock plants, but rather for its picturesque effect in the park.'[54]

About eighteen months later, the *Gardener's Magazine* also published an article about Battersea Park, written by B Ebbs.[55] It reads:

> 'When we consider that the spot less than thirty years ago was a flat, open space from the Thames to Wandsworth Road, consisting of market gardens, with a path from the Red House, Battersea, to Clapham, the transformation of cabbage, turnip, potato and carrot fields to the present beautiful park (consisting

of 173 acres) decorated with such a variety of mounds, vistas, and rare and beautiful scenery, rockwork intercepted with trees and shrubs, it is marvellous what the revolutions of time, in a few years, have added to the Londoner's pleasure, almost in the very centre of this vast and smoky metropolis.

> 'The park was begun about the year 1856. Mr Gibson undertook the planting of the park in 1858, arranging the principal lakes, mounds, lawns etc. Mr Pulham, of Broxbourne, had the arrangement of the rockwork which was finished in 1871; and Mr Roger (Mr Gibson's successor) has displayed a considerable amount of horticultural ability in the arrangement of the shrubs and trees amongst the rocks, which has made the park one of the most romantic spots in or around London.'

It all looks and sounds idyllic, but, sadly, some of the rockwork features no longer exist, so it is not possible to admire them today. The waterfalls still do exist, however. They are situated on the mound beside the lake, and it has been said that their main function may have been to partially screen the view of Clapham Junction Station from that part of the park.

Before discussing these, however, it is interesting to see what they looked like in the early 1900s. The picture in **Fig 6.1** was taken by W T Goodhew, and with it he won the Amateur Photographer Bronze Medal at the Exhibition of Members' Work of the North Middlesex Photographic Club.

It is quite evident from this picture that everything was flowing nicely in those days, but there is evidence to show that problems developed with the water supply at sometime during the next twenty or thirty years. For some reason unbeknown to the present staff, there is a framed letter hanging in the Manager's Office at Battersea Park that was written by James Robert Pulham (James 4) on 29th July 1935 to Brig. Gen. Philip Maud, CMG, CBE, Chief Officer of the Parks Department at County Hall, London. It is reproduced here in Fig 6.4, and reads as follows:

> 'In the years 1865 and 1866 we constructed the Rock formation and Waterfalls in Battersea Park.
>
> 'Mr Pulham had a look at these recently, and it appears that the water is not now run over the falls, presumably on account of running to waste. This naturally detracts from the interest of the falls, and it occurs to us that you may possibly not be aware that a pumping arrangement could be installed, to draw the water from the lake, and pump it over the falls, then using the water over again and eliminating its waste.
>
> 'This could be worked by either an electric (if any current near) or petrol motor driving a small centrifugal pump, which would be housed either under the rock or in a wooden or other building,

which could if desired be more or less hidden by planting. The initial cost and upkeep of this arrangement if properly done is relatively small, and if this suggestion should appeal to you, we shall be pleased to give you further details. We may add that there is not much noise with this pump etc, and what there is, is silenced by the noise of the water coming over the fall.

'We trust you will pardon our suggestion, but we are naturally interested in our old works, and like to see them looking at their best.'

This letter may perhaps be an indication of the way the firm's workload was declining during the 1930s, but it seems likely that they were not invited to tender for this work as a result of it. In fact, the powers that be may not have even noticed that anything was amiss with their rockwork, although it is rather intriguing that they should have decided to frame the letter and hang it in their office.

Whatever the truth about that may be, it is interesting to read the comments of two expert writers some fifty years after this letter was written. Sally Festing – in an article for the *Journal of The Garden History Society* magazine in 1984[56] – commented that:

'. . . the entire outcrop seems to be Pulham stone, textured to make it appear more interesting, like a rough sedimentary pudding-stone. There is a low wall to create falls in front of the bridge; a narrow gorge in the hillside exposing the site of the cascade, and there are lumps scattered around the main concentration to give the effect of authenticity . . . It seems likely that James Pennethorne's brick pump house, dated 1861, was used in Pulham's water scheme.'

At almost the same time that Sally Festing's article appeared, Brent Elliott wrote an article for *Country Life* in which he also commented on the rockwork at Battersea Park:[57]

'Visitors to Battersea Park in London cannot fail to notice the various rockworks which ornament the grounds near the lake. Outcrops of boulders flank some of the paths, and a defile in the hillside exposes the site of a cascade. The impression created is of a geological fault near the lake, with strata of sandstone dipping inland and exhibiting a variety of patterns of erosion on those faces open to the air.

'Obviously, these rockworks have been arranged by man, and one may reflect on the ingenuity with which they have been placed. If some of the boulders are scrutinised carefully, an even more interesting form of erosion becomes apparent. In places, the sandstone texture of the rocks has been worn away to reveal darkened surfaces of brick in the middle of the boulders.'

Very soon after these articles appeared, Wandsworth Council finally decided to commission a restoration study. It was reported that the passage of time had resulted in some areas of the rockwork becoming eroded through the action of frost and the penetration of roots, thus exposing the core material of clinker and rocks, and a four-stage strategy was devised to remedy the situation.[58]

This is the point at which things started to go downhill. The first stage involved clearing the site of vegetation and other extraneous matter. Some areas of the rockwork then needed to be cleaned to enable a more thorough examination of the surfaces, but instead of using the normal archaeological tools of hand trowels and brushes, it was

Fig 6.2 *View across the lake from the cafeteria to the rockwork cliffs in 2001*

Fig 6.3 *Sections of the Pulhamite cliffs in Battersea Park, London, in 2001*

decided to use a high pressure water jet, drawing water from the lake! One can imagine the feigned surprise when it was discovered that this process merely served to further damage the already fragile surface of the rockwork, and open up the cracks even further.

So what to do next? The answer seemed to be quick and easy. Simply cover the worst bits with gunnite – a cement-based mortar especially adapted for spray application – and hope that nobody would notice! Fortunately, somebody did. Somebody at English Heritage noticed, and decreed that, from that point on, Pulham's rockwork constructions should be 'listed', and only restored under suitably qualified and experienced supervision.

Herein lies the crux of this story. A discussion with a partner of the firm of consultants who supervised this work revealed that, up to that point, they were actually quite proud of their achievements. From a purely technical point of view, they considered that they had managed to repair the surface damage to the rockwork, and that is what they had been asked to do. What they had failed to consider was their responsibility for the aesthetics of the project, but their answer to that was that they had no previous benchmark to work to. Up to that time, no large-scale restoration of Pulham rockwork had

ever been undertaken, so they effectively had to 'learn as they went along'. Time and the cost of labour were obviously critical factors in their considerations, and it must be remembered that one is talking here about a period before National Lottery funding started to become available for this sort of work. It is consequently doubtful that Wandsworth Council would ever have been prepared to fund a restoration project involving the use of specialised craftsmen for the time required to do the job properly. So perhaps it is fortunate that this massive act of 'restorative vandalism' was inflicted on the first major project of its kind, because it may at least have spared us from several more similar instances in the future.

If one looks at some of the pictures I took in Battersea Park in 2001, it is easy to understand why I – and English Heritage – was horrified by what I saw. **Fig 6.2** is the view of the 'cliffs' across the lake from the cafeteria, and **Fig 6.3** shows two close-up views of some of the rocks. The bottom rock in the left-hand picture is relatively untouched, but the rest look as if they have been 'mothballed'. On the other hand, the *'rough, interestingly-textured sedimentary pudding-stone'* surfaces – once admired by Sally Festing – have now been completely obliterated by the 'gunnite goo' that was sprayed all over them. A Pulhamite hunter's nightmare!

Fig 6.4 *The cascade basin*

Fig 6.5 *Cascade basin and pool in Battersea Park in 2001*

Fig 6.4 shows the basin of the cascade itself, in which the smoothing effects of the gunnite coating is plain to see, but the *pièce de résistance* must be the pool into which the cascade flows. This is shown in **Fig 6.5**, and looks nothing more than a solidified mess. Fig 6.4 also provides a sorry comparison with the picture in Fig 6.1, which was taken about 100 years earlier from almost exactly the same spot.

Thankfully, one only has to study the recent, careful restoration of Dunorlan Park in Tunbridge Wells, in Kent – a real success story discussed in Chapter 5 – to realise that some lessons have been learned from this catastrophe.

Also Noted:

1866 – Bedwell Park, Essendon, near Hertford, Hertfordshire

- 7 -

AUDLEY END
NEAR SAFFRON WALDEN, ESSEX
1867

Fig 7.1 *The Pond Garden at Audley End* c.*1926* (Photo © Country Life)

Just over the northern borders of Hertfordshire is Audley End, near Saffron Walden, in Essex. During the early years of the 17th century, Thomas Howard, the first Earl of Suffolk, replaced the existing house with a vast Jacobean mansion, of which the present house is only a one-third part.[59] In 1762, Sir John Griffin – later to become Lord Howard de Walden and first Baron Braybrooke – inherited the estate.

In 1763, he engaged Lancelot 'Capability' Brown, the most eminent landscape gardener of the day, to create a park in which man and nature could coexist harmoniously and peacefully. Brown transformed the park by removing barriers to allow views across the acres of great rolling pasture that lay beyond the old formal gardens.

The land was 'graded' – i.e. remodelled to remove uneven ground – and seeded with grass to produce a smooth sweep of pasture between the house and the western ridge of the Cam valley, along which a belt of trees was planted to create a sense of seclusion.

In order to simulate the rugged Alpine scenery of France and Switzerland, the fifth Lord Braybrooke decided in 1867 to construct a rockery and two ponds in what is now known as the Pond Garden. The picture in **Fig 7.1** dates from 1926, and the fountain in the fish pond – in the centre of this picture – has now been replaced, but the original consisted of intertwining fish supporting a shell-like basin. It was almost certainly by Pulhams, as was the rose pergola along the edge of the far path.

Fig 7.2 *Otter Pool in the Pond Garden at Audley End*

There is a second pond beyond the fish pond. This is called the Otter Pool – shown here in **Fig 7.2** – because it was originally built by Pulhams to house a family of otters. The official guide to the gardens at Audley End says that the first otter was a female called Paddy, purchased by Lord Braybrooke during a fishing trip to Connemara, in Ireland. When Paddy died, she was stuffed, and is now on display in case 56 in the natural history collection in the house. The otters entered their lodge through the entrance arch in the west wall of the pool, and the keeper was able to access this via a hatch in the footpath behind the pool. The fern and moss-clad fountain in the centre of the pool was intended to imitate a natural mineral spring.

The rockery itself runs along the south wall of the Pond Garden, and is covered with climbing shrubs, as can be seen from the picture in **Fig 7.3**. To enhance the 'Alpine' theme, the rugged landscape was combined with 'raging torrents of water' by cutting a channel parallel to the River Cam, which flows a few yards away, behind the rose pergola. There is a sluice to control the rate of flow of the water – first sharp left, and then sharp right – from the main river, and the rockwork extends all the way to the weir. James 2's rocks have consequently had to take the full force of the water at the points of the elbow for nearly 150 years, and, at the time of my visit, the water was rushing through this point at quite an alarming rate, as one can see from **Fig 7.4**.

Lord Braybrooke sadly lost two of his sons in the Second World War, and the estate passed to the state in 1948 in lieu of death duties. It was first opened to the public in 1950, and is now looked after, with great credit, by English Heritage. In addition to the extensive maintenance programmes that are involved, they have undertaken a number of planting schemes involving both trees and shrubs. Even more spectacularly, they have completely restored the nineteenth century parterre and the walled kitchen garden, so that the park today retains much of the form and appearance of the magnificent 18th century landscape created by 'Capability' Brown.

Also Noted:

1868-74	– Hutton Hall, Guisborough, North Yorkshire
1869	– Pierremont Park, Darlington, Co Durham
1870	– Pavilion Gardens, Buxton, Derbyshire
1870s	– Brogyntyn Hall, Oswestry, Staffordshire
1871	– *'High Leigh'*, Hoddesdon, Hertfordshire
1871	– *'Titsey Place'*, Oxted, Surrey
1872	– *'Buckfield Keep'*, Leominster, Herefordshire
1872-75	– The Aquarium, Brighton, Sussex
1873-74	– Sundridge Park, Bromley, Kent
1873-80	– *'Park Hill'*, Streatham, London
1873	– Smithills Hall, Bolton, Lancashire

Fig 7.3 *Rock garden, at one end of rose garden at Audley End*

Fig 7.4 *Water rushing round the elbow of the rocky stream that borders the Pond Garden at Audley End*

- 8 -

SANDRINGHAM

NORFOLK

1868-1905

Fig 8.1 *The west terrace and gardens at Sandringham c.1900 – with Pulham's Otford vases on the steps* (Photo © Country Life)

The recently formed firm of James Pulham and Son soon began to earn itself a reputation for artistry and good workmanship, and, in 1868, they received a very special commission – from HRH Prince Edward, The Prince of Wales.

Prince Edward married Princess Alexandra of Denmark in 1863, and they went to live at Sandringham, near King's Lynn, in Norfolk, which Prince Albert had bought for his son in 1862 as a coming-of-age present. Alexandra was passionately fond of flowers, and decided to create a 'world of flowers' in the gardens. This turned out to be a world into which she gradually retreated later in life, as she became increasingly deaf, and Edward was out and about pursuing 'other interests'.

The gardens were designed by William Broderick Thomas – one of the leading landscape gardeners of the time – although he did not

have a great reputation for innovation. He preferred instead to follow trends, and the popular trend of the 1860s was to react against the high formality of the more traditional Victorian lifestyle. 1870 also happened to be the year in which William Robinson published his new book, *The Wild Garden,* in which he extolled the virtues of planting indigenous flowers in the garden 'in a wild state'; since this was a view that would have found enthusiastic endorsement from Princess Alexandra, it was hardly surprising that Mr Thomas decided to adopt this principle into his plans.

His first major change was to move the old ornamental lake – which lay close to the west façade of the house – and create a lawn in its place, with a grassy bank leading up to the west terrace, as shown in **Fig 8.1**. He then created two new lakes with a number of cascades and rivulets further away – the upper lake being fed by a spring, and the lower lake by a stream. Rock gardens were also becoming

Fig 8.2 *The Sandringham Boat Cave*, c.*1870s* (Picture provided by Greg Kobett)

increasingly fashionable at this time, having by now progressed from the 18th century emphasis on grottoes and cascades to far more ambitious landscape creations that incorporated rocky terrains built from both natural and artificial rock.

This trend was largely due to the work and influence of James 2, and he was chosen to create these gardens at Sandringham – the boathouse and rock cliffs overlooking the upper lake being one of his most important commissions. One of his promotional pictures of the boathouse and surrounding rockwork taken during the 1870s is reproduced here as **Fig 8.2**.

The précis notes left by James 2 on the work he did at Sandringham refer only to:

'Waterfalls, rocky stream, and cave for boat house'. [60]

Yet, there can be little doubt that he would also have been involved in the general reshaping of the lakes and gardens, because this is exactly what he did for Henry Reed at Dunorlan Park in Tunbridge Wells just a few years earlier, as discussed in Chapter 5. This suggestion is supported by Fig 8.1, a *Country Life* picture dating from *c*.1900, which shows the west terrace and gardens at Sandringham – which are now laid to lawn – with a set of Pulham's Otford vases on each flight of steps.

James 2 recorded in his booklet that, when the work was finished,

'Mr. Broderick Thomas says, writing me from Sandringham, of the boat-cave thus formed there, "'Tis quite a work of art!" "Picturesque art" is what the editor of the *Art Journal* calls it.'

He felt sure that their Royal Highnesses would be delighted with everything, and he was absolutely correct because in 1895 the firm was awarded its first Royal Warrant. This was presumably because

of its work at Sandringham, although, according to Jennifer Davies, there may possibly have been a further reason. She recalls that:

'. . . a swan might have also had something to do with the honour. Mr Arthur Pulham, now in his eighties, and the last to carry the family name, told me that when his grandfather James went to supervise the work at Sandringham, he rescued the Prince of Wales (later Edward VII) who was being attacked by a swan, and the men became friends.' [61]

Sally Festing also had this to say about the boathouse:[62]

'By comparison with Battersea [see Chapter 6] the entire lichen-encrusted outcrop looks remarkably realistic – only a close inspection reveals a distinction between relatively unweathered Pulham stone and the well-eroded, rough, and sometimes bright orange carstone, coloured from its iron concretions. The squat carstone layers lie underneath, forming a template for the much deeper Pulhamite, which is bonded together with cement. Overall, the Pulhamite comprises by far the greater proportion of the works. The roof of the cave is composed of very large slabs of it, although there is some carstone in the supporting walls.

'The carstone, probably quarried from the Wolferton pits midway between King's Lynn and Hunstanton, is a lower greensand bed. Being such a soft stone, it could probably not be excavated in nearly such large blocks as the Pulhamite.'

The view across the lake to Sandringham House as it is today is shown in **Fig 8.4**, with the huge artificial boulders and rocks that form the 'supernatural' archway of the boathouse visible on the right.

Fig 8.3 (overleaf) *The boathouse and 'The Nest' at Sandringham* (Photo by Jenny Lilly)

Just to the right of the boathouse there is a cute little summer house called 'The Nest', which was built as a present for Queen Alexandra by her Comptroller, Sir Dighton Probyn VC, in 1913, and it soon became one of her favourite retreats – hence the name with which she christened it. As can be seen from **Fig 8.3**, it has a commanding view across the lake, and **Fig 8.5** is an imposing close-up picture of the steps and cascade that lead down from it to the lake shore. **Fig 8.6** shows another section of the rocky bank of the upper lake.

Fig 8.4 (left) *Upper lake, west lawns and boathouse at Sandringham* (Photo by Jenny Lilly)

Fig 8.5 (below) *Steps and cascade leading down from 'The Nest' to the lake at Sandringham* (Photo by Jenny Lilly)

Fig 8.6 (bottom) *Rocks along the edge of the main lake at Sandringham*

91

Fig 8.7 (left)   *'The Dell', with post-Pulham figure in rocky stream*

Fig 8.8 (below)   *A section of Pulhamite rockwork along the banks of the lower lake at Sandringham* (Photo by Jenny Lilly)

The picture in **Fig 8.7** is of 'The Dell' as it was in 2000 – 'The Nest' is just visible through the trees, and the statue in the stream is a modern addition. **Fig 8.8** shows a section of the rocky bank of the lower lake.

As far as is known, the boathouse and most of the rockwork was constructed in 1868, although James 2 does record that the firm paid another visit in 1876, and there is also visual evidence that he did further work after that, probably between 1890 and 1905.

Everything in the rest of the garden seemed to reflect Alexandra's vision of 'the perfect garden'. New trees, shrubs and flowers were brought in from all around the world, and the Princess's particular favourites were the new acers from Japan, which introduced a brilliance of autumn colour into the garden that had previously been unknown. The glade of elms and Scotch pines were underplanted with drifts of daffodils and narcissi, and the 'wild garden' with lily of the valley, bluebells, primroses, snowdrops, aconites and foxgloves, followed in summer by tumbling masses of sweet briars. Nearby was the imitation of wild woodland called 'The Dell' – a spot as natural and wild as Her Majesty could have wanted it to be.

One major feature with which I believe he was involved is the kitchen garden, across the road from the main estate. According to Scilla Latham[63] – a garden historian who has been researching the gardens at Sandringham – this garden was initially laid out in 1864, which indicates that it may have been done just prior to James 2's first visit. However, it wasn't until 1903 that the Prince and Princess of Wales – later to become King George V and Queen Mary – installed the wrought iron gates shown in **Fig 8.9**, and presented them to the future King Edward VIII. The brick piers, topped by terracotta urns, lead to what used to be a rose pergola, although the crossbeams have long since gone.

Half way down the avenue, there used to be a fountain – Ms Latham showed me an old photograph that shows it to have an ornate basin, decorated with rams' heads around the rim, and dolphin figures on top. As can be seen from Fig 8.9, this no longer exists, but has been replaced by a large decorated Italian garden urn, very similar to the ones shown in Fig 3.22. All of these features were added in 1905, and are absolutely typical of Pulhams' style, so I am in no doubt that this section of the walled garden was constructed by James Pulham and Son.

Another intriguing item was the fine terracotta coat of arms on the side of the main house, pictured in **Fig 8.10**. This was put here sometime after the building was restored and extended following a fire in 1891, so could well date from *c*.1905. Once again, its provenance may be difficult to establish, but – as will be noted elsewhere in the book – there are similar coats of arms at other sites on which the Pulhams are known to have worked.

Whether or not they came back once more to construct 'The Nest' is not certain, but I can't help feeling that this, too, might well be a Pulham construction. I have so far found no documentary evidence to substantiate this, but it is certainly a nice idea.

Fig 8.9 (above) *Entrance gates to the kitchen garden* (Photo by Jenny Lilly)

Fig 8.10 *Coat of arms on the side of the 1891 addition to the main house* (Photo by Jenny Lilly)

The gardening staff numbered just under one hundred in those days, and there were still about sixty at the time of the outbreak of war in 1914, but the death of Alexandra in 1925, followed by the death of King George V in 1936, and the Second World War from 1939-45, all contributed to a steep decline in numbers, with the consequent steady deterioration in the condition of the estate. However, the gardens were thankfully restored and improved by the efforts of King George VI during the years following the war.

The current head gardener, Martin Woods, heads up a core team of only seven, although he at least has more mechanised assistance than did his predecessors. He is very proud of the gardens, and has an especially warm spot in his heart for 'his' Pulhamite. He has worked steadily to return it as nearly as possible to its original state, and is amazed at how well it has been naturally retained.

- 9 -

ST FAGANS CASTLE
NEAR CARDIFF, WALES
1872-1876

The building of the present St Fagans Castle was begun by Dr John Gibbon *c*.1580, but completed by Sir Edward Lewis, who bought it in 1616. It remained in his family until Elizabeth Lewis – daughter of his last male descendant – married Other Windsor, 3rd Earl of Plymouth in 1730.[64] The eventual heiress of this branch of the Windsor family married into the family of Clive of India, and became Windsor-Clive. A later descendant of this family became Earl of Plymouth (on the 3rd creation of the title), and the family eventually gave St Fagans Castle and its surrounding estate to the County of Glamorgan, and it has for many years now been used as the National Museum of Wales – Museum of Rural Life. The castle itself is a museum, and, in the grounds, many buildings have been transferred from all over Wales to show what rural life was like in days gone by.

It is indeed a fascinating place to visit, but the focus of this particular chapter is the rock garden – indeed, it has as much to do with the plans for the landscaping as it does with the gardens themselves. Lady Mary Windsor-Clive hired Pulham & Co. to construct a rock garden for her in 1872, but, although she agreed in principle to some preparatory work being done during that year, it seems that discussions were long and protracted, and it was not until 1876 that (most of) James 2's plans were approved, and the final work was completed.

Thanks to the Glamorgan Records Office, some fascinating documents that relate to work done for Lady Mary by the firm have been preserved. These include various invoices and correspondence, and also James 2's original coloured plan, which is reproduced as **Fig 9.1**.

It is only possible here to provide some indication of the full-sized original – in pen and watercolour – which actually measures roughly 36 x 24 ins. It is nevertheless possible to see the care and attention to detail that James 2 took with his work. (The key to the plan is reproduced at the bottom of these pages.)

What more could he do – other than append an especially composed poem to convey his vision of the completed garden? In fact, this is not quite so far-fetched as it might at first sound, because James 2 appears to have been very fond of poetry. His promotional booklet[67] contained several poetic quotations, and concluded with an original poem of no less than 25 verses!

He also appended poems to the plans he submitted to his clients, and Lady Windsor-Clive was no exception. Part of it can be seen in the bottom right-hand corner of **Fig 9.1b**, and the full script of it is reproduced overleaf:

Key to Fig 9.1a

A	Is principal waterfall about 4ft 6ins high with ford across in line of present road, which I suppose is required for occasional use, for such a narrow oblong lattice may serve to be laid, and removed as required, so as it remains to ford over, if not a low bridge across.[65]	**F**	Is upper waterfall of about 2 ft, where the stepped fall now is. This and the altered form of the banks around this Pond is proposed to alter the present formal shape.
B	A rustic footbridge – the best place to see upstream, and view waterfall at 'A'. If bridge at 'A', this may be a ford by stepping stone here at 'B'.[66]	**G G**	Are inlets from the formal arches under the wall so as to conceal them, and, with the clump formed at . . .
C	Large Ash tree, with seat under, and path round it.	**H**	A clump to hide the pier between arches, and planted as shown, so that, by raising the ground each side of this pond with soil out of stream, and planting, I hope to hide the wall, which is at present objectionable.
D	First of lower ponds, thus altered from this ugly formal shape to a naturalistic form, with another waterfall of 2 or 3 ft into next pond.	**I**	A Ford across upper stream, or maybe a second rustic footbridge.
		J	A Rocky Island.
E	Is a Yew Tree with seat, and path round it.	**K**	Island with Weeping Willow, as it is so broken of late, needs a new one. Also two or three others along course of stream.

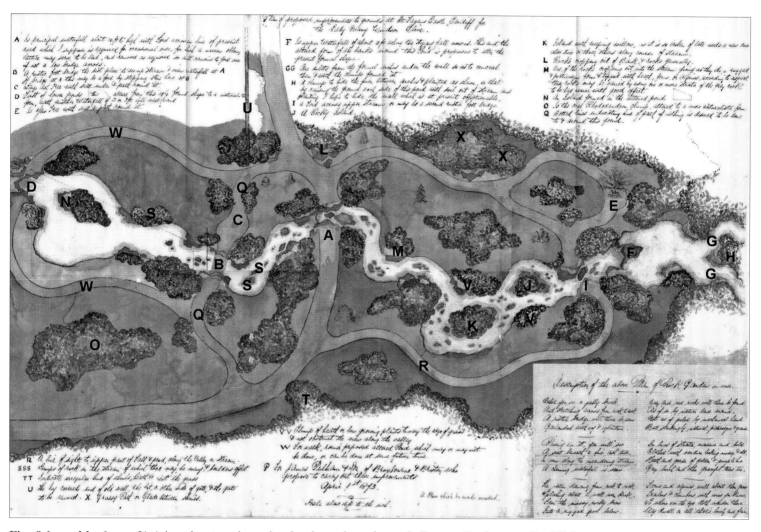

Figs 9.1a and b *James 2's ink and watercolour plan for the rock garden at St Fagans Castle, near Cardiff, for Lady Mary Windsor-Clive, dated 1st April 1873* (Reproduced by permission of the Glamorgan Record Office)

L	Rocks cropping out of bank, and rocks generally.	**S S S**	Lumps of rock in the stream, of which there may be many, and boulders effect.
M	One of the rocks cropping out into the stream, giving as they do a rugged and picturesque form, and topped with heath, ferns or Alpines, according to aspect. These rocks may be varied by using one or more strata of the grey rock, to be had nearer, with good effect.	**TT**	Indicates irregular line of shrubs, heath etc next the grass.
		U	The ivy-covered end of old wall – the bit on the other side of the gate, and the gate to be removed.
N	An island formed in the altered pond.	**V V**	Clump of heath or low growing plants to vary the edge of grass, and not obstruct the view along the valley.
O	Is the oval Rhododendron clump, altered to a more naturalistic form.	**W**	For walk around proposed altered pond, which may or may not be done, or can be done at some future time.
Q	Dotted lines indicating line of path if nothing is desired to be done to and around this pond.	**X**	Grassy path or glade between shrubs.
R	A line of sight to upper part of fall and pond, along the valley or stream.	**P**	For James Pulham and Son, of Broxbourne and Brixton, who propose to carry out these improvements – 1st April 1873. (Scale about 16ft to the inch)

Description of James 2's Plan of Rock Garden in Verse

Behold, you see a pebbly brook,
And stretching across from rock to rock
A rustic bridge will there be seen,
Garlanded with ivy and eglantine.

Passing o'er it, you will see
A seat beneath a fine Ash tree.
In view along the meandering stream
A charming waterfall is seen.

The water dancing from rock to rock,
Splashing about a well-worn block,
From the mossy rocky brow
Into a rugged pool below.

Then flowing along the valley so fine,
O'er rocky beds, it will ripple and shine
Among great boulders of other days,
Turning hither and thither many ways.

Along a circuitous path you keep.
You will, now and again, get a peep
Through a well-formed rich and grassy glade
Not as if by man were made.

There will be heaths and shrubs all evergreen
Some variegated will be seen;
Also the golden and sable yew,
Bright hollies, and plants of varied hue.

Grey and red rocks will there be found,
As if so by nature laid around,
Not as if piled by mechanical hand,
But strikingly natural, picturesque and grand.

In lines of strata, massive and bold,
Clothed with verdure, looking mossy and old,
Heath and gorse of golden and purple hue,
Grey birch and other graceful trees too.

Ferns and Alpines will about them grow,
Trailers and climbers, with ivies you know,
So where e'er the eye doth wander there,
May dwell on all that's lovely and fair.

The old roads will exist to be trodden again.
The ancient wall will also remain
Where our old, old friend, the ivy green
Helps to enrich the picturesque scene.

As a scene of picturesque beauty is a treasure,
To view it a source of frequent pleasure.
Where harmony of form and colour combined
Is by light and shade all well defined.

Excuse me, Lady, I pray thee,
If enthusiastic I appear to be,
For without a little, may lack success,
'Tis my darling theme, I do confess.

Some of these verses – especially the last – are very reminiscent of those published in his booklet, and whether or not this would qualify James 2 for the exalted position of Poet Laureate, there can be no doubt that it provides a fascinating insight into the character and nature of the man – a poetic visionary in both his work and his thoughts.

According to the correspondence that followed the completion of this plan, it seems that Lady Mary insisted on working to a very tight budget. James 2 obviously preferred to keep things as flexible as possible, so the work was put in hand, and assessed and paid for in stages. Lady Mary ignored James 2's claim for £17 to cover his initial visit and the preparation of the plan, so he eventually insisted on an advance of £50 before starting further stages of the work. These financial differences can easily explain why the completion of the garden was delayed, and perhaps also why some of the features proposed in the plan were not implemented.

The Garden Today

Much of it still remains, however. Situated in a small north-to-south valley, overlooked by the castle to the south-east, and set into grounds of some 105 acres, this is by no means a large rock garden by Pulham's standards, but it is nevertheless extremely pleasant and peaceful.

The stream flows down the valley from north to south, and the paths on either side of the upper stream – features **M** to **H** – are somewhat straighter than James 2 suggested. The planting is mainly heather, but the weeping willow – at the spot marked **M** – and the yew date from that period. There is only one long island, instead of the two shown on the plan, and the landscaping and ponds are also rather less 'picturesque' in the lower stream – features **D** to **A** – than indicated. In view of the fact that the work was carried out in phases, it is not possible to say which sections were done at which time.

The central stream and island were 'rockified' using mostly the natural stones – occasionally 'locked' together with Pulhamite – quarried from the estate during the initial preparatory stage in 1872. This is consequently not rockwork in the 'spectacular' sense – it is a charmingly natural scene of a pretty stream meandering gently down towards the ponds at the lower levels. **Fig 9.2** shows a very shallow waterfall, with flat-topped rocks jutting out from the banks on either side, and stepping stones just below. The stream passes a lovely weeping willow, spreading its boughs across the water on the southern side of the bridge – at Point **A** on the Plan – and then enters the lower ponds, where there is another set of stepping stones.

There was a major project to restore and clean the water gardens at St Fagans in 2003. The area around the upper stepping stones and small waterfall was given a new lease of life, and three trees were planted on the island, which was also graced by the addition of two Goscombe John statues, erected by the Art Department of the National Museum of Wales. Best of all, though, is the charming Pulhamite bridge and waterfall, at point **A** in the Plan, and pictured here in **Fig 9.3**.

Fig 9.2 *Stepping stones just below the very shallow waterfall, following a major restoration and cleaning project in early 2004* (Photo by Juliet Hodgkiss)

Fig 9.3 *The rustic Pulhamite bridge and waterfall at St Fagans in 2004* (Photo by Juliet Hodgkiss)

There is also an intriguing story to tell about the Italian Garden at St Fagans. There is a small fountain there that apparently dates back to 1855, and **Fig 9.4** is a picture from the National Museum Archives dated *c*.1902. It appears to have all the hallmarks of a Pulham piece, but has since been replaced by another – pictured in **Fig 9.5** – that could also have come from the Broxbourne manufactory. This one still plays, but why was it changed, and when was it installed?

Perhaps James 2 installed the original around 1855, and it was on the basis of that – and their growing reputation for the construction of picturesque rock gardens – that Lady Mary decided to invite them back between 1872 and 1876 to landscape further improvements to the gardens more distant from the house.

A Poetic Footnote

I cannot close this Chapter without quoting another 'Pulham Poem' that came my way by pure chance, soon after I started my research into the firm's work. In my Introduction to this book, I explained how my great-grandfather, William, moved to Hoddesdon in 1864-65 to begin working for Pulhams at nearby Broxbourne. His younger brother, George, moved down from Great Bardfield in Essex – their birthplace – to join him and lodge with him.

During my efforts to trace my family roots in the Great Bardfield area, I discovered a third cousin of whose existence I had no previous knowledge, and it transpired that he had recently discovered a piece of paper in his loft that, until then, had completely puzzled him. It was a poem about rockwork that was written in exactly the same style as that used by James 2 in his booklet, and in his plan for St Fagans.

A cleaned-up copy of this poem is reproduced here in **Fig 9.6**. The things that immediately intrigued me, however, were the names at the bottom, which show quite clearly that it was written by George

Fig 9.4 (above) *The fountain at St Fagans prior to 1900* (Photo reproduced by permission of the St Fagans National History Museum)

Fig 9.5 (left) *The fountain today*

Ferns and Rockwork.

By a LOVER OF NATURE.

SINCE the fern has become such a rare plant,
It makes our hearts for ferneries pant;
We love to see them natural grow
Where the gushing waters flow.

Growing amongst the rugged rocks,
Creeping o'er the projecting blocks,
Shooting forth their evergreen heads
From underneath the massive beds.

We love to wander, as if we by accident fell,
Upon some rocky stream or dropping-well;
Where we find water dropping from various heights,
In small streamlets and form stalactites.

We love to resort to some quiet nook,
Where we can enjoy a lounge with a paper or books
And to ponder over the works of Shakespeare or Burns,
To admire the rocks and lovely ferns.

Yet many an estate of this scenery is still left bare,
Because we have not been invited there.
To beautify it with our natural rocks,
Built with our patent cement in large rugged blocks.

Large stones by us are placed so exact,
That the joints appear as a natural crack;
Leaving plenty of space for ferns to thrive in,
Likewise forming rocky streams for fish to dive in.

In the beautiful fernery of the grand Aquarium
How well the rocks look as we approach near them.
We see here how well they have studied the line of strata,
And to detect it from nature 'tis no easy matter.

Have we not heard of that firm of great repute,
Who our taste is sure to suit?
To fail in their endeavours to please they seldom have done:
I am alluding to the work the Rock Makers have done.

GEORGE HITCHING.

Fig 9.6 *'The Hitching Poem'*

Hitching, and 'produced' or 'published' by William Hitching, George's older brother. This could consequently provide some clue as to how this sheet came into the possession of my cousin, whose name is also George – maybe someone passed it on to him in the belief or supposition that he might be related to the writer of the poem? The answer to this conundrum will probably never be known, but it does raise another question. Were the 'Pulham Poems' actually written by James 2 himself, or by one or both of the two Hitching brothers who worked for him during that period? It doesn't really matter, but it nevertheless conjures up the image of two, or possibly more workmen musing and making up poetry as they worked with their 'patent cement', building those 'large rugged blocks'.

Also Noted:

1870 – Singleton Hall, Singleton, Lancashire
1871-1906 – *'Highland Gardens'*, New Barnet, Greater London

- 10 -

SWISS GARDEN

OLD WARDEN, BEDFORDSHIRE

1876

Fig 10.1 *The tufa-lined entrance tunnel of the fernery at the Swiss Garden, Old Warden*

The development of the Swiss Garden at Old Warden, Bedfordshire, is thought to have been the work of the third Lord Ongley, who inherited the property in 1814.[68] Planting was simple, featuring few of the exotic plants that thrive there today. It is called the Swiss Garden because it was deliberately styled in the manner of the 'Swiss Picturesque', and is made up of a series of contrived vistas, leading the eye along evergreen alleys towards ornate or rusticated architectural features, such as the Swiss Cottage and the Indian Kiosk.

The estate was sold in 1872 to Joseph Shuttleworth (1819-1883), a Lincolnshire boatbuilder and co-founder of the successful engineering firm of Clayton and Shuttleworth, who specialised in building steam engines and agricultural machinery.[69] He pulled down the whole of the original house, and built the gothic-style Shuttleworth Mansion that stands there today.[70] He also remodelled the garden by introducing some typically Victorian touches, and commissioned the landscape architect Edward Milner to plan the new drives.

A central feature of the garden is a magnificent sunken glass-domed fernery with two entrance tunnels – each of which is lined with rough tufa, and has stained glass windows let into the sides. In plan, it is arranged in the form of a rough crucifix, with the fernery in the centre, but the entrance tunnels that span out from this are set at a very slight angle to each other, so that it is impossible to see directly from the end of one to the end of the other – thus enhancing the air of mystery.

Fig 10.2 *The rock-lined fernery of the Swiss Garden, Old Warden*

This is where James 2 became involved – either as a result of his growing personal reputation, or because Milner recommended him from the time they worked together in the Preston parks some ten years previously. The framework of the fernery was built in 1830, so the Pulhams had nothing to do with that, but there is an inscription of '1876' above the entrance door, which is presumably the date of their work on the lining of the entrance tunnels, and on the rockwork in the fernery itself. Maybe they put the sign there as an indication of their professional satisfaction for a job well done?

The Swiss Garden is not mentioned in James 2's promotional booklet,[71] but this is no doubt because it was completed after the booklet was submitted for publication *c*.1877. However, a note that appears in the English Heritage database describes it as a:

> 'Semi-circular building with glass dome. Reached along passages clad with Pulhamite stone (including stalactites) and lit with stained glass windows.'

The simple glazed entrance door provides no clue from the outside as to what may lie within, but step through, and one can immediately see why James 2 had every reason to be proud of his work. One finds oneself in the tufa-lined passageway, dimly lit from the stained glass door and a few small stained glass windows along one wall. This is shown in **Fig 10.1**, and, as one steps out of the gloom of the tunnel, one enters the dazzling light of the cast-iron dome that forms the central fernery, pictured here in **Fig 10.2**.

An article in the *Journal of Horticulture and Cottage Gardener*[72] carried an article about the Swiss Garden, from which the following extract is quoted:

> 'Almost in the centre of the grounds, and hidden from view, but for the glimpse of a dome of glass, is a glass structure with a semicircular roof. It appears to have been formed to shelter the old wisterias that cover the roof. This almost buried structure is entered by long passages, into which light is admitted here and there through stained glass windows. These arched corridors were originally of plain brickwork, but they have been transformed into stalactite caverns by Mr Pulham, of Broxbourne, who, with great skill, has imparted to the interior a singularly romantic appearance. In the walls, pockets have been formed for ferns and other suitable plants. This rugged, grotesque, and almost subterranean fernery comes as a surprise from the great expanse of smooth lawn (outside).'

Fig 10.3 *The rocky banks of the stream at Old Warden*

Moving out into the gardens from the central fernery, there are two pools, and these, too, pre-date Pulham's work. However, he must have been involved in remodelling them, because there are some Pulhamite rocks around the banks (**Fig 10.3**) and supporting the small ornamental bridge that is definitely post-Pulham. There was some restoration work in the 1990s, both around the lake and along the wall of the Punt Cave. Although carefully done, they do not have quite the 'naturalistic' or 'rustic' feel of a Pulham original.

There is also a pathway that leads into the Swiss Garden from the Shuttleworth Mansion. This is the 'Garden Walk', and, shortly before entering the garden, it passes through an underpass that dips under an old cattle track – a feature that acts as a gateway between real life and fairy tale, emphasising the other-worldliness of the Swiss Garden itself. The balustraded bridge (**Fig 10.4**) is very reminiscent in style of other Pulham bridges found elsewhere. As can be seen from **Fig 10.5**, however, there has recently been a 'repair' on the underpass side, and it is a shame that whoever did the restoration did not bother to match the colour or texture of the original bricks.

Lack of money after the Second World War meant that it was only possible to maintain the gardens at a very minimal level, and they deteriorated steadily until 1976, when the Richard Ormonde Memorial Trust decided to lease them to the Bedfordshire County Council for a period of 45 years. They restored them, and opened them to the public in 1981.

Fig 10.4 *Driveway bridge at Old Warden – note the rusticated coating of the brickwork and terracotta balusters*

Fig 10.5 *Driveway tunnel at Old Warden*
(Photo by Malcolm Amey)

- 11 -

MADRESFIELD COURT

MALVERN, WORCESTERSHIRE

1876-1879

Fig 11.1 *Watercolour of Madresfield Court* c.*1889* (Photo reproduced by kind permission of Lady Morrison)

In a way, the previous two chapters serve as a sort of 'intermission' in this study of the work carried out by James Pulham and Son, since they focus mainly on their major projects prior to the publication of James 2's promotional booklet c.1877.[73] If one pursues this line of thought, one could say that this chapter effectively marks the beginning of the second part of the story, because, from here on, there are very few specific date checks that enable the historian to establish exactly when many of the later Pulham projects were carried out.

The dates ascribed to them are therefore based either on evidence provided by local historians or archivists – or others immediately associated with the various sites concerned – or on conclusions drawn from other information available. They must consequently be accepted as tentative suggestions, and one must also accept that it is often easy to look around a site of which one has no previous knowledge, and claim that it is 'likely to be by Pulhams' on the basis that some of its features appear to carry their very characteristic signatures. It is therefore possible that someone may come along later and prove otherwise, but this should not be allowed to detract from the enjoyment of what one sees.

I have often been asked if Pulhams had a sort of catalogue of features and designs that they used or adapted for particular sites. There is evidence that some clients wanted something similar to a feature that had been created for someone else. However, basically each

Fig 11.2 *The visitors' early view of the rock garden, with dropping well, at Madresfield Court*

project was tailor-made to suit its own individual geological situation, and the financial circumstances of the client – as was demonstrated in Chapter 9, which was devoted to the development of the garden at St Fagans Castle, near Cardiff.

This chapter features the rock garden at Madresfield Court – a splendid moated Elizabethan manor at the foot of the Malvern Hills, with nearly seventy acres of beautiful gardens. It can trace its origins back to the de Braci family in the twelfth century, from whom it was handed on to the Lygon family through marriage in the fifteenth century. William Lygon was created the first Earl of Beauchamp in 1815, and the fifth Earl of Beauchamp inherited Madresfield in 1863. It was he who commissioned James 2 to construct the rock

garden in 1876.[74] **Fig 11.1** is from a watercolour of the front elevation painted *c*.1889.

This is commonly regarded as being one of Pulhams' masterpieces. The garden is built entirely of Pulhamite, and stands on three separate levels – more than 30-ft high in places.[75] Some might regard this garden as being rather more 'theatrical' than 'natural', due to the comparatively small space in which it was built. By comparison, the rock and water gardens at Waddesdon, in Buckinghamshire – discussed in the next chapter – can also be described as 'grand' in scale, but are spread over a much larger area, with the result that they are more naturally proportioned than the garden at Madresfield. **Fig 11.2** is a view that greets the visitor when approaching down the

Fig 11.3 *Underneath the Madresfield arches*
(Photo by Jenny Lilly)

Fig 11.4 *The second archway at Madresfield*

entrance path, and gives some idea of the sheer scale of the central section, with a dropping well at its base. **Figs 11.3** and **11.4** are pictures of two of the towering archways that span the path – the one in Fig 11.4 being at least 12-15 feet high, with a massive 'keystone' rock suspended in the centre that looks as if it might easily be dislodged by the vibration caused by someone either brave or foolish enough to walk beneath it. **Fig 11.5** is a close-up of the stratification 'necklace' that binds the 'rocks' together.

There is also another amusing signature here that can be found in several other Pulham gardens – a 'Pulham face'. This is not immediately obvious, but it stands out prominently once it has been noticed. It is shown here in **Fig 11.6**.

Fig 11.5 *Example of the rock stratification at Madresfield* (Photo by Jenny Lilly)

Fig 11.6 *A flight of steps and a 'Pulham Face' on the end of a rock at Madresfield* (Photo by Jenny Lilly)

Fig 11.7 *The inscription stone at Madresfield* (Photo by Jenny Lilly)

Fig 11.8 (below) *The Mercury Fountain at Madresfield* c.*1907* (Photo © Country Life)

It is interesting to note that the actual style, or 'pattern', of these striations tended to vary slightly from one Pulham rock-builder to another, so that, if one had a list of all their names, it might even be possible to determine the actual craftsman responsible for each construction. In this case, it was probably Mr J Pegram – the clue being provided on an inscription stone tucked away in a narrow crevice near the entrance (**Fig 11.7**), which reads.

> 'This work By Mr J Pulham, Broxbourne, AD 1878-79. Workmen R Pegram, Boss, J Stracey, J Jonson, Fini July 18.'

The Earl of Beauchamp was obviously happy with Pulhams' work at Madresfield, because there is a short testimonial appended to the firm's *Garden Ornament Catalogue* c.1925 that quotes him as writing:

> 'I am well satisfied with what you have done.'

Since this letter was written in 1890 – some twelve years after the rock garden was completed – it is possible that he may have been referring to another well-known Pulham artefact at Madresfield.

Fig 11.9 *'The Mercury Pool' in its immaculately-maintained gardens in 2007*

This is the terracotta figure of Mercury after Giambologna,[76] which stood in the 'Mercury Pool' in another part of the gardens – pictured here in **Fig 11.8** as it was shown in *Country Life* on 30th March 1907. Notice the quatrefoil shape of the basin, which was used in a number of Pulhams' water features. The figure of Mercury has now been removed for safety reasons, but the original basin remains today, albeit in need of some repair. **Fig 11.9** is of the basin taken some 100 years later.

The eighth and last Earl of Beauchamp died in 1979. His niece, Lady Morrison, the present occupant, has also happily taken over the duties of 'Head Gardener', and began a large-scale replanting project in 2002.

Also Noted:

1877-80	St Stephen's Green, Dublin, Eire
1878	Mesnes Park, Wigan, Lancashire
1878-98	Insole Court, Llandaff, Cardiff
1879-85	Bearwood College, Wokingham, Berkshire
1880	Heythrop Park, Chipping Norton, Oxfordshire
1880	Ware Park Manor, Hertford, Hertfordshire

- 12 -

WADDESDON MANOR
WADDESDON, BUCKINGHAMSHIRE
1881-1892

Fig 12.1 *One of the grottoes at the top of 'Tulip Patch Hill'* (Photo by Jenny Lilly)

Waddesdon Manor is, in its own way, even grander than Madresfield, because it covers a much wider area. Baron Ferdinand de Rothschild, nephew of Lionel and Charlotte Rothschild, who owned Gunnersbury Park in London – another site on which James Pulham and Son worked – built it during the late 1870s, and everything the Baron did was on a monumental scale. He was not the world's most patient man, and once he had decided that he wanted something, he wanted it in a hurry. Lord Beaconsfield is reputed to have commented, after visiting Waddesdon Manor: 'With the help of a Rothschild, the Almighty could have made the world in *much* less than seven days!'[77]

One of the features he wanted was a rock and water garden – a feature he had seen in his uncle's garden at Gunnersbury in 1874, and also in the rock garden on the Royal Estate at Sandringham in 1868 – discussed in Chapter 8 – the home of his great friend, HRH The Prince of Wales, and future King Edward VII. Both of these had been the work of Pulhams, so they came to Waddesdon with strong credentials.

There are actually three separate areas of the Waddesdon estate on which the Pulhams worked. One was around the top of the North

Drive that leads up from the front of the main house, and extends around to the top of the Aviary Garden to the north west. Another is the Water Garden, linked to the dairy – a short distance away to the north east – and the third is the 'Tulip Patch', on a neighbouring hilltop to the mansion.

Accounting records for the period[78] indicate that their first project at Waddesdon was on the 'Tulip Patch'. This was done during the period in 1881-82, when they constructed two grottoes to house some goats that the Baron wanted his guests to be able to view from across the valley, on the mansion terraces. The grottoes were brick built internally, but covered in natural rocks on the outside (**Fig 12.1**).

There is also some rockwork surrounding these grottoes, and the rocks are obviously natural, which ties in with the fact that they wanted to utilise some of the rock remaining from the decapitation of the hill on which the house was built. Unfortunately, using natural rock in this sort of structure means that it is difficult to achieve the simulated stratification effects that the Pulham rock builders so often achieved with Pulhamite.

Fig 12.3 (opposite) *The water garden at Waddesdon in 2010* (Photo by Jenny Lilly)

They had their chance to demonstrate what they could do with artificial rocks just two or three years later, however, in 1884-85. As previously noted, this was when they created the water garden in the area of the dairy, which lies just over the far side of 'Tulip Patch Hill' from the Mansion, at the foot of a neighbouring hillside on which used to be the old glasshouses. These have now all been removed, and a quaint little rustic summerhouse stands in their place, with a commanding view over the water garden, which was originally fed by springs flowing from the hills around, and also by water run off from the gigantic glasshouses directly above. Today, some water runs from a spring, and some is fed from land drainage, with the water recirculated by pumps.[79] **Fig 12.2** is a reproduction from *Country Life* that shows what the garden looked like *c.*1898, while **Fig 12.3** shows how little things had changed during the next 110 years. **Fig 12.4** looks back across the pool to the steps, and the summer house above.

Fig 12.2 *The water garden as it was* c.*1898* (Photo © Country Life)

Fig 12.4 (left)   *Looking back from the water garden to the steps and summer house* (Photo by Jenny Lilly)

Fig 12.5 (above)   *The archway over the path that runs around the water garden at Waddesdon*

There is a massive archway over the path that runs around the water garden – **Fig 12.5** – that is an excellent example of the rock-builder's craftsmanship, and must be among the best quality Pulhamite anywhere, although, incredibly, this garden was abandoned, and fell into total disrepair during the war years of 1939-45. It was then effectively forgotten until 1989, when Beth Rothschild – daughter of Jacob, the 4th Lord Rothschild – first heard about its existence from a former Waddesdon head gardener. She brought in specialist garden designers to supervise the clearance and restoration of the site, and the garden gradually re-emerged, miraculously intact. The lake edges are still sound; the mossy steps that lead down from the glasshouses have been uncovered, and the paths reinstated.

Fig 12.6 *Entrance to the Water Garden Goat Grottoes at Waddesdon* (Photo by Jenny Lilly)

Fig 12.7 *Inside the Water Garden Goat Grottoes at Waddesdon* (Photo by Jenny Lilly)

Further along the path there is another very large rock outcrop, and it is only when one gets round to the other side that one notices a gap in the rocks that is actually the entrance to another large grotto. This is shown in **Fig 12.6**, and, if one ventures inside, one discovers that the core was actually divided into two compartments – **Fig 12.7** – and it transpires that this was the new 'living quarters' to which the goats were transferred after they had outstayed their welcome at the top of 'Tulip Hill'.

Continuing along the side of the 'Dairy Pool', another large outcrop of 'rocks' comes into view – **Fig 12.8**. On close inspection, this looks quite a bit 'rougher' than the water garden archway and goat

Fig 12.8 *Rock outcrop near the 'Dairy Pool'* (Photo by Jenny Lilly)

Fig 12.9 *A series of vertically placed shells in the rock face near the 'Dairy Pool'*

Fig 12.10 *The small cascade near the 'Dairy Pool'* (Photo by Jenny Lilly)

grotto, and there is even a small 'shell-encrusted' area – **Fig 12.9** – in which a series of equally spaced shells have been inserted vertically into the cement, where one would normally expect to see them in horizontal layers. By normal Pulham standards, this area is quite casually executed.

At this point, the dairy itself is only a short distance away on the opposite side of the pool, and on one's way back to the well-kept lawns that surround it, one becomes aware of the sound of tumbling water, which comes from a small cascade built into the side of the rock borders, pictured in **Fig 12.10**.

Fig 12.11 *The central feature of the aviary at Waddesdon* (Photo by Jenny Lilly)

Some further amounts were paid to James Pulham and Son between 1886-91, and it is suggested that this was the period during which they worked nearer the house, in the area of the aviary and the top end of the North Drive.

The original aviary at Waddesdon was built between 1881-83 – at the time when the drives and formal gardens were laid out – and its design is thought to have been based on the aviary at Grüneburg, where the Baron spent his youth. There are small amounts of ornamental rockwork, both inside and around the aviary, although neither this nor the central figure – shown in **Fig 12.11** – is likely to be attributable to Pulhams. Some sums were paid out for 'rockery' between 1895 and 1898, but this time to a firm noted as 'Harpham', whose name also crops up at Sheffield Park – see Chapter 14.

Returning to the house around the top end of the North Drive, one comes to 'The Cavern', the entrance of which is shown here in **Fig 12.12**. There is a suggestion that this might originally have been an ice house, and later converted to house the massive water tank that is still there today. There are some huge rocks here – some of which may be natural – and one has to admire the care with which they were arranged to simulate a natural stratification.

The inside of this man-made grotto is railed off now for security reasons, but there are even more gigantic structures to be seen just around the corner from here, and along the main entrance drive. The huge grotto shown in **Figs 12.13** and **12.14** is quite remarkable.

The dairy, water garden, 'Tulip Patch' – and the land on which the glasshouses once stood – still belong to the Rothschild family, so some areas are only accessible to the general public on National Gardens Scheme Open Days. The magnificent mansion itself, together with the Aviary and 165 acres of the surrounding grounds, were transferred to the National Trust in 1957, so visitors today are able to see all the 'show rooms' in the house and the many features in this part of the grounds.[80]

Fig 12.12 *Entrance to 'The Cavern', a huge water tank at Waddesdon* (Photo by Jenny Lilly)

Fig 12.14 (below) *Massive rock grotto at the top end of the North Drive at Waddesdon in 2010* (Photo by Jenny Lilly)

Fig 12.13 *The already maturing rockery at Waddesdon* c.*1898* (Photo © Country Life)

- 13 -

HOLLY HILL PARK
SARISBURY, NEAR FAREHAM, HAMPSHIRE
1881-1892

Fig 13.1 *The upper lake and island at Holly Hill Park* (Photo by Dorothy Turner)

Holly Hill Park, near Fareham, is possibly the only Pulham site in Hampshire. It was on land that used to be part of the grounds of Holly Hill House, purchased in 1879 by Quentin Hogg, founder of the London Polytechnic. As so often seemed to happen in those days, the house was seriously damaged by fire soon after he bought it, and he made extensive alterations to both the house and the surrounding grounds during his reconstruction soon afterwards.

He employed the landscape designer Edward Milner – or his son, Henry Ernest Milner – to help him with this. James 2 had already worked with Milner on a number of projects, and was brought in to create two man-made lakes along the bottom of the five-acre valley gardens, together with islands, stepping stones and waterfalls, and a boathouse at one end of the lower lake. Following a further serious fire in 1886, Hogg eventually sold the site to Henry Foster in 1890.[81]

Fig 13.2 *The upper cascade at Holly Hill Park* (Photo by David Redwood)

Maps of the area show that, by 1895, the lakes had been reshaped to their present form – mainly by extending the lower lake to the east – so there is quite a strong possibility that James 2 was called back sometime around 1892, and it is also likely that the boat cave was added at that time. The property was sold again in 1947, when the grounds became increasingly derelict until Fareham Borough Council took them over in 1954.

The Council began a programme of excavation and restoration of the overgrown lakes between 1975 and 1983. Thanks to a staff of Park Rangers and the very active volunteer group of The Friends of Holly Hill Woodland Park, the Park is being very well maintained. A number of leaks began to appear in the cascades, but arrangements to restore them were being investigated when I last checked in 2011.

The entrance to the park is from the car park in Barnes Lane, and

one approaches the lakes via quite a steep path. This brings the visitor to a charming spot on the bank – pictured here as **Fig 13.1** – from where one can turn right, and proceed around the edge of the lake in an anti-clockwise direction.

A little further on, one comes to the point where the upper lake is fed by a small stream flowing down the eastern slope of the valley, fairly close to the entrance pathway. This is actually one of two tributaries of the primary stream that enters from the extreme northern end of the park, and used to run along the bottom of the valley and out to the south-west, towards the River Hamble. When James 2 arrived to 'beautify' the park, this was the stream that he converted into the two lakes one sees today.

Fig 13.2 shows the cascade between the upper and lower lakes, and, walking around the top, and back down the other side, one comes to the bridge that separates the two sections. This is not the original

119

Fig 13.3 *The new bridge supported by the Pulhamite cliff at Holly Hill Park, with the lower cascade just visible beyond* (Photo by Jenny Lilly)

bridge, but a new one put up during the clearance project between 1975-83 to replace the decrepit iron bridge that had carried the old carriageway from Sarisbury Court. The new bridge still rests upon the Pulhamite rocks beneath, as can be seen from **Fig 13.3**.

The boat cave grotto is at the south-western end of the lake. As can be seen in **Fig 13.4**, there used to be a narrow gap in the top of the cave – presumably to let in the light – which is now covered by a large flat iron-reinforced concrete slab to make it less dangerous for the occasional unsuspecting walker.

It is possible to descend into the cave itself, and the entrance to it is shown in **Fig 13.5**. Care is needed, but **Fig 13.6** proves that the effort is well worthwhile. This is an interesting variation of a Pulham cave grotto – quite similar in its way to that at Sandringham, Norfolk – pictured in Fig 8.2. This one also has an inner cave, complete with two small planting pockets, which supports the suggestion that the original purpose of the slit in the roof was to admit the daylight.

Fig 13.4 *The boat cave with the slit roof* (Photo by Jenny Lilly)

Fig 13.5 *Entrance to the boat cave grotto* (Photo by Dorothy Turner)

Fig 13.6 *Looking out through the entrance of the boat cave* (Photo by Jenny Lilly)

Fig 13.7 *The 'Fallen Tree Plateau' at Holly Hill Park*

There is a small rocky plateau nearby – **Fig 13.7** – that now has a fallen yew tree resting along the top of it. This would have been a classic vantage point to stop and view the lakes in days gone by. It may also have been the location of a flight of steps via which to enter the old boathouse – probably with a gently sloping path between the rocks to water level, and maybe entering at the point of the present 'inner cave'.

Leaving the outcrop and the boat cave behind, one can continue round the western end of the lake to the point where the water runs over another cascade (**Fig 13.8**), and into the stream that runs on into the River Hamble. The crossing here is either via a little bridge or, a few yards downstream, via the original set of stepping stones.

Holly Hill Park is quite small by general community parkland standards, but it has everything one could wish for. Peace, tranquillity, lovely sylvan views, and the constant background sound of water rippling quietly over rocks. Its team of park rangers, and the Friends of Holly Hill Woodland Park, ensure that it is well maintained, and it is well worth a visit. It also deserves to be congratulated on winning the 'Green Flag' for Outstanding Park award in 2008 – its first year of entry.

Fig 13.8 *The Southern cascade near the boat cave* (Photo by Jenny Lilly)

- 14 -

SHEFFIELD PARK GARDEN

UCKFIELD, EAST SUSSEX

1882-1885

Fig 14.1 *Sheffield Park Mansion from across the Top Lake, or 'Ten Foot Pond'*

The beautiful, 120-acre landscaped gardens at Sheffield Park, in East Sussex, offers the combination of water, trees, shrubs and flowers that has always attracted both amateur and professional gardeners. All these elements have been brought together at Sheffield Park with superb effect, and provide a profusion of colour all year round.

During the 18th Century, the estate was owned by Lord de la Warr, who created a lake from what had previously been no more than a stream in the lower part of the grounds. This is now on two levels: the 'Upper' and 'Lower' Woman's Way Ponds – a name based on the local legend that the ghost of a headless woman could often be seen wandering through this part of the garden.[82]

Lord de la Warr became burdened with financial difficulties during the 1760s, and, in 1769, sold the estate to John Baker Holroyd, who became Baron Sheffield in 1781, and Earl of Sheffield in 1816. He called in James Wyatt – one of the most fashionable architects of the day – between 1776-79, to remodel the mansion in the Gothic style, and to add an elegant crenellated lodge. A picture of the mansion, taken from across the Top Lake, is shown in **Fig 14.1**.

Baron Sheffield also sought the services of 'Capability' Brown to advise on re-landscaping the paths, trees and lawns around the estate. The extent of Brown's direct involvement is not absolutely clear, because he sent one of his assistants – a Mr Spyers – to work on the project, as a result of which paths were cleared through the woods to the east of the house, leaving – after some judicious felling – irregular belts, clumps and groves of trees that created a series of sylvan vistas that changed at every turn, and every few yards along the gently winding paths.

The lake near the house – now known as the First Lake, or sometimes the 'Ten Foot Pond' – was tree-lined, and surrounded by open expanses of grass in the typical style of Brown. Humphrey Repton then worked at Sheffield Park between 1789-90 – on one of his first assignments – during which he created a series of four small lakes in its place. The park was expanded to the north, south and east during the 1790s with new plantations of trees and pasture, but, when George Holroyd, the 2nd Earl, succeeded his father in 1821, the estate became rather neglected.

Henry Holroyd – the 3rd Earl of Sheffield – inherited the estate in 1876. He was MP for East Sussex between 1857 and 1865, but

Fig 14.2 *The Pulham Falls – previously known as the Grand Cascade – between the First Lake and Middle Lake* (Photo by David Sellman, reproduced by permission of The National Trust)

Fig 14.3 *The Pulham Falls and bridge in close-up*

his real loves were cricket and horticulture. He did much to revive the gardens, and created the present Middle Lake from two of Repton's ponds. With the aid of his head gardener, William Thomas Moore, he also laid out the basic skeleton of the planting seen today. Between 1882 and 1885, he commissioned James 2 to construct artificial waterfalls at the top and bottom of the Middle Lake, and supply the stonework for the Top Bridge. The top waterfall became known as The Grand Cascade, but has recently been equally appropriately re-christened 'The Pulham Falls', and is pictured here in **Figs 14.2** and **14.3**.

It is indeed a magnificent sight, built from natural sandstone obtained from local quarries, and it must have been quite spectacular in its heyday, when, in the evenings, lights were lit behind the tumbling water. The water flow of 'some thousands of tons of water per minute' is controlled by a massive pumping system that pumps water up from the Lower Woman's Way Pond to the storage pond – the sides of which had to be raised by about three feet to accommodate the additional flow – from where it feeds into the First Lake, and down again via the Middle Lake and Upper Woman's Way Pond. The original pumping system was installed by the specialist firm of Green & Carter, who worked with Pulhams on nearly all of their sites that incorporated water features.

Over the course of time, however, tree roots managed to penetrate some of the pipework, and a number of leaks developed. A new, upgraded system has now been installed, using electric pumps and pipework that was actually pushed through the insides of the original pipes. The cascades are not on display all year round, but the 'Pulham Falls' are switched on, especially for the benefit of visitors, for one hour from noon every Tuesday and Friday during the season. This has been a spectacular success, and crowds of people regularly congregate on the Middle Bridge to await 'the big gush'.

Fig 14.4 *The 'First Lake' side of the Top Bridge, showing the Sheffield Coat of Arms on the central plinth, and the inside view of the balustrade inset*

Fig 14.4 shows the balustraded Top Bridge – taken from the 'First Lake' side, and with the pathway view inset – which used to have six of Pulham's 'Otford' vases on the central and outer plinths, but these were removed for safety and security reasons. The Sheffield family crest is cast onto the outside surface of the central plinth – as can be seen in both Figs 14.3 and 14.4 – rather than on the inside surface (inset), where it might then have been seen by visitors

No. 463
UCKFIELD BALUSTRADE
Height 3ft.
Price per foot run £3 3 0
Piers   6 6 0
For Vase see No. 4

No. 463

Fig 14.5 *The Uckfield Balustrade, with an Otford Vase on top (from the Pulham catalogue c.1925)*

walking across the bridge. Such was the third Lord's addiction to cricket that pride of place had to go to the side that would be visible from the cricket pitch and in a direct line with the house itself.

Strangely enough, the Pulham *Garden Ornament Catalogue* (*c*.1925) lists an 'Uckfield' Balustrade, pictured here in **Fig 14.5**. One would have thought that this was the pattern used on the bridge at Sheffield Park, but it is clearly different, and much closer to what was their 'Maidenhead' pattern.

There is another bridge above the small cascade between the eastern end of the Middle Lake and the Upper Woman's Way Pond, shown here in **Fig 14.6**. There is a tragic story associated with this cascade, which originally consisted of a flight of fifteen concrete steps, culminating in a level embankment, and surmounted by a bridge. This was designed by the Earl himself, and constructed by T Harpham[83] – someone whose name is also thought to be associated with the construction of the original aviary at Waddesdon Manor – but Pulhams were called back in 1886 to reduce its height, and transform it into an imitation of a subterranean upheaval, along the lines of its counterpart at the other end of the lake.

The plan was to dynamite the formal concrete steps, and leave the debris for 'natural effect', and the gang of workmen successfully lifted the bridge, and blew away five of the steps. While boring the remaining steps and charging them with powder, however, a spark from an iron ramrod is said to have caused a powerful explosion, killing two of the team – an event witnessed by the Earl, his mother and guests from the cricket field embankment. Despite this terrible setback, the new rocky foundations were finally completed, and the bridge resettled. This is the bridge that remains today, although the original balustrading has now been replaced with iron railings.

There is a third bridge and cascade between the Upper and Lower Woman's Way Ponds that was not constructed by Pulhams, but is still worthy of note here. **Fig 14.7** shows it to be in the form of about a dozen granite steps, some of which are laid edgeways, rather like the brickwork of a wall. The idea is to break up the flow of water, rather than let it fall like a flat 'curtain' over a dam.

Fig 14.6 *The rockwork along the shallow cascade beneath the Second Bridge between the bottom of the Middle Lake and the Upper Woman's Way Pond*

Fig 14.7 *The 'Steps Cascade' between the Upper and Lower Woman's Way Ponds*

Fig 14.8 *The Pulham fountain at Sheffield Park*

Back at the mansion, there is another treat in store, in the form of a lovely Pulham fountain. One can see it from some points around the First Lake, although one needs to get up close to inspect its detail – something that the general public is not able to do. However, it is shown here in **Fig 14.8**, which shows clearly how well the detail still survives.

When the 3rd Earl died in 1909, leaving no heir, and heavily in debt, the estate was purchased by Arthur Gilstrap Soames, one of his principal creditors. Mr Soames was also a very enthusiastic gardener, with a particular love for roses and rhododendrons, and he planted the specimens for which Sheffield Park Gardens are now famous. He died in 1934, and was survived by his widow, who lived there as a tenant during the Second World War, when the estate was requisitioned by the War Office, and more than 400 Nissen huts were erected among the trees. One or two still survive today as listed buildings.

Mrs Agnes Soames handed on the estate in 1949 to her nephew, who did much to restore the gardens to their previous glory, but he was forced to sell up in 1953, when the house and gardens were separated. The parkland was acquired by the National Trust with the encouragement of the RHS. Despite the fact that there are only five full-time gardeners aided by a number of unpaid part-time volunteers, they have continued to do an enthusiastic and conscientious job in maintaining the gardens, which have been open to the public since that time; today the total number of visitors is around 150,000 per year.

In the spring, the broad lawns are covered with wild daffodils, narcissi and bluebells. Two months later, the gardens are ablaze with a multitude of flowering shrubs, like the Ghent azaleas and the banks of white, blue, purple and wine-red rhododendrons.

Standing on the Top Bridge in early summer, one will see rafts of white-flowered water lilies in the pool above the cascade, and red

and pink flowers on the waters of the Middle Lake below (see **Fig 14.9**). A little later, the long grass fringing the Queen's Walk around one of the lower lakes is dotted with spotted orchids, and is now a conservation area for wild flowers. Around the shores of the lakes is a superb range of trees and shrubs, and, over recent years, the National Trust has created a shady stream garden that includes hostas, lilies, primulas and other water-loving plants.

Many people consider the gardens to be at their best on sunny days during October, however, when the blue waters of the lakes set off the magnificent autumn colours of the tupelo trees, azaleas, maples, swamp cypresses, eucryphias and birches. The inspired planting at Sheffield Park Gardens by its various owners has made this one of the finest landscape gardens in Britain – now listed by English Heritage as a Grade I site. They provide a grand day out, especially in the autumn.

Also Noted:

1883 – Halton House, Aylesbury, Buckinghamshire

Fig 14.9 *Water lilies in The First Lake*

- 15 -

WORTH PARK/MILTON MOUNT

CRAWLEY, WEST SUSSEX

1885-1886

Fig 15.1 *The terrace and lawns at Worth Park, with the mansion beyond – with Otford vases on lower pedestals* (Photo © Country Life)

Worth Park– now known as Milton Mount – is near Three Bridges Station, in Crawley. The Worth Park Estate of around 1,400 acres was purchased *c*.1850 by Joseph Mayer Montefiore – the wealthy London banker and philanthropist, who no doubt wanted to escape to the countryside from the hustle and bustle of the city – fairly soon after the railway opened up the area.

The house was destroyed by fire in 1853, and Joseph decided to build himself a grand redbrick mansion in its place. This was completed in 1860.[84] He took a great pride in his new house and gardens, and lavished great care and attention upon them. On his death in 1880, the estate was inherited by his widow and their son, Sir Francis Abraham Montefiore, who continued to invest a great deal of money in some further embellishments to the grounds. These incorporated a number of the more formal features that were becoming favoured on the larger estates, and *Country Life* published an article about them in 1899.[85] This included some pictures that clearly demonstrate Pulham's involvement, and the following is an extract from their reviewer's notes:

'…The sunny space of garden is conspicuously beautiful, and wholly appropriate to the character of the mansion. The arrangement is broad and simple … the general character is formal … No conspicuous features seem to have been sought, but there are fine fountains, and all the garden architecture is excellent.

'The illustrations [two of which are reproduced here in **Figs 15.1** and **15.2**] will serve to reveal the character . . . Variety is sought in the adornment of several special gardens, such as the fountain and sundial gardens that we depict. These have something of the double beauty of a pleasing formality, and yet an informal charm, and it is simply delightful to look from them over the green park, with its lovely foliage, and the lake glistening below…

'The curved corridor protecting one side of the garden is very unusual, and an interesting feature. Corridors in some ways analogous exist, indeed, in other places, and we have illustrated not a few. They form resorts where one may walk, sheltered from sun or rain, to enjoy the prospect the garden affords. But the corridor at Worth Park – [known as the Camellia Corridor] – is singular in having the opening to its woodwork filled with great sheets of glass, so that, within the arches, one is looking out through windows . . . The effect of this system of construction is to form a place in which delicate things may grow. There is a trellis along the wall upon which camellias thrive, but less hardy things than these love such shelter.'

The cost burdens and manpower shortages arising from the outbreak of war in 1914 resulted in the mansion and estate being broken up

Fig 15.2 *The Camellia Corridor 1899* (Photo © Country Life)

and sold in 1915. The house and 80 acres of surrounding gardens were eventually purchased in 1920 by a girls' boarding school that had previously been situated on a hill near Milton, Gravesend, and they decided to bring with them their original name of Milton Mount College. The College continued to operate until it closed in 1960, and Crawley Council purchased the house and grounds in 1963. The house was eventually demolished in 1968, and replaced by the present Milton Mount Council flats, although the gardens to the original house remain comparatively intact.

The *Pulham Garden Ornament Catalogue* (*c*.1925) includes an illustration of the 'Worth Park Sundial' – shown here on the left of **Fig 15.3** – so this must have been made for the Sundial Garden referred to in the extract from the *Country Life* article quoted above. The vases shown in Fig 15.1 also come straight out of the catalogue, and the balustrading is an upside-down variation of the Warlingham Balustrade, shown on the right of Fig 15.3.

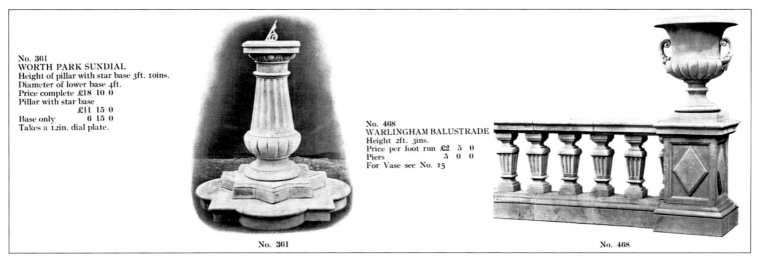

Fig 15.3 *Worth Park Sundial and Warlingham Balustrade* (from Pulham Catalogue)

Fig 15.4 *View from roof, showing the Sundial Garden in the foreground, with the Dutch Garden and the Fountain Garden beyond, bordered by the Camellia Corridor on the left, possibly* c.*1923* (Photo provided by Margaret Clark)

Fig 15.5 *The Fountain Garden at Worth Park, probably* c.*1912* (Photo provided by Margaret Clark)

Fig 15.6 *The frame of the 'Camellia Corridor' – or 'Camellia Walk' – in 2003*

Fig 15.7 *The 'planter' in the old Fountain Garden in 2003*

An 'Old Miltonian' – who has for several years acted as the college's official archivist – was able to show me a collection of other pictures ranging from 1912 to 1948 – one of which is reproduced in **Fig 15.4**. This was taken from the top of the house, and shows the circular Sundial Garden in the foreground, with the Dutch Garden and Fountain Garden beyond. The Pulham sundial can be clearly seen in the Sundial Garden, and the wooden structure that bounds the left-hand border is the Camellia Corridor referred to in the *Country Life* article. **Fig 15.5** shows the Fountain Garden as it was *c*.1912.

I visited Milton Mount in 2003, and **Fig 15.6** is a picture of the Camellia Corridor as it was at that time. It had recently been restored, although the glass front panels and the roof had long since gone. I am unable to vouch positively for its provenance, although I do know that Pulhams had an established team of joiners and carpenters working at the manufactory around this time, and I cannot imagine that anyone else would have been brought in specifically to construct this feature while the Pulham craftsmen were working elsewhere on site.

As can be seen from **Fig 15.7**, the fountain in the Fountain Garden is still there, although the basin has since been converted to a planter. The sundial has long since gone – this was auctioned off, along with almost all the vases and other garden furniture at the time of the college closure in 1963. These gardens lead through to the front of the house, which is surrounded by its grand balustraded terraces,

Fig 15.8 *Aerial view of house and gardens, showing tennis courts and round pool and fountain, probably* c.*1937* (Photo reproduced by permission of Margaret Clark)

Fig 15.9 *Large pond and fountain with main steps leading to terrace behind,* c.*1948* (Photo reproduced by kind permission of Margaret Clark)

while the pleasure gardens at the back (**Fig 15.8**) contain the tennis courts and a large round pool with a fountain in the centre – **Fig 15.9**. At first sight, this seems to be very large for a Pulham fountain, and lacks the tall centrepiece with cascading tiers that generally forms their central feature, but it fits perfectly into its surrounding circle of carefully pruned trees.

There is an ornamental lake on the far edge of the estate, and a rockwork feature at a corner near where the house used to be. These

are both examples of Pulham's craftsmanship, even though the rockwork is only comparatively small, and not a particularly notable example. It is shown here in **Fig 15.10**.

The postscript to this story contains some mixed messages. The wooden Camellia Corridor was vandalised in 2004, although, luckily for the residents of Crawley, they have some very lively and energetic councillors who are doing their best to stimulate people into action. A group of 'Friends of Milton Mount' has been formed,

Fig 15.10 *The rock cliff at Worth Park / Milton Mount*

and have applied for a Heritage Lottery grant to assist with the proper restoration of all its features.

They have even put up a commemorative plaque to James Pulham – the first and only one I have seen so far – pictured here in **Fig 15.11**. It credits James 3 with the work, and dates it in the 'mid-1880s'. I have consequently noted the dates as 1885-86, although it is quite possible that the work may have been spread over two or more visits.

Also Noted:
1886-93 – Bletchley Park, Bletchley, Buckinghamshire
1887   – *'Juniper Hill'*, Mickleham, Dorking, Surrey

Fig 15.11 *Memorial Plaque to James Pulham 3's work at Worth Park*
(Photo by Margaret Clark)

- 16 -

'THE DELL'

ENGLEFIELD GREEN, NEAR EGHAM, SURREY

1888-1913

In his spare time, Baron Sir John Henry Schroder – head of the German merchant banking family who were also associated with the Baltic Exchange, home of shipping insurance – was a distinguished collector and grower of orchids. He even had one named after him – *Calanthe Baron Schroder,* described as:

'A deciduous Calanthe, for which the culture is easy — grow it when it wants to grow, and rest it when it doesn't.'[86]

He won three gold and ten silver medals at the Royal Horticultural Society shows for his exhibits between 1891 and 1904, and was also a councillor and beneficiary of the Society, earning himself the name of 'Father of the Hall' after he found and contributed towards the cost of their present headquarters in Vincent Square, London.[87]

His home was at 'The Dell,' in Englefield Green, near Egham in Surrey, which he bought during the 1880s. He extended the house to make it rectangular, with a central courtyard, and created 50 bedrooms, a billiard room, drawing room, a hall of pictures, and servants' quarters.

As might be expected, he also lavished a great deal of care and attention on his gardens, where he used to grow grapes, peaches, nectarines and melons in a group of large greenhouses, which may possibly have been built by James 2, although there is no known

evidence to substantiate this. His extensive gardens and collections gained a wide reputation, as is demonstrated by this quote from the *Gardeners' Chronicle*:[88]

'The beauties of Baron Schroder's gardens are well known to most gardeners in Europe and America. Year by year, the liberality of the Baron, and the care of his gardener, Mr H. Ballantine, add new beauties to it – the last, the extensive rockeries, being one of the most attractive. In their construction, Pulham has done his work well, artistically winding and sinking or raising the rockery, and introducing pieces of water in several places with considerable effect. The rockery has been fortunate in being skilfully planted; the capping of these massive rocks being especially well done.'

This article was published in 1891, so an estimated construction date of 1888 cannot be far from the truth. It is a relatively small Pulham garden, but it nevertheless evokes almost magical images in the mind of the visitor.

Baron Schroder died in 1910, and his estate was divided up and sold in three parcels. Security flats were built on the portion of the land that incorporates the rock garden, and, luckily, some of the owners were very interested in what they had inherited, because they have lovingly uncovered and restored the previously overgrown garden to something approaching its original splendour. A former resident told me that some of the trees in the gardens – in particular, a 300-year old oak – had been identified as once being part of the nearby Windsor Great Park.

The view that one gets when entering the rock garden is shown in **Fig 16.1**, and this is classic Pulham. A shady path winds away into the distance, with a few scattered outcrops of rock along the sides that are only small to begin with, but gradually get larger until, as one walks further down the path, they develop into massive outcrops that look completely 'natural' in their formation. **Fig 16.2** shows a section of these rocks, while **Fig 16.3** is a picture of a massive rock archway, through which one can catch a glimpse of the stream that flows beyond.

Fig 16.1 (opposite page) *The entrance to the rock garden at 'The Dell'*

Fig 16.2 (above) *A little further down the rocky path*

Fig 16.3 (right) *A rock arch leading to the stream*

One doesn't just have to look, however. Pass through and round the back of the arch to where the stream widens out into a pool, with a series of stepping stones, from which the picture in **Fig 16.4** was taken – the entrance path being on the far side of it. Returning through the archway, one continues along the path, which follows the line of the stream, and finally crosses over it, via a small stone bridge – shown in **Fig 16.5** – that looks as if it has come straight out of a book of fairy tales. The stream flows into a small rocky pool, with a large, round, castellated water tower on the far side.

In fact, this bridge may have a story of its own to tell, because I was recently given an old photograph of the water tower at 'The Dell' – shown here in **Fig 16.6** – which shows a rustic wooden bridge that was a typical Pulham construction during the 1880s. The present stone bridge must consequently be a more recent replacement, dating perhaps from the 1910s, or even somewhat later. The water tower can be clearly seen in the background of this picture, and the contemporary photograph (**Fig 16.7**) shows it still in good condition; the trees around it have just got bigger in the meantime.

Fig 16.4 (above)   *The pool at 'The Dell'*

Fig 16.5 (below)   *The fairy-tale bridge and rock outcrops at 'The Dell'*

Fig 16.6 (right) *The old bridge and water tower at 'The Dell' c.1900.*

Fig 16.7 (below) *The castellated water tower*

Due to the fact that 'The Dell' stands high on a hill, it was necessary to pump the water up from the valley on one side, and feed it down into the garden on the other but, instead of just building any old tower, James 2 decided to render the outside with cement, and simulate the stonework of a crenellated mediaeval tower! That is what was meant by 'taking pride in your work' in those days.

This marks the furthest extent of the rock garden, and **Fig 16.8** looks back along the stream and the path from the bridge. Returning down the outside of the garden, one can look back over the pool from the top of the 'cliff' – **Fig 16.9** – and get a more comprehensive overview of how well the current residents are looking after their Pulham heritage. A number of planting pockets can be clearly seen here, while **Fig 16.10** takes a last, lingering look at the back of the 'cliff' behind the pool, on the way back towards the houses.

Fig 16.8 *Stream and rocks near the bridge at 'The Dell'*

Fig 16.9 *The pool from above at 'The Dell'*

One rather disturbing aspect of my return visit in 2005 was that some of the Pulhamite had been pressure-sprayed. This was in an attempt to 'clean' the surfaces, but the downside to this is that it also washed away the patina that had formed over the previous 120 years.

This is exactly the procedure that completely wrecked the rockwork in Battersea Park during an early attempt at Pulhamite 'restoration' during the 1980s, as discussed in Chapter 6. In that instance, the high-pressure water jets removed so much of the surface cement that they had to find a way of repairing it – and the method they chose was to spray it all over with gunnite! Fortunately, the 'spray cleaning' at 'The Dell' was undertaken with much more care, and only minimal damage was done to the rock surfaces. It has, however, in my opinion also removed some of its weatherworn charm.

Pulhams were invited to return to Englefield Green some time after creating Baron Sir John's rock garden at 'The Dell,' because there is another garden on the 'third parcel' of the original Dell Park estate, at what is now called 'Oaklands'. This garden is shown in **Fig 16.11**, and, during my visit in 2000, I was lucky to meet an old local gardener, who was then well into his 90s. He remembered the garden from his youth, and told me that, as a boy, he often saw the ageing Baron Bruno Schroder – the son of Baron John Henry – being brought in his bath chair to sit in this piece of garden, which is quite a long way from the main house.

It is impossible to put an exact date to this, but it is a fascinating piece of anecdotal evidence which would put the construction of this piece of garden into the early 1910s – i.e. just before the First World War. I am therefore suggesting 1913 – possibly at the same time the new bridge was built in 'The Dell' – which means that the guiding

Fig 16.10 *The back of the Pulham garden from the lawns at 'The Dell'*

hand would have been James 3. This picture provides an interesting illustration of the way rock garden styles had changed over the period of 25 years that had elapsed since the original garden at 'The Dell' was constructed. There are no massive Pulhamite rock constructions here. This is a typical 'natural rock' garden that was far more economical to construct, and far less labour intensive than bringing in the rock builders.

Also Noted:
1889 – Piggots Manor, Letchmore Heath, Radlett, Hertfordshire
c.1900 – *'Leonardslee'*, Horsham, West Sussex

Fig 16.11 *A path in the park – second 'Oaklands' development, c.1924*

- 17 -

ROSS HALL PARK
GLASGOW, SCOTLAND
1890-1891

One of the best surviving examples of the Pulhams' work in Scotland is surely to be found in Ross Hall Park – a small park of just over 30 acres, set amidst the White Cart Water in the Crookston area on the south side of Glasgow. In fact, due to the absence of any definitive record of Pulhams' work after 1877, this garden could easily have remained 'unknown' outside its immediate vicinity had it not been for its recent 'rediscovery' in which Christopher Dingwall – the then Scottish Conservation Officer of the Garden History Society – played a significant part.

Ross Hall Park is now owned by the City of Glasgow Council, and takes its name from the Ross family, who originally owned Hawkhead Castle, in Paisley. Hawkhead was later owned by the Cowan family, and it was in 1877 that James Cowan J P – Chairman of the West Renfrewshire Conservative Association; President of the Renfrewshire Agricultural Society, and wealthy head of Messrs Cowan & Co., carriers and contractors to several railway and shipping companies – moved to the Crookston area, and built the large red sandstone baronial mansion that he named Ross Hall. An enthusiastic connoisseur of the arts, he ensured that his new home was designed to display his rich collection of silver, jewellery, porcelain, books and paintings at its very best.[89]

Fig 17.1 *A rock path in the gardens at Ross Hall, Glasgow, c.1920* (Photo reproduced by permission of RCAHMS)

Fig 17.2 *The lake in Ross Hall gardens,* c.*1920* (Photo reproduced by permission of RCAHMS)

In 1890, he commissioned James 2 to 'reconstruct the garden, regardless of expense', and the little rivulet that once flowed through the estate was transformed into:

'. . . a layout of artificial lakes and rockwork, waterfalls and grottos, furnished with a great variety of plant life.'

This quotation is taken from a letter written by James Cowan's nephew, Lachlan, to his uncle while he was away from home on a journey round the world.[90] In another letter, dated October 1890, he wrote:

'How is the lake at Ross Hall getting on? I expect that I shall hardly know it when I come back, and am looking forward to seeing it nearly completed.'

It looks like it was a long job, because, one year later – in October 1891 – while staying in Yokohama, waiting for a letter of credit to arrive that would relieve him of his rather impecunious state, and allow him to resume his travels, he wrote:

'I expect Ross Hall must look very pretty, now that you have at last(!) got the pond and rockeries finished, at which I don't suppose you are very sorry.'

James Cowan was a bachelor, and the estate was put up for sale when he died in 1908. The sales catalogue had this to say about the gardens:

'Naturally beautiful, owing to the undulating nature of the ground, and the large number of fine old beech and other trees

with which they are furnished, the gardens and grounds at Ross Hall, which extend in all to 31.188 acres, are unique. They have been laid out regardless of expense, with extensive artificial lakes and rockwork, with waterfalls, grottos, bridges, rustic arches and caves, furnished with masses of the finest of Alpine, aquatic and other rare plants in endless profusion, embellished with beautiful trees and shrubs, and laid out with beautiful walks, forming one of the finest gardens of its kind in Scotland.'

This estate was later purchased by Sir Frederick Lobnitz – head of a shipbuilding family – who lived there for forty years and is also reputed to have carried out 'extensive reconstruction, extension and modernisation of the gardens'. It is rumoured that the pool was originally designed as a bathing pool, between 6ft and 8ft deep, and that the family had hot water piped into it from the house, but it is not known whether the Pulhams were involved in this stage. **Figs 17.1** and **17.2** show a rocky pathway, and a view of the lake, taken during the 1920s.

In 1948, the estate was sold to the Glasgow Corporation, and the mansion is now used as a hospital. Some of the fine features of the grounds were restored and opened up to the public as Ross Hall Park. They were maintained to a fairly basic standard, but the overgrowth of vegetation, root and frost damage – and even vandalism – all contributed to their general deterioration over the years. Fortunately, a group of local people got together to form the Friends of Ross Hall Park, and their continued hard work, with the help of funds put aside by the City Council, resulted in the implementation of a conservation plan aimed at restoring this outstanding example of Pulham's work to its former glory.

Fig 17.3 *A close-up of some shell-encrusted 'rocks' in Ross Hall Park* (Photo by Catriona Morrison, and reproduced by kind permission of the Carts River Valleys Project)

Fig 17.4 *The boathouse in the rock pool at Ross Hall Park during the first stage of the restoration project in 2006* (Photo by Ian Fraser)

Fig 17.5 *Overview of the former bathing pool, showing an incongruous free-standing rock stack which has a central knuckle-shaped stone on top, indicating that it may well have had a larger stone slab fitting on to it. Restored in August 2010* (Photo by Ian Fraser)

Fig 17.6 *Part of the restored rockwork, looking from the former bathing pool back towards the entrance through the grotto*
(Photo by Ian Fraser)

Fig 17.3 is a close-up of some of the 'shell-encrusted rocks', and **Fig 17.4** is a picture of the boathouse grotto in the rock pool after it had been cleared of overgrowing ivy during the initial restoration stage in 2006. The surface damage to the rockwork was repaired in 2010, although the depth of the bathing pool was reduced for health and safety reasons. The results of this work are shown in **Figs 17.5** to **17.8**.

The next phase of the project is to replant a number of the planting pockets using James 2's *List of Recommended Plants* as a guide. This will ensure that historically appropriate species will be used, together with some of their modern equivalents – such as dwarf ferns, grasses and trailing plants – that will tolerate the climatic conditions of the grotto and garden. The longer-term goals are to improve access to the rock garden by installing a footpath to a viewing area that wheelchairs can use, and to add new directional and information signage.

Also Noted:
1891-94 – Gisselfeld, Denmark
1891   – Carpenders Park, Watford, Hertfordshire
1891   – *'The Acacias'*, Reading, Berkshire

Fig 17.7 *Restored rockwork around the entrance path to the former bathing pool* (Photo by Ian Fraser)

Fig 17.8 *Footpath leading to the kitchen garden through the rock arch. The roof of the arch is constructed using a massive sandstone slab* (Photo by Ian Fraser)

- 18 -

EWELL COURT HOUSE

EWELL, NEAR EPSOM, SURREY

1892-1914

Fig 18.1 *The back of Ewell Court House, c.1937. Note the Pulham Exhibition Fountain, and the large glasshouse on the left of the house* (Photo reproduced from the Epsom and Ewell Borough Council's Charter Day Celebration booklet)

Alexander Bridges – a wealthy man with other properties in Surrey – bought Avenue House, in Ewell, in 1730, and, in 1754, applied for a licence to use the water running through his land as a source of power to make gunpowder. This was granted, and he built four waterwheels – each driving two gunpowder mills – along the River Hogsmill from Ewell village to just beyond where it was joined by the tributary from Avenue House.

The mills were closed following a series of accidents and the passing of the Explosives Act of 1875, and, for a time, Avenue House remained empty. One of Alexander Bridges' descendants – John Henry Bridges – inherited it on the occasion of his marriage in 1879, and it was not long before he had a new house built on the site. It was a three-storey, red brick structure in the 'Old English' style, with Elizabethan decorative elements, and incorporated parts of the old Avenue House, after which it became known as Ewell Court House.[91]

He had some further work carried out later, including the establishment of several new glasshouses in which to grow all his own

Fig 18.2 *The 'fountain flower bed' in 2008. The base of the fountain is the original, but a large vase replaces the fountain itself.*

produce. These were shown on the 1896 OS Map, which indicates that they must date from between the early 1880s and 1896 – which prompts me to suggest *c*.1892 as the likely date – and can be seen on the left of **Fig 18.1**, which dates from *c*.1937. These structures no longer exist, but they look similar to others constructed by James Pulham and Son – some of which are pictured in this book.

The large fountain that stands in the centre of this picture has already been noted in Chapter 3. Fig 3.12 shows a medal-winning Exhibition fountain, and Fig 3.13 is of a very similar one, called the Ewell

Fountain, that was pictured in the *Pulham Garden Ornament Catalogue* *c*.1925. **Fig 18.2** shows the flowerbed that stands in its place today – the basin surround and fountain base are still there, but a large vase now stands where the main fountain used to be. (Note that the four 'Preston' vases that stand on the four corners in the catalogue picture are no longer there – in fact, they had already been removed by the time of the 1937 picture.)

Pulhams did another major piece of work during their visit to Ewell Court House *c*.1892 – this time around the lake that had been created

Fig 18.3 *Lake and island at Ewell Court House*

Fig 18.4 *Remains of the cascade*

Fig 18.5 *The rocky stream meandering through the trees at Ewell Court House after clearance of overgrowth* (Photo by Carol Hill)

many years earlier – possibly *c*.1690, when Avenue House was first built, and the Bourne Stream was dammed on its way through the grounds. The idea was to realign the shores to form a boating lake - complete with boathouse and island, as shown in **Fig 18.3** – and to build a Pulhamite cascade, over which the water tumbled into a 'rocky stream that gently meanders through the trees on its way to join the River Hogsmill.'[92]

This was just the sort of work with which the firm had gained their reputation – in fact, this would have been around the same time that they constructed a very similar scheme in Holly Hill Park, in Fareham, Hampshire, as discussed in Chapter 13. **Fig 18.4** shows the current state of the cascade between the lake and the stream, and **Fig 18.5** is of the stream 'gently meandering through the trees' after the recent clearance of the overgrowth.

Sometime after that visit, Pulhams returned again to Ewell Court House – this time to construct a hexagonal, domed 'grotto fernery' beyond the centre panel of the back wall of the glasshouse shown to the left of Fig 18.1. It extended out into the kitchen garden, but evidence of this structure first appeared in the 1907 plans, which indicates that it must date from sometime during the early 1900s – say *c*.1904.

Time took its normal toll on the house and grounds during the latter years of the 20th Century, and there was a time when they were in danger of being purchased for redevelopment, but a group of local heritage enthusiasts banded together under the name of the Ewell Court House Organisation, and worked tremendously hard to help restore the facilities. Under the supervision of (the now late) Professor John Ashurst D.Arch, RIBA, EASA (Hon), and with the help of the local Council, they have succeeded in restoring the grotto, and are now working progressively to return the remaining features to the service and pleasure of the local community. They are off to a good start, because the house is now a popular venue for weddings and other functions.

Things have also been happening apace with the fernery. Funds were raised for its complete restoration – the tufa was cleaned; the irrigation system restored; the pockets replanted, and new gates installed – and it was officially 'reopened' by Cllr Jan Mason, Mayor of Epsom and Ewell, in 2009. **Fig 18.6** is a view of the fernery, and **Fig 18.7** is of a scene at the 'handover ceremony'.

The lake, island and stream are next on the list, with efforts being made to raise further funds for the restoration of the island. This will be followed, in stages, by the restoration of the lake and stream,

Fig 18.7 The Handover Ceremony of the Pulham grotto, with Chris Grayling MP, Margot Ashurst (widow of the late Professor John Ashurst), Jan Mason (Mayor of Epsom and Ewell), and Don Scott (Ewell Court House Organisation)

Fig 18.6 *The restored fernery grotto at Ewell Court House*

and then, hopefully, by the restoration of the magnificent fountain, and its reinstatement as the centrepiece of these lovely gardens. Ewell Court House is a heart-warming example of what can be achieved with the drive and enthusiasm of local people interested in the preservation of their local heritage.

Also Noted:
1892-97 – Aldenham House, Elstree, Hertfordshire

- 19 -

BAWDSEY MANOR

BAWDSEY, SUFFOLK

1892-1900s

Fig 19.1 *Bawdsey Manor from the air, c.1930s. The Pulhamite path extends along the length of the 'cliff', about half way up*

Bawdsey, on the Suffolk coast, lies about eight miles down the River Deben from Woodbridge, where James 1 was born and began his career as a stone modeller in the early 1800s. This is a unique example of Pulhamite construction because, although James 2 often used the word 'cliff' to describe what we might today regard as a 'retaining wall', there is no other word with which he could have described his work at Bawdsey. Looking at the aerial photograph in **Fig 19.1** – which was probably taken at some time during the 1930s – one can see the cliff going down to the beach along the edge of the property. It is about 300 yards long, and 40ft high, and it is all artificial Pulhamite rock, with a path running along the length of it, about half way up. This must be a 'cliff' to end all artificial cliffs.

Sir William Cuthbert Quilter – a stockbroker, financier and Liberal-Unionist MP – moved to Bawdsey in 1886, and built himself:

'. . . a fine new mansion situated on an eminence, and commanding a splendid view of the sea.'[93]

Fig 19.2 *Entrance to the gardens at Bawdsey*

Figs 19.3a and b *The Round Garden, on the site of a Martello Tower, c.1910* (Photo © Country Life), *and, below, in 2011* (Photo: Ellie Johnson)

Fig 19.1 shows that it was a complex mixture of prevailingly Gothic styles, including turrets and cupolas, and it is said that, during the time of Sir William Cuthbert's residence, Lady Quilter was regarded as the 'Head Gardener' on the estate,[94] and responsible for the design of the gardens, so one can assume that it was probably she who commissioned the Pulhams to work their magic here.

Access to the gardens from the outside is achieved by means of a door that is set right into the face of some very large 'rocks' – as pictured in **Fig 19.2**. This was a fairly common Pulham device, as will be seen from other examples pictured throughout this book. This one opens into a rock-lined tunnel – rather similar to the entrance tunnel to the fernery at the Swiss Garden, Old Warden (Fig 10.1) – with the gardens at the other end of it.

These are divided into a number of separate 'compartments', one of which is called the 'Secret Garden', constructed on what was originally the site of a Martello tower, built in 1810. This particular tower was demolished in 1819, and one of Pulham's tasks was to convert the site into a lovely secluded garden, with a rock-lined

entrance path, and centred on an Italian urn where the tower used to be. **Fig 19.3a** shows it as it used to be, while the way it looks now – after some considerable effort has recently been invested in its comprehensive restoration – is shown in **Fig 19.3b**. A glimpse of it

Fig 19.4 *The old water garden – 'Next Garden' – at Bawdsey in 2011, with the remains of the Rose Garden pergola on the right* (Photo: Ellie Johnson)

Figs 19.5a and b *The cliff path at Bawdsey, c.1910* (Photo © Country Life) *and in 2011* (Photo: Ellie Johnson)

Fig 19.6 *A grotto along the cliff walk at Bawdsey, 2011* (Photo: Ellie Johnson)

Fig 19.7 *The rose pergola leading to the cliff path, 2011* (Photo: Ellie Johnson)

can also be seen in the centre-right of the aerial picture in Fig 19.1. Close by is the 'Next Garden' – which has a rectangular lily pond in the centre, as can be seen in **Fig 19.4** – adjacent to this is the Rose Garden, where the pergola (**Fig 19.7**) used to have a slatted wooden roof. Both of these gardens have recently been restored. Beyond the rose walk is a gate to the cliff path that enables the visitor to see the shell-speckled 'rocks' of the cliff at close quarters.

Figs 19.5a and b compare the view along the cliff path as it was *c*.1910 with what it was in 2011, after the excess growth had been cleared, and the planting pockets replanted. It is still possible to get along it, and discover some typical Pulham 'signatures' – like the small grotto pictured in **Fig 19.6**.

There are even more tantalising suggestions of Pulham's influence inside the house, where there are some magnificent plaster ceilings in some of the downstairs rooms. Two of these can be seen in **Figs 19.8a and b**, both of which show a remarkable resemblance to those in other houses where the Pulhams are known to have worked – such as those at Rawdon House, in Hoddesdon (Fig 2.4). Since it is not known for sure whether the firm was still doing this sort of work during the 1890s, it is impossible to prove whether or not these features at Bawdsey can actually be accredited to them.

Also Noted:
1892-97 – Aldenham House, Elstree, Hertfordshire

Figs 19.8a and b *Two plaster ceilings at Bawdsey*

- 20 -

BELLE VUE PARK

NEWPORT, WALES

1893

Fig 20.1 *The Belle Vue Park cascade,* c.*1920* (From 'The Life and Work of an English Landscape Architect' by Thomas Mawson)

Fig 20.2 *The rocky stream in Belle Vue Park, Newport, 2006* (Picture by David Morris)

Belle Vue Park in Newport, South Wales, is a triangular south-facing area on a steep slope near the centre of the town of Newport, and was donated to the town in 1891 by Lord Tredegar in the hope that its construction would help to relieve the high level of unemployment that existed in the area at that time. A competition was held for its design, and was won by Thomas Mawson, who was only 32 at the time.[95] This was his first commission to design a public park, and he later became famous for his love of the informal, 'natural' style of park and garden design.

The park was officially opened in 1893, and the central feature in its main section was an ornamental water garden, starting from a cascade at the top, from which a rocky stream flowed down through pools and more cascades, and under a bridge at the bottom – a typical Pulham woodland scene, in fact. **Fig 20.1** shows this feature in all its original glory *c*.1920, while **Fig 20.2** is a picture taken soon after its restoration in 2004-06, enabled via a generous Heritage Lottery Fund grant that was awarded to the park as a whole.

There are a number of other features in the park that point to the suggestion that the water garden was not the only one for which Pulhams were responsible. There was a fountain near the top of the park, and a bridge at the bottom of the stream, both of which bore very typical Pulham hallmarks, although neither appears in the *Pulham Garden Ornament Catalogue*.

The wooden bridge shown in **Fig 20.3** is actually a recent replica of the original bridge that was constructed in 1893. That bridge was later replaced by a balustraded stone bridge, but this, in turn, was removed during the Heritage Lottery restoration programme of 2006, and the current wooden bridge erected in its place.

Fig 20.3 *The lower stream, crossed by a replica of the original bridge, constructed with the aid of a Heritage Lottery grant in 2006* (Photo by Charles Hawes)

Fig 20.4 *The Belle Vue Pavilion following restoration in 2007* (Picture by Charles Hawes)

Right at the top of the park there is a grand balustraded terrace, with a bandstand (**Fig 20.5**) and another terrace above, on which is built a pavilion and glass-roofed tea house, shown in **Fig 20.4**. These would all have been built to Mawson's designs, but there are so many familiar features about them – such as the balustrading around the terrace and the steps, and the rusticated walls – that one cannot avoid the conclusion that James Pulham and Son must have been involved in the whole of the construction project.

Another feature that helped to confirm this in my mind was the terracotta plaque just above the door of the pavilion – **Fig 20.6**. It carries the Newport Coat of Arms, which is still beautifully clean and crisp, and just like ones at Sandringham (Fig 8.10) and Madeira Walk in Ramsgate, Kent – the next site to be discussed.

Also Noted:

1893   – *'The Hendre'*, Monmouthshire
1894-98 – Hanley and Burslem Park, Stoke-on-Trent, Staffordshire

Fig 20.5 *The Belle Vue Park bandstand following restoration in 2007* (Photo by Charles Hawes)

Fig 20.6 *The terracotta moulding of the Newport Coat of Arms above the door of the Belle Vue Park Pavilion*

- 21 -

MADEIRA WALK

RAMSGATE, KENT

1894

Fig 21.1 *The rockwork at the bottom end of Madeira Walk and Albion Place, c.1900* (Photo provided by Terry Wheeler)

By the latter part of the 19th century, the advent of the railways was beginning to affect the lives of people who had hitherto had to rely on their local parks for fresh air, relaxation and entertainment. By now, they could travel by train to spend their leisure time at the seaside.

One of the first coastal towns to cater for this change of lifestyle was Ramsgate, on the east coast of Kent. The Council of the Borough wanted to change the appearance of their town from that of a busy fishing port to one with picturesque gardens and promenades that would welcome its new visitors, and they attempted to do so in several stages of development that included four visits from the Pulham rock builders. Only the first stage will be dealt with here, because the later return visits did not take place until the 1920s, and will be more appropriately discussed in Chapter 41.

The Council produced a brochure in 1887 in which they outlined a plan for a new road system that would connect the town's west and east cliffs. The first road would run south west from the harbour up

to the West Cliff – it is now called Royal Parade – and was completed in 1893.[96] It consists of a series of ornamental arches under the road – they were, and still are, used to house boating workshops and so on – and another set of arches running along the landward side of the road, supporting the West Cliff Arcade. To the best of my knowledge, Pulhams were not involved in this stage of the project.

The second road was to wind up from the other side of the harbour to the East Cliff. This road is now known as Madeira Walk, and the plan was to create a long, sweeping highway that would take the traffic from the steep, narrow thoroughfare of the still-existing Albion Hill, and make it look as if it had been cut through a steep gorge, especially near the harbour end. One only has to walk up (or down) Madeira Walk to know that James 2 was involved here, and, indeed, I have a copy of the contract that was issued to Messrs Pulham and Son by The Mayor, Aldermen and Burgesses of the Borough of Ramsgate for this work. It is dated 5th April 1894, and begins: [97]

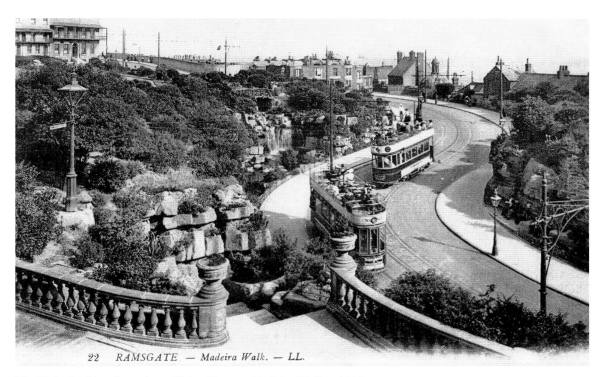

Fig 21.2 *Looking down from Albion Place to Madeira Walk,* c.*1910* (Photo provided by Terry Wheeler)

'The Contractor shall execute in an artistic substantial and workmanlike manner the works indicated in the plan hereunto annexed and comprising the formation of artificial rocks on both sides of the New Approach Road to the East Cliff at Ramsgate, the chalk being first excavated and broken back for the purpose of the Corporation, such rocks to be formed of the Contractors' Pulhamite Stratified Rock.

'Commencing at the low end facing the Royal Hotel the Rock will necessarily be very upright at first and will therefore be made to appear as part of the Cliff cut back, breaking back further up and getting the rock more broken about a fissure or cleft to be formed in the rock sufficiently wide to form a series of easy steps and landings from the New Road to Albion Place (at the top of Albion Hill) and further up the hill cropping and masses of rock to be formed with here and there slopes for turf and planting down between as in nature and in sight of the bend of the road a waterfall and watercourse to be formed to add picturesqueness and interest, this to appear to start from a cleft in the rock . . .

'The construction of the whole of the rock to be of brick burr and other suitable rough material and to have plenty of hollows and pockets for planting in. The whole surface to be covered with the Contractor's special Pulhamite cement of different quiet tones of colour . . . so that when done the rocks will appear massive and bold and form a picturesque, naturalistic winding road through a split in the rock.

'The Contractors to provide all skilled labour all personal and other supervision and the whole of the aforesaid Pulhamite Cement for the whole of the creation of the rock formation and steps herein named and shown and rail carriage, but all other material including cement other than the above Pulhamite cement, unskilled labour, scaffolding, carting, turfing, planting and proper protection to be provided by the Corporation free of charge to the Contractor.'

Between four and six months was envisaged for the task, and the cost of the work would not exceed £770. Nearly one hundred years after this contract was issued, Sally Festing referred to this project in an article for the *Journal of The Garden History Society*.[98] She wrote:

'...Moving eastwards, audacious, gaudily tinted rocks lead backwards on either side of Madeira Walk. On one side there is a small park with a waterfall, "to add picturesqueness and interest"; on the other, caves and tunnels ...Colour bands in green, pale pink, peach, and mauve, stuck with white shells are in appropriate festive spirit, though they show no attempt to copy naturalistic tones. They are planted with berrying shrubs, pelargoniums and other bedding plants.'

Fig 21.1 is from an old photograph, and shows a tram moving up the hill of Madeira Walk, past the bank of rockwork below the old route of Albion Hill, with Albion Place at the top, and **Fig 21.2** looks down from Albion Place to Madeira Walk, near an 'outcrop' opposite a bend about half way up the hill. It is quite easy to assess from these pictures why a new, wider road, with a shallower gradient, was considered necessary to link up with the East Cliff.

Fig 21.3 (above) *The Pulhamite rockwork at the bottom end of Madeira Walk*

Fig 21.4 (left) *Balustrading terminal, with the Ramsgate Coat of Arms, at the foot of Madeira Walk and Albion Hill*

Fig 21.5 (below) *Looking across Madeira Walk to the steps leading up to Albion Place* (Photo by Anne Rowe)

Fig 21.6 *Steps from Madeira Walk to Albion Place*

I am confident that the balustrading that borders Albion Hill would also originally have been by Pulham, although most of it has now been replaced – a lot of it was damaged by bombs during the First and Second World Wars. The original terracotta terminal still stands at the bottom, however, and proudly carries the Ramsgate Coat of Arms moulded into it, as can be seen here in **Fig 21.4**. This is just like the Newport coat of arms on the pavilion in Belle Vue Park, Newport, as discussed and illustrated in the previous chapter.

I had a special reason for wanting to see the rockwork along Madeira Walk, because I have a strong feeling that my great-grandfather, William Hitching, may have been involved in its construction. I can't prove it, but will explain why I think this during the course of

my description of the other Ramsgate sites in Chapter 41.

Fig 21.3 is a picture of the extreme lower end or Madeira Walk as it is today, with the road sign showing clearly on the right. The bands of *'different quiet tones of colour'*, or the *'green, pale pink, peach, and mauve'* described by Sally Festing – whichever way one wants to view them – are not now very evident, but everything is still in good condition, with only a few places in need of restoration work. The rocky bank continues round the bend of the road, and up the *'series of easy steps and landings'* specified in the contract as leading up to Albion Hill. The picture in Fig 21.2 looks down from the top of these steps, and **Fig 21.5** looks at them from across the road – **Fig 21.6** being a view upwards from the bottom.

Fig 21.7 *Steps up from Madeira Walk (opposite Albion Place)*

Fig 21.8 *Rock-lined path and tunnel leading from Madeira Walk.*
(Photo by Anne Rowe)

Fig 21.9 *A postcard of the waterfall, rocks and pool in Madeira Walk,* c.*1920* (Photo provided by Hazelle Jackson)

Fig 21.10 *The waterfall, rocks and pool in Madeira Walk, 2005*

There is another flight of steps opposite here, on the inside of the curve, as shown in **Fig 21.7**, but, as can be seen in **Fig 21.8**, this leads to a service area at the rear of some houses, with a little tunnel at the far end that leads back out to Madeira Walk, at the point from which Fig 21.5 was taken.

A few yards further up the hill from here, on the opposite side of the road, are the small waterfall and pool; the central feature of this part of the road, they can be clearly seen in Fig 21.2, just where the two trams are about to pass. **Fig 21.9** is reproduced from an old postcard,

showing people looking down at the floodlit display. The lights are not used now, but the water pumping system has recently been completely overhauled and restored, and is now working again as effectively as it was when it was originally installed, as is evident from **Fig 21.10**.

Also Noted:
1894-96 – *'Kingswood House'*, Sydenham Hill, Dulwich, South London
1895-99 – St James's Park, London

- 22 -

DEWSTOW HOUSE

CAERWENT, MONMOUTHSHIRE, WALES

1895-1912

Fig 22.1 *Henry Oakley (in waistcoat and boater) and guests in his rose pergola*, c.*1935* (Photo reproduced by kind permission of Mrs Howells)

Fig 22.2 *Edward Pearce, the head gardener, at work in the Lion Grotto*, c.*1935* (Photo reproduced by kind permission of Michael Naish)

Dewstow House, near Caerwent, is not far from Chepstow in Monmouthshire, and one of the incredible things about this garden is that it was only rediscovered in 2000, after lying buried for nearly sixty years!

Henry Roger Keene Oakley – a director of and shareholder in the Great Western Railway – bought Dewstow House in 1893, and lived there until his death in 1940.[99] He was a rather eccentric recluse, and almost obsessive about keeping himself to himself.[100] When he died in 1940, the property was inherited by Stanley Naish, and later

passed through various hands until it was eventually broken up into 'parcels' during the 1950s.[101]

Most of these were sold individually as houses and smallholdings, but the main bulk of the estate was made up of Dewstow Farm and Dewstow House – with the portion upon which stood Dewstow House being rather like a slice in the 'cake' of Dewstow Farm. William Harris – who had previously worked for Stanley Naish as Head Bailiff – purchased the farm, and Dewstow House was sold separately.

The Harris family continued to farm the land until 1987, when they decided to move over into the golf industry. The Dewstow Golf Club opened its doors in August 1988, and has expanded progressively since that time. When Dewstow House came back onto the market in 2000, William's son Elwyn, and his family, decided to buy it, with the result that the whole estate is now back together again, almost in its entirety, for the first time in sixty years. Dewstow House thus became the home of Elwyn's son, John Harris.

Fig 22.3 (right) *The small Italian Garden at Dewstow* (Photo by Jenny Lilly)

Fig 22.4 (overleaf) *The South Garden at Dewstow* (Photo by Jenny Lilly)

Soon after moving in, John and Elwyn noticed something strange in the garden and grounds. There were pieces of rock projecting through parts of the soil – some close to the house, and some further away, down the slope towards the road. As they began to move the soil away, more rocks were uncovered, and the more soil they moved the more rocks they found. They then noticed that the corners of a few of the protruding rocks had chipped off, and, beneath the natural-looking surface, there appeared to be bricks.

Thankfully, they realised that they had bought into a slice of English and Welsh garden heritage, and decided to proceed with great care and caution. They eventually uncovered not just a very large surface rock garden – complete with streams, cascades and pools – but a labyrinth of underground tunnels, caves, grottoes and ferneries! It took them three years of meticulous digging and excavating to uncover and restore the basic structures of the gardens, and they appointed a head gardener – with special responsibilities for replanting the restored gardens – and two assistant gardeners to look after them.

There was no doubt that the gardens had been created by James Pulham and Son, and, based on the knowledge that quite a lot of Pulhams' patrons called them in to landscape their gardens within a few years of taking over a new property, it seems likely that at least part of this work would have been done around 1895, although there is evidence that the total project was spread over two or three sections, spanning a number of years. So why have the gardens suddenly come to light again after so many years – and what happened to them in the meantime?

William Winter – who once lived on the estate – explains that his family stayed on at the Lodge for about a year after the property was inherited by Stanley Naish in 1940, and recalls how, sometime during his ownership, someone covered the whole area of the gardens – including the subterranean features – with thousands of tons of topsoil from the nearby motorway development.[102] It is quite possible that this was in response to a request from the Ministry of Agriculture to maximise the output from his land, and Mr Naish may even have been paid to do so in order to create more grazing land for his cows.

Fig 22.1 is one of the only known photographs of Henry Oakley himself – he is the elderly gentleman in the waistcoat and boater, standing with some guests in his rose pergola – and **Fig 22.2** is a picture of the underground Lion Grotto – so called because one of its fountain heads is in the form of a lion's head. The man at work with his ferns is Edward Pearce, head gardener to Henry Oakley.

Thanks to John Harris and his family, it is now possible to get some idea of what the gardens looked like in Henry Oakley's day. I first visited the gardens at Dewstow in 2001, when the restoration work was well under way, and then again in 2005, when it was nearly complete. The transformation was remarkable, and this has to be one of the jewels in the Pulham crown. The gardens are effectively split into two main areas that, for ease of reference, can be referred to as the South Garden and the North Garden. Each of these is in turn divided into a number of different 'compartments'.

The South Garden includes a small low-walled Italian Garden, pictured in **Fig 22.3**, near which is a stream that tumbles over a rocky cascade, past the summer house, and into the 'Engine Pond', and **Fig 22.4** is a picture of the South Garden as the path meanders over the stream. The 'Engine Pond' – which was apparently once used as a swimming pool – is so called because it includes the pump house that circulates the water through the whole system.

Fig 22.5 shows the Pulhamite façade of the pump house on the left, with the summer house visible at the far end of the pond. One of the pumps carries the date of 1911, so this provides a clue to the probable date for the construction of one part of the gardens. My estimation is therefore that the South Gardens at Dewstow were landscaped during phase 1 – probably around 1895, perhaps under the direction of James 2 – and the North Gardens during phase 2, around 1912, when James 3 would have been responsible.

The stream runs from here into the lily pond, and then into the beautifully laid-out duck pond, which can be seen in **Fig 22.6**, with its small grotto or boat cave at the far end. It then continues along the edge of the gardens – **Fig 22.7** – to the cascade at the far end,

Fig 22.8 *Work under way on the waterfall and stream in the South Garden in 2001*

Fig 22.9 *The South Pool waterfall* (Photo by John Harris)

Fig 22.10 (below) *Steps leading up to the gazebo* (Photo by Jenny Lilly)

Fig 22.11 (above) *The Bog Garden at Dewstow*

Fig 22.12 (above right) *Inside the South Tunnel at Dewstow* (Photo by Jenny Lilly)

Fig 22.13 (right) *The dropping well and stepping stone pathway leading through the archway to the North Garden* (Photo by Jenny Lilly)

Fig 22.14 (overleaf) *The Alpine garden* (Photo by Jenny Lilly)

and this was the point to which the course of the stream had been traced by the time of my first visit in 2001. **Fig 22.8** shows the team hard at work removing the topsoil from the rocks at the waterfall, but compare this with **Fig 22.9**, which illustrates – far better than words can describe – the transformation that had taken place by 2005.

On the way back towards the house, one passes over the spot where Henry Oakley had his pergola – which no longer exists – and the steps that lead up to the gazebo (**Fig 22.10**). A little further on is the Japanese-style bridge that passes over the Bog Garden, which is shown in **Fig 22.11**. The entrance to the South Tunnel is just visible behind the rocks at the far end of the pathway, and part of the tunnel is pictured in **Fig 22.12**. There is a flight of steps at the far end of the tunnel that leads back up to the surface.

The tour of the North Garden starts at the handsome balustraded entrance bridge, near the visitors' car park, and there is a small pool just below the bridge, fed by a stream that runs down to this part of the garden through a picturesque rustic archway. To get through here, one has to walk along a little path of stepping stones set into the stream, at the other end of which is another small Pulhamite rock garden, with a dropping well on the right – **Fig 22.13** looks back from here through the archway.

A flight of steps leads up into a large area that has been laid out as an Alpine garden (**Fig 22.14**), but, just opposite the dropping well, one should take a close look at the Pulhamite rocks, because there is a narrow cleft, at the end of which is an unobtrusive black wooden

Fig 22.15 (left) *Door leading to the subterranean Fern Grotto* (Photo by Jenny Lilly)

Fig 22.16 (below) *Inside the Fern Grotto* (Photo by Jenny Lilly)

gothic-style door – **Fig 22.15**. By now, this should not be a tremendous revelation, because this was a fairly common Pulham invitation to the visitor to step through, and prepare for a surprise in the space beyond . . .

They would not be disappointed, because the door leads right back underground into the Fern Grotto, shown in **Fig 22.16**. The walls are all lined with Pulham's tufa rock, and there are planting pockets all around, brimming with a wonderful selection of ferns. A small waterfall feeds the pool to one side, and the water flows off from here to join the stream on its way to the pool by the entrance bridge. At the far end of the grotto, a tunnel – **Fig 22.17** – beckons, suggesting another surprise in store. This time, it leads to an even larger grotto – **Fig 22.18** – with more tunnels seeming to lead off in all directions! This is called the Tufa Grotto, because there is tufa rock all around – much of it masked by another splendid array of ferns and other plants.

Fig 22.17 *Inside the North Tunnel* (Photo by Jenny Lilly)

Fig 22.18 *Inside the Tufa Grotto* (Photo by Jenny Lilly)

Fig 22.19 *Inside the Lion Grotto at Dewstow* (Photo by Charles Hawes)

And then, on to the final point of the tour – the Lion Grotto where Mr Pearce was in charge one hundred years ago. As can be seen from **Figs 22.19 and 22.20**, its balustraded pools, fountain, fern-clad tufa covering the walls and pillars, and planting pockets everywhere, make it a place in which to linger and savour a unique experience. These gardens are now open to the public, and should not be missed.

As one leaves the Lion Grotto, and makes one's way to the steps at the end of the passage that leads back to the gardens, there is a patch of wall where the ashlar-style rendering has broken away, and it has been deliberately left like this to help illustrate the craftsmanship of the Pulham workmen. This is shown in **Fig 22.21**, while **Fig 22.22** is a picture of a section of the ceiling in one of the rooms of Dewstow House. Could this also be Pulhams' work – I doubt that we shall ever know.

Fig 22.20 (right, top) *The Lion Grotto at Dewstow*

Fig 22.21 (right, centre) *A patch in the ashlar coating of the tunnel wall*

Fig 22.22 (right, below) *The ceiling in one of the rooms of Dewstow House*

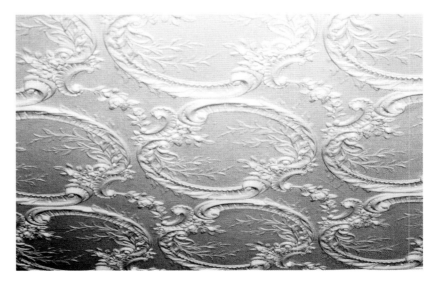

- 23 -

BLAKESLEY HALL

BLAKESLEY, NORTHAMPTONSHIRE

1895-1908

Fig 23.1 *Side view of Blakesley Hall, c.1910. Notice the fountain, balustrading and vases that are almost certainly by Pulham*

The manor and estates at Blakesley, near Towcester, Northamptonshire, have a long history and have had several owners, the last of whom was Charles Bartholomew. Charles purchased the property in 1876 as a gift for his son, Charles William Bartholomew, who acquired the title of Lord of the Manor.

Although Charles William spent little time there before his father's death in 1895, he then proceeded to make up for lost time. He set off almost immediately to spend large portions of his father's fortune on the estate and village, and was well known as a local benefactor.[103]

One of his 'improvements' was to commission James 2 (or 3) to construct an ornamental stream – complete with a waterfall, cascade, lagoon, stepping stones and rustic bridges – in his pleasure grounds. He did this very cleverly by cutting a canal that branched off from the Black Ouse – a stream that ran down through the village – about 200 yards or so above the Hall, and feeding it into a holding lagoon in the far south-west corner of the estate. He then created an artificial 'Back Brook' down the southern boundary, lined it on both

sides with Pulhamite, and fed it back into the Black Ouse at the lower end of the village, some 600 yards below its starting point. Charles William's guests were even able to participate in a quiet afternoon's punting on the picturesque 'upper stretch' of the stream.

He was also apparently a great railway enthusiast, and built a miniature railway line around the estate for his guests to ride on. He even built a branch line to the local station in order to facilitate the delivery of all the stone and other materials directly to the site.

It is not exactly clear when the work was actually done, but the large-scale Ordnance Survey map of 1900 shows the stream and the waterfall, which means that it must have been somewhere around 1895-98. **Fig 23.1** is a picture of the side of the house, with an unusual pool in the shape of a Maltese cross, and **Fig 23.2** shows the waterfall as it was c.1910. **Fig 23.4** was taken in 2004, and features a number of large planting pockets interspersed among the rocks, which are generally still in very good order. There is even a small crocodile (**Fig 23.3**) hiding near the bank.

Fig 23.2 *The waterfall at Blakesley, c.1910*

Fig 23.3 *A crocodile lies in wait*

Fig 23.4 *The remains of the waterfall in 2004*

Fig 23.5 *The balustraded bridge over the stream*

Fig 23.5 shows the balustraded bridge that crosses the stream just below where the house once stood, and it is known that Pulhams built this in 1907-08. Based on observations at other sites, I am confident that there was originally a rustic wooden bridge at this point, and later replaced by the present balustraded bridge.

There is a garage and part of a workshop complex near the stables that once housed an electricity generator. This is in the vicinity of a chalybeate spring, and there is another interesting item here, too: the remains of the old farm manager's cottage, shown in **Fig 23.6**, that is situated at the corner of the meadow on which Charles William Bartholomew grazed his cows.

The internal walls can be seen through the open doorway, and these are built from normal house bricks, but the external walls are not. At first glance, one might think that they might be Pulhamite-coated

Fig 23.6 *The farm manager's cottage, the outside walls of which are built from hollow pre-cast blocks*

Fig 23.7 *One of the two seats near the bridge at Blakesley Hall*

bricks, sculpted into this very pleasant, old-style 'rough hewn' finish, but they are actually hollow, pre-cast concrete blocks, and my initial instinct was that these may also have been cast by Pulhams. The cottage was apparently built around the time that the firm was on site, and they would certainly have had the facilities to produce such blocks if they wanted to, but it has been suggested to me that they may perhaps have been cast by a firm called Hitch, who owned a brickworks near Ware, in Hertfordshire – quite close to the Pulham manufactory. 'Hitch Bricks' were apparently quite well known around the turn of the 20th Century, although few known examples of them survive today. Perhaps this is one more that can be added to the list, although I am personally inclined to stick with the idea that they actually came from the manufactory in Broxbourne.

The Secret of the Seat

There used to be two terracotta seats in the grounds, and, although nothing quite like them is illustrated in the *Pulham Garden*

Ornament Catalogue, they have a distinct 'Pulham look' about them, and they also match the piers at the end of the balustrading of the bridge (Fig 23.5), near where they were originally placed.

When I first visited Blakesley in 2002, there was only one of these seats left in its original position – shown here in **Fig 23.7** – because the present owner had decided to move one of them to 'somewhere safer'. That obviously worked well, because, two years later, in 2004, he decided to move the second one, and pair them up again in their new situation. It may seem a drastic way of doing things, but the seat was too heavy to lift, so he cut it up in pieces, and put it back together again in its new position – something that, it should be noted, he was well qualified to do.

Despite its weight, the seat was hollow, and, during dismantling, something very strange was noticed tucked away inside the frame. It was a bottle, inside of which was an old envelope that had been unstuck and folded flat, just like one of those bottles that are

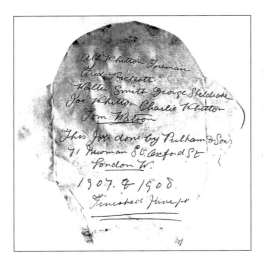

Fig 23.8 *The 'Message in the Bottle' that tells us when the Pulham work was done, and by whom*

sometimes found washed up on the shore from a shipwreck! And sure enough, there *was* something written on this piece of paper. It wasn't an S.O.S. message, but a list of names, with a date at the bottom, and it is reproduced here as **Fig 23.8**.

It was actually a list of the names of the Pulham craftsmen who worked on the site, and it concluded with the date of 1907-08. So there it is – the question answered in just about the most romantic way possible. The team foreman was Alf Whitton, and his team consisted of Fred Rickett, Walter Smith, George Sheldrake, Joe Whitton, Charlie Whitton and Tom Watson, and there is a note at the bottom that confirms the provenance of the work beyond any doubt. It reads:

'This job done by Pulham and Son, 71 Newman St., Oxford St., London W. 1907 and 1908. Finished June 1st'

What more could one ask? Not a lot, really, but there was indeed a bonus, because, tucked away further down inside the shell of the seat, was an old piece of wood, and this, too, had writing on it – on both sides, in fact! It is shown here as **Fig 23.9**.

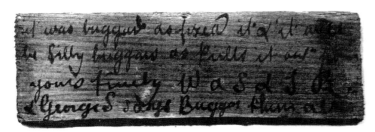

Figs 23.9a and b *The old piece of wood that the team obviously never thought would see the light of day again!*

One side carries the signatures of Walter Smith, George Sheldrake and Fred Rickett, and on the reverse there is a rather cryptic message that reads:

'It was buggers as fixed it, and it will be silly buggers as pulls it out! From Yours Truly, W.A.S and T.W.'

So Walter Smith and Tom Watson obviously thought that neither the bottle with its message, nor the piece of wood, would ever be retrieved from their hiding place, but they were wrong . . .

Oh, and there was a postscript:

'George S says Bugger them all!'

One wonders what they would have said if they had known that, in one hundred years' time, someone would actually be reading it!

Blakesley Hall was demolished for safety reasons in 1957, and the grounds are now owned by Philip Burt, a descendant of a friend, associate and respected confidante of Charles William. It was when Philip began to tidy up the grounds, and clear away the undergrowth, that he uncovered the stream with its banks lined with very large rocks, the surfaces of some of which had slightly chipped away to reveal what appeared to be a brick-based core. It was Pulhamite – although he didn't know it at the time. His ambition is to rebuild the Hall – as far as possible to its original plans – and then see it used as a family home, in just the same way that it was in the past. At the time of my last visit in 2010, he had uncovered – and was in the process of restoring – the Maltese cross pool near the side of the house.

1898: Death of James Pulham 2

James 2 died after a very short illness – in fact, he was working until one week before his death on 11th August 1898 – and the following two obituaries provide a few clues about his personal and professional reputation at that time. The first, published in the *Gardeners' Chronicle*,[104] reports that he died at his home, Clyde Lodge, Tottenham. The Tottenham Street Directory for 1898 shows Clyde Lodge as being at 42a Clyde Road, and it is interesting to note that the map of the area shows the property backing onto a nursery, so perhaps he moved in order to gain access to a facility that enabled him to grow some of his own plants? The house no longer exists, although the house at No. 30 probably dates from that period, and the stone face – which may or may not be Pulhamite – is pictured in Fig 2.1d.

Fig 23.10 *The memorial to James 2 in St Augustine's churchyard, Broxbourne*

of
Hannah
the Beloved Wife of
James Pulham
of This Parish
who Died December 26th 1873
Aged 58
Not Lost But Gone Before
And of
Hannah Jane
the Beloved Wife of
James George Bensted
of Waltham Abbey
Daughter of the Above
who Died December 7th 1874
Aged 30
Her Sun is Gone Down While it Was Yet Day
Charles Percy Bensted
Born Dec'r 1st, Died Dec'r 18th 1874
Also of the Above Mentioned
James Pulham
Who Died at Tottenham
August 11th 1898
Aged 78

Now the Labourer's Task is O'er;
Now the Battle Day is Past;
Now Upon the Farther Shore
Lands the Voyager at Last.
Father, in Thy Gracious Keeping
Leave We Now Thy Servant Sleeping

The obituary goes on to say:

'Many of our readers, and especially those who have had dealings with Mr Pulham in the capacity of garden architect and constructor of rockeries, waterfalls, lakes etc, will regret to learn of his death, which took place on Thursday, August 11, at the age of 78 years. The funeral took place at Broxbourne churchyard on Monday (15th). We are informed that the business will be carried on as heretofore under the same title.'

The second obituary – in the *Hertfordshire Mercury*[105] – reads:

'We regret to announce the death of Mr James Pulham (the head of the well-known firm of Pulham and Son) terracotta manufacturers and rock workers, of Finsbury Square and Broxbourne, which took place, after about a week's illness, on the 11th inst at Tottenham, where he had resided for the last fifteen years. The late Mr Pulham was born in Woodbridge, Suffolk, in 1820, and commenced his business in Tottenham, and afterwards moved it to Hoddesdon, and subsequently to Broxbourne, where it has been carried on for the last 45 years.

'He was actively employed until within about a week of his death, and it is through his untiring industry and perseverance, maintained through a long life, that he succeeded, with the assistance of his son (Mr James Pulham) in raising the business to the eminent position it now occupies as one of the leading firms of its kind in the kingdom . . .'

This confirms that James 2 moved out of his home in Broxbourne around 1883, and handed it over to his son, James 3, while he moved back to Tottenham – the place where he spent much of his childhood, and where he first took over the business on the death of his father, James 1. Before saying one's final farewell to James 2, however, there seems to be one last, sad story of a much more personal nature to record. It is told on his tombstone in St Augustine's churchyard in Broxbourne, Hertfordshire, pictured here in **Fig 23.10**.

This tells how James 2 survived his wife, Hannah, by some twenty-five years. She died on Boxing Day, 1873, which was sad enough in itself, but the following Christmas season must have been just as bad for him, because his daughter, Hannah Jane Bensted, died on 7th December, 1874. This was evidently as a result of childbirth, because her baby, Charles Percy, was born just six days earlier, on 1st December, and died on the 18th, only 17 days old. This series of tragic events must have made the family home seem very empty for James 2, and could well have been one of the reasons for him deciding to hand the production side of the business over to James 3, and move away to Tottenham to concentrate on the London office.

Also Noted:

1896 – Knebworth House, Hertfordshire
1896-97 – Wotton House, Dorking, Surrey
1898 – Mount Stuart, Isle of Bute, Scotland
1898-99 – Sunningdale Park, Ascot, Berkshire

- 24 -

FRIAR PARK

HENLEY-ON-THAMES, OXFORDSHIRE

1898-1912

Fig 24.1 *The Alpine Garden and 'Mini-Matterhorn' at Friar Park, c.1910*

James 2 died on 11th August 1898 after a very short illness, which meant that he sadly just missed out on being involved in one of the firm's greatest achievements. On the other hand, one could say that James 3 was lucky in that Friar Park, at Henley-on-Thames, was the first project for which he was solely responsible, and thus marked the beginning of a new era in the firm's history. It couldn't have got off to a more auspicious start, because their work here is truly 'fantastic' – in the literal sense of the word.

Friar Park was once the home of Sir Frank Crisp – a brilliant, eccentric man who lived at the same time as Henry Oakley, in Dewstow, discussed in Chapter 22. Unlike Mr Oakley, however, Sir Frank was anything but reclusive.[106] He had an irrepressible sense of fun, and a taste for the bizarre. He bought Friar Park in 1896, and replaced the old house with a sprawling 120-room mansion. It is an eclectic blend of French Renaissance and Gothic Revival architecture – complete with turrets, towers and gargoyles

– that bears more than a casual resemblance to the Palace of Versailles. He was also a gardening enthusiast, and his gardens contained many attractions for his guests to admire and enjoy. In fact, he was one of the first people to introduce garden gnomes into England, and is reputed to have placed many hundreds of them around his gardens.

He was an acknowledged expert on Alpine plants, and sought to provide an appropriate setting for his outstanding collection. He imported thousands of tons of huge rocks with which to build a massive 'natural rock' alpine habitat for them in the eastern section of his estate, and – never having been known for doing things in moderation – decided to construct a 30-ft high replica of the Matterhorn as its centrepiece. It was reputably topped with a piece of rock from the summit of the Matterhorn itself, and a little tin chamois could even be seen cavorting on the slope.

A short article appeared in *Country Life* about the rock garden at Friar Park in 1903.[107] It read as follows:

> 'Rock gardening is imitative, but made ridiculous when the desire is simply to throw together in meaningless confusion brick-ends and the refuse of a mason's yard – that is rock gardening gone mad. At Friar Park, the great boulders and stones are arranged so naturally that the effect is dignified, and the flowers are given just those places in which they rejoice in alpine pass and mead. No formal walk mars this garden. The path winds through the stones heaped on either side until an open space permits things of ruder growth than others to ramble at will, and a knowledge of where to place the alpines leads to surprising success. Saxifrages crawl into the paths, and Sun Roses open wide in the hot sun, their stems dropping like a gorgeous curtain over some sun-baked rock surface.'

The rocks for the 'Matterhorn' were supplied by the firm of James Backhouse and Son, of York, and Sir Frank's head gardener, a Mr Knowles, was detailed to arrange them under the guidance of Mr W A Clark – Backhouse's chief foreman, and specialist in rare Alpine plants – who came down from York to supervise the planting.[108]

This is not an exclusively Backhouse garden, however, because there are several features here that bear all the hallmarks of Pulhams' involvement. In fact, I have recently been given a copy of a diary that was maintained by Fred Rickett, one of the Pulham rock-builders – he was one of the team who left their names on the piece of paper hidden in the seat at Blakesley Hall (Fig 23.8) – and he noted that they started work at Friar Park in October 1898, and stayed until 1901, during which time they constructed:

> 'Caves (dry and water), water pools, lake and Matterhorn, including Ice Cave and Glacier.'[109]

Sir Frank died in 1919, and the estate was taken over by a Catholic convent and parochial school. By the 1950s, however, the gardens were derelict, and the nuns had insufficient funds to do anything about it. The school closed in 1969, and, just as it was about to be sold to developers, it was discovered by George Harrison, 'The Quiet Beatle', who immediately fell in love with it, and bought it in 1971.

Most people remember George for his music, but he consistently claimed that gardening was his true love. He renovated the mansion and hired ten gardeners and a full-time botanist to scrupulously restore the grounds to their previous glory. His widow, Olivia Harrison, is now making sure that they stay as perfect as George would have wished them to be.

The Matterhorn Rock Garden

I was invited to visit Friar Park in 2005, but was specifically asked not to take photographs. However, I have been fortunate enough to obtain some old postcards of the gardens as they were during their early years, and I hope that these – together with my written description of this wonderful place – will help to convey the sense of magic and fantasy that were obviously the objective of Sir Frank Crisp when he engaged James 3 to bring his dreams to life.

The first thing one sees when entering the East Rock Garden is a delightful little waterfall and pool. I had seen Pulham waterfalls and pools like this before, but the rocks around here were exceptional. They were massive things, some of which must have measured more than one cubic metre, and weighed several tons.

This is just near the base of Crisp's 'Matterhorn' – an incredible replica of Zermatt's majestic Alpine peak. It is difficult to imagine that, about one hundred years ago, a team of men – presumably with comparatively basic lifting equipment – were responsible for the individual placement of all these rocks. The 'mountain' itself is now capped with white alabaster chips, and the little tin chamois no longer cavorts over the slopes.

A flight of steps leads about halfway up the 'mountain', from where the pathway runs down between the lichen-covered rocks, around the edge of a pool, and into the bottom of a charming valley, where one can stand, or sit, and look back along the way one has come. This is the point from which the postcard published *c*.1910 – **Fig 24.1** – was taken, and it shows the huge rugged rockscape, with the stream running down into the pool at the bottom.

Very little has changed since those days, except that the Matterhorn now shows up against a backdrop of the trees that have grown up since Sir Frank's day. Overall, this is a typical Backhouse 'natural rock' garden on a grand scale, although James 3 obviously got involved during the early stages of construction, because the water features would have had to be laid out before the rock building was completed.

Fig 24.2 *Inside the Ice Grotto at Friar Park,* c.*1910* (Postcard provided by Denise Theophilus)

Fig 24.3 *Looking down the lake at Friar Park from the lawns,* c.*1920* (Postcard provided by J Gardiner)

There are a series of grottoes beneath the Matterhorn – which I was unable to explore for safety and security reasons – and another one near the top. This one has a wooden door let into the rock face – just like the one at Dewstow, shown in Fig 22.15 – and the rocks immediately surrounding it are Pulhamite. Inside, the walls are smooth and white, as is also the floor-to-ceiling pillar that stands near the door, whereas, in a fernery grotto, these would have all been rough, like tufa. There is a pool in the centre of the floor, and 'stalactites' are suspended from the roof. This is the Ice Grotto, and the postcard reproduced in **Fig 24.2** provides a unique impression of what it looked like in its prime – the stork had long since departed by the time of my visit.

One of the guidebooks to the gardens, written by Crisp himself, claimed that more than 20,000 tons of stone were used on the site, and the complete job was spread over a period of at least seven years. This was because, as well as being extremely meticulous by nature, Sir Frank was also a hard taskmaster. Everything had to be 'just right', and James 3 returned to make 'alterations to the Matterhorn' in both 1902 and 1906.

The Lakes, Grottoes and Japanese Garden

And this was just the beginning. An article in *The Garden Book*,[110] noted that James 3's work at Friar Park included:

> ' . . . create the waterfall in the rock garden, and the rocky banks
> around the lakes.'

This is confirmed by the inclusion of the word 'lake' in the short extract from Fred Rickett's diary referred to above. This hardly does it justice, because it is, in reality, a beautiful landscaped man-made lake – with rockwork visible around the edges – that lies on the opposite side of the meticulously manicured lawn from the rock garden. When looking down the lake from the lawn, one gets the impression that it is one continuous expanse of water, with an arched – almost Japanese-style – bridge spanning a neck of the lake towards the left-hand side, as can be seen in **Fig 24.3**.

When one looks back up the lake from the bottom, however – across the lawns towards the house – one can see that it is not one flat expanse of water at all. There are actually two cascades spanning the lake, thus effectively splitting it up into three levels. The entrance to a small cave can be seen on the right-hand end of the top cascade, and there is a set of stepping stones that completely spans the width of the lake at the foot of the lower one. It seems that Sir Frank was as meticulous in his planning of this part of his garden as he was about the Alpine meadows around the Matterhorn, and this part of the project could also have been spread over a number of years.

An old postcard from c.1920 – reproduced in **Fig 24.4** – shows this view from the bottom bank of the lake, with the stepping stones clearly visible, leading over to the left, just below the Japanese lantern. Another view of the stepping stones – with a lady walking across them – is reproduced in **Fig 24.5**. This is taken from the side, and, if one looks closely, it is also possible to see that there is a ridge – or shelf – of stone that runs just below the surface of the water at the top edge of the lower cascade, over which the water flows on its way to the stepping stones below. In fact, if one studies Fig 24.3 closely, one can see two people walking across the stepping stones, just level with the bridge. From here, their legs are not visible beyond the cascade.

The rocky edge of the top cascade is visible towards the left of Fig 24.5, and the entrance to the cave is on the far bank. Careful inspection shows that the front of this cascade is not one continuous 'wall' of stone – it is actually a 'shelf' supported by a series of pillars that allow the water of the middle lake to flow between them. In fact, the 'cave' at the far side is the mouth of a tunnel through which a boat can pass, with the gaps between the 'pillars' acting like windows in a wall.

Fig 24.4 *The mansion, lake, cascades and stepping stones at Friar Park, c.1920* (Postcard provided by Denise Theophilus)

Fig 24.5 *The set of stepping stones below the top cascade in the lake at Friar Park, c.1920* (Postcard provided by James Gardiner)

These pictures help to illustrate Sir Frank's mischievous sense of humour, and his desire to impress. The story goes that, after wining and dining his guests, he loved to assemble them on the lawn, and, while they were admiring the view down what they assumed to be one large lake, he would ring a bell as a signal to his butler to walk across the line of stones – or shelf – below the lower cascade, to make it appear as if he was 'walking on water' across the lake with a tray of drinks.

Fig 24.6 *The Japanese Garden, c.1912* (Photo provided by Peter Crook)

The path that leads along the bottom edge of the lake is bounded on the opposite side by the bank of a steep gorge, along the bottom of which is a rapidly flowing stream that winds its way over a series of waterfalls. There is also a Japanese Tea House on the opposite bank, and, at the far end of this path, a small bridge spans the stream as it leaves the bottom neck of the lake on its way down into 'The Gorge'.

Crossing the bridge, the path leads to the Japanese Garden – an old photograph of which is shown in **Fig 24.6** – and, just to the right of this, behind where the old Nippon lantern used to be, a flight of steps leads down into the ground, at the foot of a short slope. The whole character of this part of the garden – together with the Tea House on the opposite side of 'The Gorge' from here – gives the impression that it was probably constructed sometime between 1908 and 1914. It is impossible to put an exact date on it, but – as will be discussed later – this was the period when the Pulhams were earning themselves an enviable reputation for their construction of Japanese gardens. This could therefore be the time when the whole lake was re-landscaped, and the cascades and stepping stones inserted.

There is another one of those 'Pulham doors' at the bottom of the flight of steps – again let directly into the rock face – and the short passage on the other side leads towards an opening in the rocks, through which one steps onto a sort of railed landing stage on the edge of an underground pool in a massive grotto. This is another world – a world of pure fantasy. The walls of the grotto are all clad in tufa, and there are several tufa pillars reaching up to the roof – just like the ones in the Lion Grotto at Dewstow – from which hang more 'stalactites'.

This is the Blue Grotto, named after the suffused light that filters in through blue glass windows in the roof. A stream flows into the grotto through a tunnel on the opposite side from the landing stage, lit by a series of electric lights controlled from a switch near the door. The stream continues out on the opposite side, through another section of the tunnel, and into another grotto.

Mere words can only provide a superficial impression of the real experience of seeing this for oneself. It is quite enchanting, and it is difficult to pull oneself away. It is also difficult to resist the temptation to compare this with the subterranean grottoes at Dewstow, but that would not be realistic, because those are adorned with a beautiful array of ferns, whereas there are no ferns in sight in the Blue Grotto at Friar Park.

Legend has it that, as a finale to his evening's entertainment, Sir Frank liked to take his guests on a boat trip. Starting from the cave entrance on the right-hand side of the middle lake, he would row them through the tunnel beneath the overhang of the top lake, from where they could look through the 'windows' between the pillars, and out through the overflowing curtain of water.

The tunnel bears left as it reaches the far side of the lake, and makes its way beneath the lawns and into the series of grottoes, which are actually built below the mound on which the Japanese Garden is placed. In Sir Frank's day, one of these grottoes contained skeletons and mirrors; another featured vines and illuminated glass grapes; a third contained a selection of mini-crocodiles, whilst a fourth housed part of his celebrated collection of garden gnomes. **Fig 24.7** is a

Figs 24.7a and b

Top right: *Inside the Crocodile Grotto at Friar Park* (postcard reproduced by permission of Mrs Olivia Harrison)

Right: *The Gnome Grotto* (postcard provided by Denise Theophilus)

composite picture of two old postcards that have come my way, showing sections of the Gnome Grotto and the Crocodile Grotto as they used to be in those days.

This Edwardian 'fantasyland' is a triumph of imagination and ingenuity, but still depended on the craftsmanship and virtuosity of the rock builders to translate this dream into reality. As far as can be ascertained, there are very few published references to the Pulhams' involvement here, apart from the brief note quoted from *The Garden Book,* but it will be clear by now that I have some very positive feelings about this.

Having seen the features that they created in several other gardens, my personal opinion is that James 3 actually did much more than *'create the waterfall in the rock garden, and the rocky banks around the lakes'* at Friar Park. Apart from the rocks brought in by Backhouse to build the Matterhorn rock garden, I am convinced that Pulhams should be credited with almost everything in these truly incredible gardens.

In fact, I can go further than that, because I was recently contacted by a near relative who is descended from my grandfather's brother,

John William Hitching. She tells me that her grandmother often spoke warmly of her 'Uncle William', and loved to hear his tales of when he worked on the grottoes at Friar Park. We are not able to say, however, whether he was in charge of the project, or was there as assistant foreman.

Sir Frank Crisp is not the only person who has to be thanked for this totally enchanting and eccentric piece of our garden heritage. It might have been lost forever had it not been for the intervention of George Harrison, who devoted the final years of his life to overseeing its complete restoration from its previous state of dereliction, and, since his death in 2001, his widow, Olivia, has continued to supervise its maintenance with great diligence and care.

Also Noted:

1899	– Coombe Wood, Croydon, Surrey
1900s	– Stoke Park, Guildford. Surrey
1900-01	– Bushey House, Bushey, Hertfordshire
1901-05	– *'Davenham'*, Malvern, Worcestershire

- 25 -

MERROW GRANGE

NEAR GUILDFORD, SURREY

1902-1907

Fig 25.1 *A shady rock-lined path leading into the rock gardens at Merrow Grange* (Photo by Jenny Lilly)

Between 1894 and 1927, Merrow Grange, near Guildford, was the home of Francis Baring-Gould, formerly a Director of the De Beers Diamond Mining Company and Chairman of the Kimberley Central Company in South Africa.[111] It is not known where he acquired his love for gardening, but it became an occupation about which he was both passionate and knowledgeable. He tended his gardens at Merrow Grange with great care and enthusiasm, and some idea of what he achieved can be gained from Saville's sales catalogue of 1929, which records:

'The delightfully laid out gardens and grounds are a very charming feature of the property. Fine trees, extensive rose gardens and walks are unique, and it is planted with specimen trees, shrubs and plants. There are grottoes, lily ponds, a Fernery, Dutch and rose gardens, lawns – including two excellent tennis lawns – and a woodland walk to a dell with a lake, where a boat is kept.'

All but about eight acres of the estate were auctioned off in 1929, in parcels of land that were then mainly covered by houses built during the 1930s. Merrow Grange itself, and its remaining gardens along

the southern boundary of Epsom Road, was converted into an auxiliary hospital during the latter years of the Second World War. In 1945 it was purchased and run as an independent girls' school, but the gardens became neglected and overgrown, and, by 1979, few people would have been aware of what was there until an article on garden restoration appeared in the *Sunday Observer Magazine* which referred to Merrow Grange, and commented that:

'. . . conservation volunteers are keen to work in the gardens of grottoes, woodland walks and fairy dells . . . it is exceedingly spooky, with unreal overtones of a macabre film set.'

In fact, these gardens contain some of the finest examples of Pulham's work that still exist today, and, in an article for the *Journal of The Garden History Society*[112] in 1983, Sally Festing recorded that they were constructed by James 3 *c*.1907. They included:

'. . . a sunk garden [probably known as the Dutch garden], a rectangular green open space with a central lily pond set within the trees to the west, and ornamental rockwork in the wooded parts. A two-arched cave, conservatory grotto seat and an ornamental rocky

Fig 25.2 *Further down the pathway at Merrow Grange* (Photo by Jenny Lilly)

pond surrounded by bamboos and Chusan palms; it is one of the prettiest parts of the wooded complex. The south front remains much as he left it, with a large 'Pulhamite' cave at the end of the grass, and informally planted specimen trees.'

It is likely that 1907 could well be the date of completion, but it is known that work was in progress on the rockwork and fernery between July 1902 and February 1903.[113]

A three-storey block of apartments with garages in this area of roughly 3.5 acres – now called 'Fairlawns' – was built in 1985, with the stipulation that most of the listed Pulham features were to remain intact. This split the remaining site into two sections, with the Grange in one part, and the new apartment block in the other. Merrow Grange house itself was then sold in 1993, and is now also a development of houses and apartments.

Provision was made in the conditions of the 'Fairlawns' development that part of the Edwardian gardens, including a fernery, should be restored, but restoration is one thing, and maintenance can be quite another, and it didn't take long for the gardens to become overgrown again. Luckily, however, the owners of some of these new flats have taken a great interest in their inheritance, and have put a tremendous amount of back-breaking work into bringing the gardens back to life. They continue to maintain them, and have achieved amazing results, so that, by the time of my visits in 2005, almost all of the superfluous

overgrowth had been stripped back to reveal the original features in all their glory, and replanting was well under way. By 2010 it had again become a question of routine maintenance.

Entry to the garden is through an iron gate, from where the path meanders gently down into the wooded area beyond, but it isn't long before small outcrops of rock begin to appear along the edges – a device that Pulham often used. As the path rounds a bend, the rocks gradually increase in size and guide the visitor to a rockwork screen ahead, as shown in **Fig 25.1**. If it were not for the pigeons in the trees overhead, this would have formed a delightful refreshment area.

The path then winds back in the general direction of the apartments, by which point the rocky structures are sometimes head high, as can be seen in **Fig 25.2**. Turning through a small gap in the rocks – on the left of which is a small pool and cascade – it reaches the main pool (**Fig 25.3**), which is only a few feet away from the apartments themselves. As can be seen from this picture, the water is clear; a new birdbath has been placed on the central Pulhamite rocks, and the small cascade and pool is in the background. The surrounds have been cleared of surplus growth, which is a tremendous tribute to the work that the residents have invested in this project.

Fig 25.3 (overleaf) *The circular pond and small cascade near the new development of flats* (Photo by Jenny Lilly)

Fig 25.4 *Dropping well in garden* (Photo by Jenny Lilly)

Fig 25.5 *Planting pockets and a tilting rock alongside the path*

Figs 25.6a and b *The Merrow Balustrade* (Photo by Jenny Lilly)

a (right) *The Merrow Balustrade, as pictured in the* Pulham Garden Ornament Catalogue c.*1925*
b (below) *A length of balustrading along the boundary*

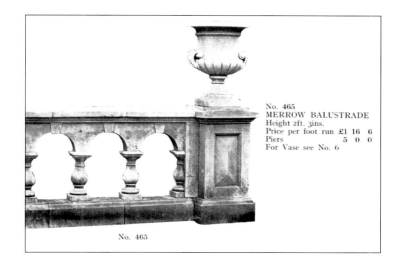

No. 465
MERROW BALUSTRADE
Height 2ft. 3ins.
Price per foot run £1 16 6
Piers 5 0 0
For Vase see No. 6

No. 465

These pictures – Figs 25.2 and 25.3 – show that the rocks at Merrow carry their own distinctive 'signature'. The surfaces of the 'rocks' themselves, and of the intermediate stratifications, all have quite pronounced horizontal grooves that are more pronounced than in most of the other Pulham gardens that I have seen – apart, perhaps, from the stratifications at Madresfield Court (Fig 11.5). The 'rock builder' responsible for this particular construction obviously had his own ideas about how the surfaces should be sculpted. Compare these with the more 'natural looking' rock surfaces at Buckingham Palace in Figs 30.7 and 30.8, for example.

Towards the western boundary of the 'Fairlawns' development is a dropping well – shown in **Fig 25.4** – and, along the northern boundary, there is another large area of rockwork that includes a number of planting pockets. There is also a 'tilting rock' near the edge of the pool (**Fig 25.5**), and this is similar to another that I have seen elsewhere.

Just near here there is a short length of balustrading that marks the edge of what is now an adjoining property. As can be seen from **Fig 25.6b**, it has been beautifully cleaned, and the *Pulham Garden Ornament Catalogue c.*1925 indicates that it was originally designed and produced especially for Francis Baring-Gould – for a cool £1-16-6d per foot!

There is a rather strange sunken twin-arched 'shelter' in the middle of one of the lawns, the real purpose of which has never been ascertained, it is pictured here in **Fig 25.7**. Another feature near here is effectively a smaller version of one of the main attractions at both Dewstow and Friar Park (discussed in Chapters 22 and 24 respectively). A flight of steps leads down to an iron door, which may at one time have been wooden, set into an archway, and leads to a tunnel (**Fig 25.8**). The floor dips quite steeply at first, and it then levels out, and one is immediately struck by the many tiny specks of light that reflect from the beams of one's torch. This is caused by thousands of tiny mica crystals that were embedded into the rough tufa-like cement used to surface the walls, and the picture in **Fig 25.9** gives some idea of this effect.

There are several tiny niches embedded into the wall surfaces that have either the end of an old electric cable sticking out, or the remains of some candle wax. These mark the points where lights

Fig 25.7 (above) *A sunken twin-arched shelter in the lawn* (Photo by Jenny Lilly)

Fig 25.8 (right) *The entrance door to the fernery tunnel at Merrow Grange*

Fig 25.9 *Inside the tunnel, in which the occasional fleck of mica can be seen* (Photo by Jenny Lilly)

and candles had once been placed to light the way, and are obviously the reason for the sprinkling of the mica granules. The new string of lights provides an impression of how magical this must have looked one hundred years ago.

The tunnel twists and turns for about forty yards before rising again into a small cave that once had 'stalactites' hanging from the roof, but these have since been broken off. This, in turn, leads out onto the basement floor of a large, sunken fernery, where the walls are about fifteen feet high. One wall is covered with tufa and Bargate sandstone, and contains numerous planting pockets, while the one on the side of the curved stairway only has the core brickwork.

The 'basement' floor is covered with a mosaic of red glazed terracotta tiles that have remained almost intact since they were laid more than 100 years ago. The stairway curves up to the ground level, where a rock-edged causeway stretches across to link the entrances on either side, as shown in **Fig 25.10**. The glass has long since gone from the iron-framed roof.

If one crosses the causeway, and leaves the fernery via the opposite exit, one would pass the entrance to the old boiler house, which is cunningly concealed in an archway near the entrance. One of Mr Baring-Gould's gardeners would have had to stoke the boiler every day to maintain the heat and humidity required in the fernery. Passing through here into the open, one enters a small rock-lined area with a massive 'archway' at the far end that leads out into the rock garden. **Fig 25.11** looks through the archway from the garden side. In fact, this is not strictly an archway, because there is a small gap between the two overhanging rocks that almost – but not quite – meet in the centre.

The main feature of the rock garden itself is 'The Mound', which stretches behind the point from which Fig 25.11 was taken. This was created from the earth displaced from the excavation of the

Fig 25.10 *The causeway across the fernery at Merrow Grange* (Photo by Jenny Lilly)

Fig 25.11 *The rock 'archway' leading from the garden fernery. There is actually a small gap between the two overhanging rocks across the top of the arch* (Photo by Jenny Lilly)

tunnel, and is another area where the residents have done a tremendous amount of restoration and clearing out of 'tired' and self-seeded surplus growth. The rather quaint 'conservatory grotto seat' referred to in Sally Festing's article used to be perched on top of it, but this has since been blown down by the storms, and is now lying rather forlornly on its back.

There is a large Pulhamite grotto near the centre of the six-foot high fence that marks the boundary between 'Fairlawns' and the Merrow Grange development. It is just like the boat cave at Heatherden Hall (Fig 29.4), but the residents of the 'Fairlawns' flats can only see the back of it – as shown in **Fig 25.12**. Those at the Grange, on the other hand, can relax in the cool of the grotto itself, if they wish, but are unable to access the steps that lead up to the sunbathing patio at the top. Incidentally, is that a 'Pulham face' – or possibly two – in **Fig 25.13**?

The Grange residents also enjoy the benefits of a balustraded terrace, with another neat grotto at the 'Fairlawns' end. This is pictured in **Fig 25.14**.

This marks the end of the 'Fairlawns' tour, but the Saville's sale catalogue of 1929, also refers to:

'... a woodland walk to a dell with a lake, where a boat is kept...'

This was actually in the northern area of the original estate that was sold off for housing development during the 1930s. The 'woodland walk' was built over many years ago, but the 'dell' – which, in reality, used to be an old chalk pit before Mr Baring-Gould asked Pulhams to convert it into a small Italian water garden and boating lake – still exists in the grounds of a house now called 'Dellwood'.

The recent owner is another who can be proud of his restoration abilities, as can be seen from **Fig 25.15**. The central feature of this part of the garden is the small 'lake' and its three-arched 'Italianate' bridge, on which the original rusticated balustrading sadly had to be replaced for safety reasons. The lake was shaped to represent a miniature copy of Lake Como, and an imitation 'mountain skyline' was built around the top of the pit to enhance the illusion when viewed from the level of the lake. This was constructed in sections set at different distances from the edge of the pit to provide a three-dimensional effect, and **Fig 25.16** shows one section that used to

Fig 25.12 (above left) *Steps leading up to the plateau at the top of the cave at Merrow Grange* (Photo by Jenny Lilly)

Fig 25.13 (above right) *Is that a face in the rocks at Merrow Grange?* (Photo by Jenny Lilly)

Fig 25.14 (right) *The Terrace Grotto and balustrade at Merrow Grange* (Photo by Jenny Lilly)

Fig 25.15 *The restored Italian water garden at Dellwood in 2007* (Photo by Mick Hibberd)

form one wall of a glasshouse, fernery or gardener's bothy – its original function is not clear, because whatever used to be there no longer exists.

It is a pity that all the Pulham features at Merrow Grange had to be split into three separate sections, because it means that none of today's residents can enjoy all of them without making 'special arrangements' with their neighbours in order to do so. But at least everything is now beginning to come to life again. There are pleasures in store at every turn, although, as private property, these gardens are not generally open to the public.

Also Noted:
1901 – *'Ballimore Gardens'*, Otter Ferry, Argyllshire, Scotland
1901 – Kelvingrove Park, Glasgow, Scotland
1902 – *'Dutton Homestall'*, East Grinstead, Sussex

Fig 25.16 *A section of the escarpment screen around the top of the Italian Garden at Dellwood*

- 26 -

ABBOTSWOOD

STOW-ON-THE-WOLD, GLOUCESTERSHIRE

1901-1920

Fig 26.1 *The Spring Garden pool at Abbotswood*

Fig 26.2 *The small waterfall and pool below the house at Abbotswood*

Abbotswood is situated on a hill overlooking the River Dikler, and was purchased by Mark Fenwick – a wealthy member of an ex-banking family who later became Managing Director of the Consett Iron Co. Ltd. – in 1901. In the following year, he commissioned Sir Edwin Lutyens to make extensive alterations to the house, and design the formal gardens immediately surrounding it.[114] These included the terraces, gazebos, a formal lily pond and a canal garden. Mark Fenwick was passionately fond of gardening, and was once described by Lord Redesdale[115] – himself a 'past master of flowers and arboriculture', and whose wild garden at Batsford Park is close by – as:

'. . . by far the best all-round amateur gardener that I know. His knowledge of his plants and their possibilities is really consummate. . . . He has worked at Abbotswood in such a way as to combine the formality of an Italian architectural garden with the broader and wilder lines of the natural woodland scene, the one fading into the other by the skill of imperceptible gradations. I would like to see what he would do on a large scale. I feel sure that it would be something very beautiful and very practical.'

That letter was written in 1913, and obviously refers to the formal terraces and gardens immediately surrounding the house, and the 'naturalistic' rockwork below. One only has to look at these features to conclude that they are Pulhams' work, but evidence has recently come my way to prove that they were on site here during the early months of 1903.[116] Having been there once, it is more than likely that he returned to do other work at different times – in fact, from the evidence contained in Lord Redesdale's letter, I have a feeling that he probably started work here somewhat earlier than 1903 – possibly *c*.1901.

By the 1920s, when Fenwick was an old man confined to his wheelchair, he was still developing new areas of the garden beyond Lutyens' terraces, and he engaged the assistance of a young Russell Page (1906-85) to help him create a spring garden with a stream tumbling through a series of miniature waterfalls at the front of the house on its way down to the lower gardens at the back. [117]

My suggested date for this is consequently 1920, although this is only approximate. It does mean, however, that, by this time, James 4 would have been responsible for working with Page on this part of

Fig 26.3 *The double waterfall in the lower gardens at Abbotswood*

the garden, and it is interesting to note the differences between the character and 'feel' of the rugged, naturalistic rockwork in the lower rear gardens, and the sparser, 'natural rock' placing in the Spring Garden at the front, which tends to illustrate how the styles gradually changed during this period.

The Spring Garden descends the hill on the left as one approaches Abbotswood along the entrance drive. It is a delightful sight and, on further investigation, one can see that the stream emerges from higher up the hillside, and is then diverted into three channels that flow separately down the hill. Two of them join up again before flowing over the small waterfall into the pool by the drive – shown

in **Fig 26.1** – while the third takes a separate course, and descends nearer to the entrance of the drive.

The stream then flows from here, under the drive, and down through the lower gardens into the river at the foot of the valley. Just below the house there is another, quite small waterfall – shown in **Fig 26.2** – as the stream broadens out into another pool, and then flows over a much more spectacular double fall into the rushing stream below. This is shown in **Fig 26.3**, and it is quite possible that there may be at least some natural rocks here, brought in from a local quarry, but, like so many of Pulhams' constructions, the imitations are so good that it is not always easy to tell.

Fig 26.4 *The lily tank garden at Abbotswood*

Fig 26.5 *The sunken pleasure garden, with typical Pulham-style pool and summer house* (Photo by Bridget Fox)

Fig 26.6 *The old paved garden and pergola at Abbotswood* c.*1913* (Photo © Country Life)

Fig 26.7 *The sundial at Abbotswood* (Photo © Country Life)

The more formal features of the Abbotswood gardens are also well worth mentioning here, because I am sure that these are also by Pulham. One is the lily tank garden, shown in **Fig 26.4**, and another is the old paved garden. The lily tank garden is a rather special feature in that, when viewed from the lower lawn, over a wall about five feet high, the reflection of the semi-circular feature in the wall of the house gives it a fully circular appearance.

The paved garden with its rose pergola no longer exists, but the old issue of *Country Life* referred to earlier includes some very good pictures of it – one of which is reproduced here in **Fig 26.6**. Just

beyond here is the sunken pleasure garden and summer house (**Fig 26.5**), and another *Country Life* picture shows three figures supporting a (Pulham?) sundial (**Fig 26.7**), with the paved garden pergola visible in the background. All these features seem 'familiar' after seeing a number of similar features at other sites on which the Pulhams are known to have worked, and I have no hesitation in suggesting a Pulham provenance for these, too.

The lovely gardens at Abbotswood are open to the public on 'occasional' charity open days, and under the 'Yellow Book' National Gardens Scheme. They are well worth a visit.

- 27 -

BATSFORD PARK AND ARBORETUM

MORETON-IN-MARSH, GLOUCESTERSHIRE

1902

Fig 27.1 *Bridge and rockwork waterfall near the entrance to Batsford Arboretum*

Some five miles up the A429 from Abbotswood – discussed in Chapter 26 – lies one of the true jewels of the Cotswolds.

Algernon Freeman-Mitford – later the 1st Lord Redesdale, and grandfather of Nancy Mitford the novelist – travelled widely in China and Japan as an attaché to the foreign legation during the 1860s, and became fascinated with the plants and cultures he found there, developing a particular interest in bamboos. He inherited Batsford Park in 1886, and within six years had demolished and completely rebuilt the mansion.

The gardens at Batsford Park extend over the hillside overlooking the house, and, inspired by his observations of the Oriental landscapes, Algernon Freeman-Mitford explored his ideas of combining conventional parkland with a garden landscape. He completely transformed the park, creating a 'wild garden' that was later described as 'one of the most remarkable examples of its kind in the world'.[118] He became an accomplished and respected plantsman and an acknowledged authority on bamboos. He also built an artificial

watercourse some 600 metres long from the top of the west side of the gardens to the lake at the bottom, using sandstone from the local quarry at Bourton-on-the-Hill, about a mile or so away.

There are some natural springs around the 65-acre site, but these were allowed to run away, and the water was pumped round the system by a pump installed in a field at the bottom, near the lake. He also incorporated some other major features that can still be seen today, including a Japanese Rest House and the Hermit's Cave.[119] These features were referred to in an article in *Country Life* dated 4th July 1903, so it seems likely that one can date the work as *c*.1901-02, which is just about the time when Pulhams completed the first stage of their work at Abbotswood, the home of Lord Redesdale's friend, Mark Fenwick.

Within a few yards of the entrance to the park, the path passes a typical 'Pulhamesque' rustic scene, with water flowing over a rocky waterfall, and under a low-sided bridge, the brickwork of which is coated with cement to simulate a mediaeval stonework effect. This

Fig 27.2 *Lower stream and bridge at Batsford Arboretum*

is shown in **Fig 27.1**, with the rockwork of the waterfall visible behind it. The water flows down from the stream above, over the fall, and under the bridge on its way down through the lower stream to the lake below.

Turning right at the bridge, one can proceed down the path beside the lower stream and look back at the arch of the bridge – shown in **Fig 27.2**. A lower section of this part of the stream is shown in **Fig 27.3**, and the unusually low rate of water flow that day enabled me to study the rocks at close quarters. There is an obvious sense of stratification here, and my conclusion was that this is a combination of natural rock, bonded with a comparatively small amount of Pulhamite.

Fig 27.3 *The rock-lined course of the lower stream at Batsford Arboretum*

Fig 27.4 *The path beneath the lower waterfall at Batsford Arboretum*

The stream runs down through the trees until it falls over a large rock that overhangs the path, and cascades into the lake. **Fig 27.4** shows the overhanging rock, which now has to be supported 'for safety reasons'. It is easy to imagine that, in full flow, this bridge would once have provided a magical view through a veil of falling water – this may well have been the feature that inspired the creation of the tunnel that runs below the cascade in the lake at Friar Park (described in Chapter 24).

Returning to the bridge near the entrance, one can proceed to explore the upper reaches of the stream. It is a fairly steep upward climb, passing several small cascades on the way, and it is not long before the stream widens slightly into what is charmingly known as the 'Sisters' Pool', shown in **Fig 27.5**. No spectacular rock formations here – just a few discreetly placed rocks along the banks, and one cannot help wondering if this might have been named as a result of it being a favourite point of relaxation for the Mitford sisters.

Fig 27.5 *The Sisters' Pool at Batsford Arboretum*

Fig 27.6 *The Hermit's Cave at the top of Batsford Arboretum*

Fig 27.7 *The Japanese Rest House at Batsford Arboretum*

At the very top of the path is a much more typical example of the Pulham rock style – a large, cavernous grotto known as the Hermit's Cave, shown in **Fig 27.6**. No-one seems to know exactly why it is there, but that didn't seem to matter too much in those days. Perhaps they just happened to have a few tons of rocks, rubble and cement left over when they got to the top, but, whatever the reason, it provides one with a cool resting place in which to regain one's breath after the steep climb, and to study the craftsmanship of the Pulham rock-builders at close hand. This is mostly Pulhamite, with narrow bonding stratifications that separate the main 'rocks', but if one doesn't consider oneself to be too well up in geology – or perhaps feels in need of a rest – one can just relax and admire it.

Returning downhill, there is a clearing over to the left in which stands a rather unusual building with a wide veranda and oriental-style overhanging roof. This is the Japanese Rest House – shown here in **Fig 27.7**. It is in such good condition that it almost looks new, though in fact it is original, and only the roof and ceiling have received restoration work (in 2006).

James 3, who would have been responsible for this work, is known to have shared Lord Redesdale's enthusiasm for Japanese plants and gardens, and Batsford must be one of the best remaining examples of this genre.

The Batsford Estate was sold in 1919 to Gilbert Alan Hamilton Wills, later to become the 1st Lord Dulverton. The gardens suffered mixed fortunes over the next fifty years, but Frederick Anthony Hamilton Wills, the 2nd Lord Dulverton – generally known as Anthony Hamilton Wills – took a renewed interest in them. He had a great passion for trees, and was almost solely responsible for advancing the status of the estate to that of an arboretum of international repute. In 1984, he ensured its future by founding a charitable trust and donating the park to its care and safe keeping. Lord Dulverton died in 1992, and the Arboretum has been administered and developed as an educational resource by the Batsford Foundation since that date.

- 28 -

DANESFIELD HOUSE

MEDMENHAM, BUCKINGHAMSHIRE

1901-1903

Fig 28.1 *The parterre, looking up towards the house and terrace at Danesfield House*, c.*1906* (Picture reproduced by permission of Brian Miller)

Fig 28.2 *The parterre, looking down from the terrace at Danesfield House*, c.*1906* (Picture reproduced by permission of Brian Miller)

Built on the site of an Iron Age fort, Danesfield House occupies a commanding position overlooking the River Thames near Marlow-on-Thames, with the Chiltern Hills beyond. The present house was built by Robert William Hudson, and is the third property to have been built within this magnificent setting. Robert was the son of Robert Spear Hudson, the Victorian soap magnate and manufacturer of 'Sunlight Soap'.

Robert engaged Romaine Walker FRIBA to rebuild the house in the north-western corner of the prehistoric ramparts, in the style of the Italian Renaissance, and faced with locally quarried rock-chalk. Building began in 1899, and was completed in 1901 – all totally regardless of expense, with the result that it became an architectural showplace. It is assumed that the construction of the surrounding terraced gardens of some 65 acres began c.1901-02, and was completed c.1903, although it is possible that the house's subsequent owner, Mrs Arthur Hornby Lewis, may have made some changes later.[120]

During the Second World War, Danesfield House was requisitioned by the Air Ministry for the RAF to set up a Joint Service Imagery

Intelligence (IMINT) Unit, to be known as RAF Medmenham, so that Danesfield House became to IMINT what Bletchley Park was to Signals Intelligence (SIGINT). In 1948 it was bought by the Air Ministry to become the Divisional Head Quarters for the 90 Group RAF (Signals) – the house was the officers' accommodation, with the Grand Banqueting Hall being used as the Officers' Mess. The house became a country house hotel and spa in 1991, and is a Grade II listed building.[121] Restoration and renovation of the surrounding gardens began in mid-1989, and they have been meticulously maintained ever since.

I first became aware of Danesfield House by complete chance. Some friends of mine happened to call in there for lunch one day, and immediately contacted me in a state of great excitement. 'You must look at it,' they said, 'There is a lovely rock garden there, and we are sure it is a Pulham garden.'

Even then I was not prepared for what I saw. The gardens are a wonderland of the Pulhams' work, covering a wide spectrum of styles from the picturesque cement-lined rocky stream to a formal Edwardian terrace and Italian Water Garden.

Fig 28.3 *Looking over the parterre in 2010, with the River Thames and the village of Hurley in the background* (Photo by Jenny Lilly)

To say that Danesfield House is an imposing building hardly does it justice. From whichever side it is viewed, it is truly magnificent. There is an imposing entrance drive and forecourt, and a beautiful wide, open terrace at the south-facing rear that overlooks the curve in the River Thames, far below at Hurley, not far from Marlow-on-Thames. The gardens drop steeply from the terrace, and remain almost as pristine as they were 100 years ago.

In fact, there are two fascinating photographs in the hallway that are able to confirm this point. They date from *c*.1906, and show the parterre below the high terrace – one taken from below, and the other from above. They are reproduced here in **Figs 28.1** and **28.2**, with Fig 28.1 showing the imposing nature of the house, with its high terrace, and Italianate Orangery extending along the complete length of the centre portion.

Fig 28.2 looks down across the terrace to the parterre and valley below, while **Fig 28.3** shows the same scene as it is today – practically unchanged, apart from the fact that the topiary is not now quite as extensive or extreme as it was in its early days. The balustrading

Fig 28.4 (above) *The orangery terrace, balustrading and steps at Danesfield House* (Photo by Jenny Lilly)

Fig 28.5 (opposite) *The parterre fountain at Danesfield House* (Photo by Jenny Lilly)

around the terrace, with its ball terminals and seat half way up the steps are still in remarkably fine condition, as can be seen in **Fig 28.4**.

The first thing that caught my attention when I looked down from the terrace was the fountain in the centre of the parterre, shown in close-up in **Fig 28.5**. A careful comparison with Fig 28.2 shows that it is clearly the same fountain, although, like the balustrading, it still looks quite new, which is something that one would not expect after 100 years. This is because everything was cleaned during its recent restoration, and has consequently lost its original patina, which is a shame.

The fountain has an unusual 'trefoil' – three-leaved – shape, which I have never seen before, and is not illustrated in Pulham's *Garden Ornament Catalogue*. However, there can be no doubt about its authenticity. One only has to look at the fine detail of the work – from

the tip of the fountain, past the tracery around the rim of the centre bowl, to the seated figures at the base – to see that it carries all the characteristics of a genuine Pulham piece. Everything is as crisp and clean as it must have been on the day it left the manufactory.

Moving down to the bottom of the path, one has an uninterrupted view of the Thames below. The path splits here along the top of the high bank, and the branch to the left leads to the show gardens – the first of which is a small rock garden built into the bank. **Fig 28.6** shows the entrance steps that lead upwards alongside a lovely rock garden built around a series of pools and small cascades. This is really a restored version of the original, but the restoration work has obviously been carried out very sympathetically. Most of the stone here is natural, however, so it is difficult to tell whether the original may have contained any Pulhamite constructions.

Fig 28.6 (overleaf) *The small rock garden at Danesfield House* (Photo by Jenny Lilly)

Fig 28.7 *The Italian water garden at Danesfield House* (Photo by Jenny Lilly)

Figs 28.8a and b *The Cupid figure and lower gateway to the Italian water garden*

The next stop is at the Italian water garden, shown in **Fig 28.7**. This is a lovely period piece, with a tall barley-twist column in the centre of the pool, surmounted by a figure of Cupid. Once again, there has been quite a lot of restoration work in this garden, but the column is original, as is also Cupid at the top of it – the column having been cleaned, whereas Cupid has not. Some of the ball terminals and the marble benches are recent replacements, and the stonework facing to the surrounding walls is a recent restoration, but carried out extremely well. The whole atmosphere of this garden is one of tranquillity and wonder.

Fig 28.8 shows a close-up view of Cupid, and of the steps to the garden that lead down to the path that winds through the lawns to the lower gardens. This 'gateway' is in a lovely old semicircular promontory that juts out from the escarpment of the Italian water garden to overlook the expanse of the ground below, and the first thing that comes to mind when viewing it from below is how perfect it would have been as Juliet's balcony. The facing of the supporting wall is beautifully rusticated, and great care was obviously taken with the mouldings of the doorway itself – even to the detail of the rosettes at each top corner.

Fig 28.9 *The Maidenhead balustrade above the lower arched gateway and along the east border of the Italian water garden* (Photo by Ellie Johnson)

Fig 28.10 *The wall fountain in the Italian water garden* (Photo by Jenny Lilly)

Now take a look at the balustrading from the floor of the balcony itself, shown in close-up in **Fig 28.9**. This is a completely different pattern to the balustrading that runs along the front of the terrace – in fact, this one is illustrated in the *Garden Ornament Catalogue* as the 'Maidenhead Balustrade' (inset), and, despite its pristine appearance, is again quite original.

Another feature in the Italian water garden that must be mentioned before one proceeds down into the lower grounds is the wall fountain, shown in **Fig 28.10**. These are also included in the Pulham catalogue – although not to this exact design – and this is an excellent example.

The lower grounds contain a magnificent rock and water garden, laid out in a steep valley. Starting from a mass of rocks at the top, a cement-lined stream tumbles over a series of small cascades, and flows through pools to the bottom, from where it is circulated back to the top by a ram pump. **Fig 28.11** shows the 'pump house pool', where the pump house itself is hidden down a flight of steps behind the juniper bush.

Climbing – rather than walking! – up the slope from the bottom pool, one can return through the archway and up the steps to the Italian water garden, from where a flight of steps to the right leads to the sunken garden, along the edge of which the Maidenhead Balustrade continues from 'Juliet's balcony'.

Returning up a steep lawn to the house from here, one reaches the side of the terrace, where something else catches the eye. The balustrading here – shown in **Fig 28.12** – is unlike the one that runs along the front of the terrace, and also different to the Maidenhead

Balustrade along the edge of the sunken garden and the Italian water garden. It is, however, very similar to others that have been noted elsewhere.

And now back to the terrace itself. It is beautifully spacious, with room for several tables for eating or drinking *al fresco*, as can be seen in **Fig 28.13**. The thing that attracted my main attention here, however, was the splendid Italianate conservatory that stretches along the whole length of the central part of the building. This is straight out of the *Pulham Garden Catalogue*. In fact, the illustration in the catalogue is of the Italian garden at Warren House, Kingston upon Thames, Surrey – not very far away from Danesfield – and that will be discussed in Chapter 32. That garden also survives today in pristine condition, and the arches and columns along the front are almost identical to the ones on the Danesfield conservatory, which is now used as the 'Orangery Terrace Brasserie'. This provides a good clue as to its probable original use as an orangery – indeed, an extremely grand one at that.

But don't just stop there. Take a careful look at the balustrading above. This is yet another example – the fourth in total – of a Pulham balustrade at Danesfield, and is another pattern that has been noted elsewhere. A very similar one is at Knebworth House, in Hertfordshire, although this one at Danesfield is far more extensive and better preserved. In fact, everything is wonderfully preserved at Danesfield, which should figure near the top of the visiting list for anyone interested in the work of James Pulham and Son.

Also Noted:

1903 – *'Oak Hill'*, Ipswich, Suffolk

Fig 28.11 *Looking back up the stream and its cascades*

Fig 28.12 *The balustrade and side steps leading to the terrace at Danesfield House* (Photo by Ellie Johnson)

Fig 28.13 *The Italian orangery loggia with balustrade above at Danesfield House* (Photo by Jenny Lilly)

- 29 -

HEATHERDEN HALL
IVER HEATH, BUCKINGHAMSHIRE
1902-1905

Fig 29.1 *The balustrading along the terrace at the back of the house at Heatherden* (Photo by Sarah Couch)

The previous chapters will have illustrated that, as from the early 1890s, James Pulham and Son were gradually expanding their portfolio from the 'naturalistic' garden landscaping for which they had earned such an enviable reputation over the previous fifty years. This was just about the time when James 3 began to take over the reins of the business, although this is unlikely to have been the only reason. The firm's patrons were beginning to request more formal and flamboyant features, and the gardens at Worth Park, near Crawley, in Sussex – discussed in Chapter 15 – where the formal gardens were probably constructed during the mid-1890s – is one example of this. Danesfield House, discussed in the last chapter, is another.

Many wealthy landowners – mostly from the realms of business and commerce – were buying country estates on which to build magnificent new houses, and they wanted beautiful gardens to go

with them. The current fashion favoured the elegant and extravagant formality that was so characteristic of the Edwardian era – formal features, such as balustraded terraces, 'Dutch' and 'Italian' gardens etc. James Pulham and Son were only too happy to satisfy these demands, and Heatherden Hall is one such example.

The first recorded owner of Heatherden Hall was Dr Drury Levin,[122] although nothing much is known about who he was or what he did. Whatever he did must have been quite rewarding, however, or he wouldn't have been able to afford such a large house and gardens in this lovely part of Buckinghamshire. The second owner of Heatherden was the famous cricketer, K S Ranjitsinhji, after which the house remained empty for some time before being purchased by Lt Col Grant Morden – a Canadian former multi-millionaire, and MP for Chiswick – 'early in the 20th century',[123] which can presumably be taken as being *c*.1902-05.

Figs 29.2a and b *A face above the ground floor windows, and a gargoyle head above the top floor windows at Heatherden*

Grant Morden spent in excess of £300,000 – equivalent to more than £5 million in today's money – on enlarging and refurbishing the house and estate. He engaged James 3 to build most, if not all, of the garden features, although he was not destined to gain much enjoyment from them because he was declared bankrupt during the great depression of the 1930s. Charles Boot, a building tycoon, purchased the estate at a knock-down price, and converted it into a country club for the rich and famous.

Boot's dream, however, was to turn the land into a film studio. He renamed it 'Pinewood', because of the number of trees that grew there, and teamed up with Methodist miller and millionaire J Arthur Rank to finance the project. The rest, as they say, is history, but the fortunate thing, as far as this book is concerned, is that the gardens have been well maintained, and are almost the same now as they were when they were first landscaped by James 3.

The first piece of evidence for this can be seen on the balustraded terrace along the back of the house. It is pictured here in **Fig 29.1**, which can be compared with Fig 3.7, showing it as it was illustrated in the firm's *Garden Ornament Catalogue*, published *c*.1925. Another feature on the house itself is a set of gargoyle figures and faces, as shown in **Fig 29.2**. The face on the left is above the ground floor windows – slightly reminiscent of the face in Fig 2.1d – while the head on the right is above the top floor windows – could these be Pulham figures?

Moving away from the house, one comes to the formal garden, in which there is an ornamental fountain and Pulham seat, pictured in **Fig 29.3**. The curved seat can be seen clearly in the background to the right, and the base of the fountain is centre left. At the time of my first visit in 2008, the fountain had been emptied for cleaning, and the top removed for safe storage, but this was brought out especially for my second visit in 2009, as shown here, with the detail still crisp and clean. The inset illustration is of the 'Don Fountain', taken from the *Garden Ornament Catalogue* – it is not identical, but it is obviously very similar in style.

Figs 29.3a and b *Fountain and seat in the formal garden at Heatherden*

Figs 29.4a and b (above) *Outside and inside the boat cave at Heatherden* (Photos by Sarah Couch)

Fig 29.5 (below) *The back of the boat cave at Heatherden, showing a flight of steps leading up to the sun-bathing patio at the top*

Fig 29.6 *The Pulham bridge at Heatherden*

Further on, one comes to a small man-made lake, with rocky banks, a small island, and a boat cave at the right-hand end. **Fig 29.4** shows a composite view of the entrance of the cave from across the lake, and out from its interior. A flight of steps can be seen on the right-hand side, leading up to a sunbathing patio along the top, and a similar flight of steps is shown at the back of the cave in **Fig 29.5**, with the entrance to the cave on the left.

The boat cave is typical of several that Pulhams constructed around this period – notably the ones at Sandringham (Chapter 8), and Holly Hill Park, near Fareham, Hampshire (Chapter 13) – although this may well have been one of the first they constructed with a sunbathing patio on top. As can be seen in Fig 25.12, however, the 'land-based' grotto at Merrow Grange was also built on this principle.

The main attraction here, however, is the ornamental balustraded bridge that spans the other end of the lake. It is modelled on the one illustrated in the *Garden Ornament Catalogue* as the 'Kingswood Balustrade' – see Fig 3.6 – except for the fact that the actual balusters are the Blakesley pattern. The bridge at Kingswood no longer exists, so this one at Heatherden – shown in **Fig 29.6 –** may well be a unique surviving example.

Many famous films have been made at Pinewood Studios, including the James Bond and 'Carry On' series. Heatherden Hall also played the part of Scrumptious Mansion in *Chitty Chitty Bang Bang*, in which Sally Ann Howes, as Truly Scrumptious, sang her love song, 'Lovely Lonely Man', from the top of this arched bridge.

- 30 -

BUCKINGHAM PALACE
LONDON
1903-1904

Fig 30.1 *Rocky banks to an island in the lake at Buckingham Palace* (Photo by Jenny Lilly)

Several excellent books have already been written about the history of the gardens at Buckingham Palace, in Central London – one example being *The Garden at Buckingham Palace* by Jane Brown[124] – so there is no need to repeat all the background details here.

A central feature of the gardens is the lake, with its two islands, and trees planted along the edges. It was commissioned by King George IV, and constructed by William Townsend Alton, the Royal Master Gardener, and founder of the Horticultural Society in 1804. The huge quantity of spoil was then used to build a tall bank along the opposite side of the lake from the Palace, in order to screen the King's view of the Royal Mews.

This has always been known as 'The Mound', and represents my own particular interest in the gardens at Buckingham Palace, since King Edward VII commissioned James 3 to construct some rockwork on it in 1903 – some 35 years after he commissioned James 2's work at Sandringham (discussed in Chapter 8). James Pulham and Son were thus awarded their second Royal Warrant, and my grandfather, Frederick Hitching, had the distinction of being put in charge of this project.

Fig 30.1 shows the rocky banks to one of the islands in the lake, and the structure here shows natural rocks placed on a Pulhamite base. Initially, the island was completely round, but it was decided to make it look more naturalistic by adding the rocks around the edge.

Fig 30.2 (above) *The rusticated facing and natural stone coping of the 'large' rustic bridge that crosses to an island in the lake* (Photo by Jenny Lilly)

Fig 30.3 (right) *The rocks beneath the 'large' bridge to the island in the lake* (Photo by Jenny Lilly)

Figs 30.2 and 30.3 show the larger of the two rustic bridges that cross to the islands. It is a typical example of Pulham's 'rusticated' style, where ordinary brickwork is rendered with cement that is then sculpted and incised to create the impression of rough-cut stone blocks. It is built on a concrete 'bowl' foundation that almost mirrors the arch of the span itself, and is topped with a coping of natural stone.

Fig 30.4 (opposite page, top) *The 'small' bridge, where The Royal Family posed during the 1950s* (Photo by Jenny Lilly)

Fig 30.5 (opposite page, bottom) *Beneath the 'small' bridge to the island in the lake* (Photo by Jenny Lilly)

The 'small' bridge is shown in **Figs 30.4** and **30.5**. This is the bridge that features in a famous photograph taken during the mid-1950s – many readers will recall the Queen and Prince Philip looking over the parapet at their young children, Prince Charles and Princess Anne, seated on the rocks at its base.

And then, of course, there are the outcrops of rock on 'The Mound' itself. This is not a large site by Pulham's standards, although it obviously has a special significance as far as this book is concerned. **Figs 30.6 to 30.8** are pictures of various 'rock' outcrops that are scattered around – all of them are man-sculptured Pulhamite, and illustrate the great care and attention that was paid to achieving their 'natural' appearance. There were no templates for the 'rock builders' to use – each rock has its own unique stratifications and 'character', and, when the lighting and the shadows are right, some of them reveal the elusive glimpse of a 'Pulham face'. These can be seen in several locations, and it doesn't take a great stretch of the imagination to find them in each of these pictures.

The head gardener at the time of my visits in 2000 and 2002 was Mark Lane, who had been in the post since November 1992. He, like his predecessors, had realised the importance of the Pulham legacy, and had implemented a programme of conservation and replanting. The convenient planting pockets are now filled with a good selection of both evergreen and deciduous trees and shrubs, as well as some cascading plants, like *Jasminum officinale* and *J. parkeri*. Previous planting – and probably original to the rock's installation – are *Arbutus* x *andrachnoides* and *Euonymus europaeus*, while new plantings include *Berberis aristata*, *Pittosporum daphniphylloides*, *Lonicera* x *pseudochrysantha*, *Corylopsis glabrescens* var.*gotoana*, and *Magnolia* 'Ann'.

Also Noted:
1905-13 – London Zoo, Regent's Park, London
1906-07 – River Gardens, Belper, Derbyshire
1906-11 – 'Luton Hoo', Luton, Bedfordshire
1907-25 – Cotham Park, Bristol, Avon
1909 – Ardross Castle, Alness, Ross-shire, Scotland
1909-12 – Gatton Park, Reigate, Surrey

Figs 30.6a and b *A rocky outcrop on 'The Mound' at Buckingham Palace – the right-hand 'face' is a close-up of the rock at the far end of the left-hand picture* (Photos by Jenny Lilly)

Fig 30.7 *A naturalistically-sculpted outcrop along the back path of 'The Mound', with another 'face contender' on the left* (Photo by Jenny Lilly)

Fig 30.8 *Another outcrop on 'The Mound' – is that another face on the end of the overhang?*

- 31 -

'RAYNE THATCH'

BRISTOL

1908-1910

Fig 31.1 *View of the swimming pool from the veranda at Rayne Thatch* (Photo by Kyriakos Kyvelos)

James Pulham and Son often returned to the sites of their earlier work, but this was not because this work was unsatisfactory, or needed repair. In fact, it was generally just the opposite – their patrons liked their work so much that they wanted to extend the landscaping that had already been done. HRH Edward, The Prince of Wales – later to become King Edward VII – was one such person, and Mr Walter Melville Wills, the multimillionaire tobacco magnate, was another.

His home was at Bracken Hill, in the Nightingale Valley on the Somerset side of the Clifton Gorge, just below the Clifton Suspension Bridge, and he also used his estate office as a 'holiday house'. This was known as 'Rayne Thatch', and was on the opposite side of the road to Bracken Hill, nestled into the banks of the Gorge itself. The Wills family also owned a hunting lodge on an estate called Abbots Pool, in Abbots Leigh – just over two miles west of Bracken Hill – that he bought in 1915.

Figs 31.2a and b *The path leading from the house around the swimming pool*

He commissioned the Pulhams to build several sections of Pulhamite and natural stone rockwork and formal gardens on all these sites between *c*.1908 and 1927, and started by asking them to landscape the gardens of Rayne Thatch that, from the road, looks like a single-storey, white, thatched cottage. In reality, however, it is a two-storey house built into the steep northern side of the Clifton Gorge. Wills also owned a lodge in the Highlands of Scotland, and it was on this that the spacious, oak-panelled lounge on the first floor of Rayne Thatch was modelled.

There is a wide veranda around the sides of Rayne Thatch that overlooks the gardens and the wooded valley beyond. It is a truly magical view, and has a very special and personal fascination for me, because the 'rock builder' in charge of its construction was my grandfather, Frederick Hitching. He often used to speak of the time he worked at the home of 'Mr Wills, in Bristol', and I am proud to say that this must be one of the finest Pulham gardens to be found anywhere.

It is built around five pools at different levels, linked by water cascading gently down from one level to the next. The second pool was built specifically as a swimming pool, graded from 'deep' at one end to 'shallow' at the other, and has a grotto boathouse at the deep end – farthest from the house – with a grass-covered patio above for sunbathing and diving. This can be seen from the view in **Fig 31.1**, which is taken from the veranda, but even this does not do full justice to the view, since the rockwork pools also extend down the side of the house, behind the camera.

Starting from the veranda, the path leads round the garden in a clockwise direction, and one comes first to a steep gorge on the left-hand side of the pool, between two massive cliffs of rock that must be around nine feet high. The left-hand view in **Fig 31.2** shows the path as one enters it from the house, and the right-hand view is looking back towards the house, with 'Big Derek', my brother-in-law – who is about 6ft 8ins tall – admiring the rocks.

225

Fig 31.3 (opposite page, top) *View back to the house from the path around the pool*

Fig 31.4 (opposite page, bottom) *View back along the left-hand path to the house from the top of the steps leading to the sunbathing strip above the boathouse at Rayne Thatch* (Photo by Kyriakos Kyvelos)

Fig 31.5 (right) *Looking back through the boathouse grotto*

The path rises up from here, and **Fig 31.3** shows the view looking back towards the house, just near the steps that lead up to the sunbathing roof of the boathouse. **Fig 31.4** looks back down the path from the top of the steps and, moving on from here, round the back of the large pool, one comes to the back of the boathouse – complete with boat – shown here as **Fig 31.5**.

The path meanders round the top end of the garden from here, and then turns back towards the house. And there, tucked away around a tight corner in the path, and nestling into the rock face, is the pump house – a small building with a typical Pulhamite 'ashlar' rendering around a small gothic doorway. The basic construction is actually brick, and **Fig 31.6** shows the small chip above the door where the cement coating has been frosted away.

Inside, the pump draws the water from the lowest pool, and passes it up to the highest one, which is adjacent to the pump house. It flows down from here to the main pool, and completes its circuit down through the three small lower pools. The pump working there today is actually the third generation to have been installed, and the 'retired' pumps – including the one installed by my grandfather – still lie in a corner of the room.

Fig 31.6 *The pump house doorway, with a small section of 'ashlar' coating above the door frosted away*

Fig 31.7 (above) *Looking back across the pool to the house from the pump house*

Fig 31.8 (right) *Returning to the house through another archway*

When I first saw the pump house, I suddenly had the feeling that I had seen it all before. My thoughts immediately went back to a vision of my grandfather, in his white apron and wielding his trowel, just as I had seen him so many times when I was a child. I could feel him standing beside me, having returned to check over his handiwork of so many years before, and repeating something that he had said to me countless times during my early years: "There you are, my boy! If a job's worth doing, it is worth doing well. A job well done is always done, but a job half done is never done!" I have never forgotten it.

Returning down the right-hand side of the main pool, one can pause to look across to the house (**Fig 31.7**) before one passes through another archway, shown in **Fig 31.8**, and on past three small pools to the lowest one. This is actually just in front of the kitchen window – from just outside of which the picture in **Fig 31.9** was taken.

Walking round the corner of the house, one returns to the point below the veranda from which the circuit started, and the two stone

Fig 31.9 (right) *The cascade into the bottom pool, just outside the kitchen window*

Fig 31.10 (below left) *Pulhamite base and cladding of pillars supporting the veranda*

Fig 31.11 (below right) *Fred Hitching's inscription stone at Rayne Thatch*

pillars that support the upper floor are shown in **Fig 31.10**. They are both encased in Pulhamite stone, and it is reassuring that a recent structural survey concluded that they are every bit as safe and secure now as they were when they were first built.

On the inscription stone (**Fig 31.11**) is something of special interest to me: the initial and date ('FH-1910') carved into the cement by my own grandfather, Fred Hitching, one hundred years ago.

These inscription stones are very rare, and I think that this must have been an indication of how proud he was to have been associated with this garden as the foreman in charge of its construction. It was a very proud moment for me, too, and many thoughts passed through my mind as I looked at the rough carving of his initials. I wonder what he might have said had he known that his own grandson would find this stone in one hundred years' time, and that so many people would be interested to read about his work.

There was an article in the *Bristol Evening Post* some years ago,[125] in which the reporter described the lavish lifestyle enjoyed by Walter Melville Wills during his days at Bracken Hill. It seems that he loved to hold weekend house parties, and that these often used to overflow from the main house to his 'holiday house' over the road. One can easily see why, and I asked the owners if they had a favourite time of year in their garden.

They found this rather difficult to answer, but eventually concluded that it was perfect all the year round: in the summer they could have barbecues, with lighting around the pools, and in the winter – especially in the snow and frost – it "looks like fairyland!" "It doesn't really matter what time of year it is," they said. "This is just such a magical place to be." I couldn't agree more – except perhaps to add that, to me, it has a very special magic about it. The owners I met that day have now moved on, but the house is still in good private hands. This does mean, however, that it is not open to public access.

- 32 -

WARREN HOUSE
KINGSTON UPON THAMES, SURREY
1908-1912

Warren House is located on the Coombe Estate – one of the wealthiest areas in Kingston upon Thames since Victorian times. The Duke of Cambridge bought 535 acres of land here in 1837, but sold 16 acres of it to Hugh Hammersley – a Partner of Cox & Co., bankers and army agents in London – in 1865. Hammersley immediately commissioned the building of a new red brick mansion that he called Warren House.[126]

It so happened that this piece of land was almost completely intersected by a tongue of land that had already been leased from the Duke of Cambridge by Veitch and Son – the famous nurserymen who already had nurseries in Exeter and Chelsea – for the display and sale of their many rare specimens of flowering trees and shrubs, such as acers, magnolias and azaleas. The Coombe Wood Nursery also became famous for its Japanese Water Garden.

Hammersley managed to purchase the lease for this land 'sometime during the 1870s', thus consolidating the complete area of land that surrounded Warren House. He obviously agreed that the nursery should be allowed to continue in operation during the term of the lease, because it did so until it closed *c*.1913.

Hammersley died in 1880, and the next owner was George Grenfell Glyn – the second Baron Wolverton – who died in 1887. On the death of his wife in 1897, George Holford bought the house, and lived there until 1907.

The next owner was Sir Arthur Paget, GCB, KCVO, who commanded several battalions of the British Army during the Ashanti, Sudan, Burma and South African wars. Most of the notable features of the house and grounds were added during his tenure – including the Winter Garden, with its grotto, and an Italian-style loggia. His many house guests included Mr Gladstone, King Edward VII and Queen Alexandra, King George V and Queen Mary, and King George VI.

It is known that James 3 was one of the contractors who worked in the gardens, because the firm's *Garden Catalogue c.*1920 contains a picture of the Italian loggia that they built 'for Sir Arthur Paget'. A photocopy of this picture is reproduced in **Fig 32.1**.

Warren House remained in the hands of the Paget family until 1954, when it was acquired by ICI for use as a conference and training centre. It changed hands again, and was reopened in 1988 after a major refurbishment that resulted in its becoming one of the most prestigious conference venues in the world. Parts of the gardens were parcelled off at that time, and a block of security apartments was built on the piece of land once occupied by the old Coombe Wood Nursery. That section is now called 'The Watergardens', because the Japanese Water Garden still exists, and will be discussed in detail in the next chapter.

The fernery at the side of the house is all that now remains of the old Winter Garden. It is shown here in **Fig 32.2**, and the common understanding used to be that this was all the work of the firm of Messenger & Co., who were well-known builders of conservatories and glasshouses during the 19th and early 20th centuries. However, one only has to compare this with other sites to accept that, although Messengers doubtless built the structure of the winter garden, the fernery itself was the work of Pulhams.

There is a small fountain in the main formal gardens at the back of the house, shown in **Fig 32.3**. This is typically Pulham, although it is unusual in that the basin is octagonal, rather than round or quatrefoil. Another feature is the six-seater Norbiton Seat, pictured in **Fig 32.4**, which shows just how crisp and pristine the details are after 100 years of use.

Fig 32.1 *The Italian Garden at Warren House, Kingston upon Thames* (Picture reproduced from the *Pulham Garden Catalogue*, c.*1920*)

Fig 32.2 *The Winter Garden fernery at Warren House* (Photo by Jenny Lilly)

Fig 32.3 (above) *The octagonal fountain at Warren House* (Photo by Jenny Lilly)

Figs 32.4a-d (right) *The Norbiton Seat at Warren House* (Photo by Jenny Lilly)

One passes this on the way to a small sunken walled garden, with steps that lead down from the main garden above. The balustraded wall around it is another example of the Merrow balustrade – see Fig 25.6 – which provides an interesting comparison with the Kingswood balustrade – illustrated in Fig 3.6 – that surrounds parts of the roof of the house. On inspection, it can be seen that the Kingswood balusters are actually two Merrow balusters – one inverted below the other. **Fig 32.5** shows the two balustrades at Warren House, inset with another catalogue picture of the Kingswood balustrade. The focal point of this garden is a wall fountain in a small pool, which is pictured in **Fig 32.6**, alongside the catalogue illustration of another one.

Figs 32.5a-c *Merrow balustrading along the wall, and Kingswood balustrading on the roof of Warren House, with the illustration of the Kingswood balustrade from the Pulham Garden Ornament Catalogue inset*

All of these features are maintained in remarkably good condition, and were surprise bonuses during my visit. The part that I had really been looking forward to seeing was the Italian loggia illustrated in the *Pulham Garden Catalogue* – Fig 32.1 – and, finally, there it was! As can be seen in **Figs 32.7 and 32.8**, it still looks as good as it did one hundred years ago, and is one of the most pristine examples of Pulhams' later work that I have seen – all thanks to the efforts of its small but enthusiastic team of Warren House gardeners.

Figs 32.6a and b *The wall fountain illustrated in the* Pulham Garden Ornament Catalogue, *and the one at Warren House*

Fig 32.7 *The loggia in 2008*

Fig 32.8 *The Italian loggia at Warren House 2010* (Photo by Jenny Lilly)

- 33 -

'THE WATERGARDENS'
KINGSTON UPON THAMES, SURREY
1911-1915

The Edwardian era ended in 1910 with the death of King Edward VII, after which King George V and Queen Mary came to the throne. James 3 was by then in his late sixties; garden fashions were still moving on, and it is quite likely that James 4 was beginning to exert more influence on some of the firm's major business decisions.

The British interest in Japanese plants in the late 19th century was a logical extension to the mounting fashion for new exotic plants brought home from overseas by such itinerant plant-hunters as John Gould Veitch and Henry Veitch. James Pulham and Son were keeping up with the trend and, in fact, they included a range of Japanese garden ornaments in their *Garden Ornament Catalogue* *c*.1925 – reproduced here as **Fig 33.1**.

Most of these gardens were constructed during the years leading up to the First World War in 1914, and, whenever I have enquired about the origins of those that I have seen, I have invariably been told the same story – i.e. "To the best of our knowledge, workers were brought over from Japan especially to supervise the construction of this garden." I see no reason why the Pulhams could not have been involved in some way, however, since they generally seemed to be working on other parts of the site at around the same times. Their knowledge and experience in rockwork would certainly have been complementary to that of the Japanese workers, so perhaps they were each able to learn something from the other. I have not yet been able to find any positive documentary evidence to substantiate this theory, but the evidence of my own eyes leaves me in little doubt about the part Pulhams are likely to have played.

So strong was this trend that John and Henry Veitch opened a third nursery especially to showcase their many rare specimens of flowering trees and shrubs. Part of it was laid out as a Japanese-style water garden, apparently inspired by the 'Willow Pattern' plate design.

The location they selected was on the tongue of land that dissected the grounds of Warren House, Kingston upon Thames – as discussed in the previous chapter – that was purchased by Hugh Hammersley in 1865, and subsequently acquired by Sir Arthur Paget when the lease on the nursery expired in 1913.[127] It was situated in an area of undulating ground known as 'The Warren' – later to become Coombe Wood – and consisted of a series of small lakes – believed to have once been old gravel workings – linked by streams that were fed by a number of underground springs.[128]

Some of the land was sold off when the new Warren House Conference Centre was established in 1988, and two blocks of private apartments were built on the land where the Coombe Wood Nursery previously stood. This development is known as 'The Watergardens' because of its Japanese-style garden. Thankfully, the garden still exists, and is maintained by the residents in superb condition.

Fig 33.1 *Selection of Japanese lanterns advertised in the* Pulham Garden Ornament Catalogue, c.*1925*

It was pure chance that led me to 'The Watergardens'. As noted in Chapter 32, I happened to notice a picture of the Italian Loggia Garden at Warren House while browsing through the *Pulham Garden Catalogue*, so I checked the Warren House website. Not only did I discover that it was still there, and in excellent condition, but the history page also referred to a Japanese garden:

> 'This unique garden is thought to be the oldest Japanese garden in existence today in the British Isles. In its maturity, it is now even more beautiful than when first planted all those years ago.'

The garden extends over some three acres in quite a steep valley, and the visitor is presented with a number of route options via which to explore the many incredible and unique features. The head gardener is a great tree enthusiast, and is extremely proud of the many rare specimens under his care. Acers abound, and there are several examples of the 'pocket handkerchief tree', as well as many other rare species.

A welcoming Japanese gateway signifies the entrance to the gardens – shown in **Fig 33.2** – and the sound of water tumbling over rocks encourages the visitor to step through and wander down the path.

Fig 33.2 (above) *The main entrance – or exit*

Fig 33.3 (below) *The stream tumbling over small cascades past a (recently replaced) Japanese ornament* (Photo by Jenny Lilly)

And there, on the left, the source of the sound becomes evident, as can be seen in **Figs 33.3** and **33.4**. There is a lovely rock-lined stream running alongside the path, with the water tumbling over a high cascade beneath a bridge, and downwards over a series of small cascades to a pool at the bottom. A perfect 'Pulhamesque' woodland scene.

Fig 33.4 (top left) *The middle cascade near the main entrance* (Photo by Ellie Johnson)

Fig 33.5 (left, centre) *Some 'Pulham Faces' in a cleft in the cliffs* (Photo by Jenny Lilly)

Fig 33.6 (left) *The top cascade*

Fig 33.7 (above) *The Japanese tea house* (Photo by Jenny Lilly)

Fig 33.8 (overleaf) *The pool, with its bridge, fountain and two cranes* (Photo by Jenny Lilly)

The pool is surrounded by a multitude of trees and plants. As can be seen in **Fig 33.7**, a high fountain plays near the centre of the pool, and the bridge to the right leads to a lovely Japanese teahouse. There are two crane ornaments in the pool, but both these and the teahouse are recent replacements.

Proceeding up the valley, one comes to a rock 'cliff' that encloses a small area with a narrow ravine on the opposite side. There are typical Pulham planting pockets, and one can immediately see a couple of 'Pulham faces' – **Fig 33.5** – which are among the best examples of this 'signature' that I have seen.

Passing between these rocks, one comes to a narrow bridge over another stream, with a double waterfall and small pools on the left – **Fig 33.6** – above which another bridge is just visible. That one crosses the stream as it leaves the high pool.

Returning downhill, one reaches a junction in the path that leads over the stream towards the exit, but there should be no hurry to get away. Pause at the bridge, look up the stream to the left, and one can absorb one of the most perfect Pulham woodland scenes that one could find anywhere. Anyone who finds this difficult to believe needs only to look at **Fig 33.9**.

This garden provides a wonderful, tranquil experience, and yet it is extremely exciting, because it must certainly be among the very best examples of its type anywhere today.

There have been a number of reviews of the Coombe Wood Nursery over the years, in which it is generally assumed that Veitch created this garden. An issue of *The Garden*,[129] for instance, says that, at the time of Hammersley's acquisition in the 1870s:

'. . . it was already laid out as a Japanese Water Garden. James Veitch had created a series of lakes linked by streams fed by the many underground springs which are a feature of this part of Kingston. The garden was inspired by the plate design of willow pattern china, and included many ornaments, Japanese-style bridges and summer houses, all surrounded by trees, shrubs and ferns in a design which was completely new to Britain.'

From the visual evidence available, however, there can be no doubt that Pulhams were involved here, but the question is when? The Warren House website, and other sources, claim that this was *'thought to be the oldest Japanese garden in existence today in the British Isles'*, which again implies that it was all created during the early years of Veitch's time at Coombe Wood. There is no reference to it in James 2's promotional booklet, however,[130] which means that Pulhams were not there before 1877. If Hugh Hammersley had anything to do with it – which seems doubtful – following his purchase of the lease *'sometime during the 1870s'*, then it must have been between 1877 and 1880, since that is the year in which he died.

Since Pulhams do not appear to have become involved in the creation of Japanese-style gardens until the early 1900s, I had to wonder if this could also have been the time when they worked at 'The Watergardens'. This appears to fly in the face of the above reviews, but there are two pieces of evidence to support this theory – the first being that they are known to have worked for Sir Arthur Paget at the adjacent Warren House *c*.1908-12. The second is that they almost certainly constructed the Japanese garden at Gatton Park – not included in this book – that was visited by Harry Veitch and other members of the local gardeners' association sometime before May 1910.

I contacted Dr Jill Raggett – the leading authority on Japanese gardens in the British Isles today, and currently Reader in Gardens and Designed Landscapes at Writtle College – to obtain her reaction to my theory. In response, she sent me a copy of part of her notes on the Coombe Wood Nursery.[131]

'. . . There have been suggestions that a Japanese-style garden was laid out in the (Coombe Wood) nursery of the 1870s

(Pattison 1989-90). The evidence does not seem to be available to support these statements, though there was clearly a series of Japanese-style gardens and features at the adjoining property of Warren House (G.F.T. 1921:132), part of which was constructed on the northern corner of Veitch's Nursery (Ordnance Survey, 1933).

'Coombe Wood Nursery was being completed in the October of 1865, with "the grounds open for their free inspection and promenade at all times (Sundays excepted)", with no mention of any Japanese features (see *Surrey Comet*, 1865, 21 October: 1). There was a range of articles that commented on the collection of Japanese plants growing at the nursery, from hardy bananas and bamboos to maples. . . . One such article describes the "rare beauty and interest" of the Japanese plants introduced by Veitch, and there may well have been plants in the nursery that evoked in the minds of visitors thoughts of Japan (*Country Life* 1899, 12 August: 166). However, there was no evidence of an area within Coombe Wood Nursery being called "Japan", or of the use of Japanese ornamentation. By 1913, a small series of pools had been expanded in the central portion of the nursery and a footbridge had been constructed (Ordnance Survey 1913), but whether the area was enhanced to give a feel of Japan must remain conjecture for the time being.

'Though no evidence has been found that there was a Japanese-style garden at the nursery, there were a wide range of plants with a Japanese origin that could be seen by the public. By 1921, a portion of the nursery adjacent to Warren House had been purchased, and a "new Japanese garden" had been created (G.F.T. 1921: 132). . . . The portion of the nursery that joined Warren House has survived, now known as The Watergardens, with plants that date back to the Coombe Wood Nursery . . . An article in the Surrey Comet (1981, 14 February: 4) may have led to the confusion over the existence of a "Japanese water garden" constructed by Veitch's nursery.'

So there it is. My conclusion is that Veitch grew and displayed his collections of Japanese plants from the date his nursery opened in 1865, and maybe the natural springs, streams and lakes on the site were used as central features around which to create the 'atmosphere' of a Japanese garden. He visited Gatton Park in May 1910 to see the Japanese garden that had just been constructed by James Pulham – with the aid of thirty unemployed workers – and was very impressed with it. Perhaps Sir Arthur Paget was also among the visitors.

This would put the date of 'reconstruction' to around 1911-15, and, in view of the fact that Veitch closed his Coombe Wood Nursery *c*.1915, it seems likely that it was funded by Paget, and included as part of the work being done at Warren House at that time. In fact, I have now discovered evidence that Pulhams constructed the pergola during March 1912,[132] so I am confident that these estimates are not far from the truth. But one doesn't worry too much about dates when one wanders through these beautiful gardens – they are simply timeless.

Fig 33.9 *An early view of the stream running down through the Japanese water garden* (Photo by Jenny Lilly)

- 34 -

'THE NODE'
WELWYN, HERTFORDSHIRE
1911-1932

Fig 34.1 *The steps and balustrading from the sunken garden to the terrace at 'The Node'* (Photo from the *Pulham Garden Ornament Catalogue*, c.1925)

Fig 34.2 *The rose pergola at 'The Node', looking back towards the house and terrace* (Photo from the *Pulham Garden Ornament Catalogue*, c.1925)

'The Node', near Welwyn, in Hertfordshire, derives its name from the Saxon words, *'atten ode'*, meaning 'at the mound', or 'funeral pile', although no Saxon remains have yet been found within its boundaries. Neither is there any record of a house on this site until 1638, but there must have been one, since a deed of that date refers to three or four previous occupants by name, including a John Brocket.[133]

The property passed through several hands until 1849, when 'The Node' was purchased by William Reid – a partner in the giant brewing firm of Watney, Combe and Reid – who lived there until his death in 1867. 'The Node' then changed hands again a number of times before Charles Alexander Nall-Cain – a millionaire brewer from Liverpool – purchased it in the early 1900s. He later became the first Lord Brocket – which indicates that he might have taken this name from John Brocket.

Nall-Cain was responsible for some major developments of the gardens, although Lady Brocket is known to have been an enthusiastic gardener, so it was probably she who commissioned the Pulhams to construct the terrace garden and the sunken garden adjacent to the house, and the rock and water gardens beyond. The *Gardener's Magazine* carried a tribute to James 3 in 1912, in which this was noted as being one of his recent works,[134] and the Pulhams were obviously proud of their work here, because the firm's *Garden Ornament Catalogue*, c.1925, contains two photographs of it.

The first of these, reproduced as **Fig 34.1**, was taken from the sunken garden, and shows the steps, balustraded wall, terminals, vases and animal figures along the edge of the terrace. The balustrading here is the Milton balustrade – see Fig 3.8 – and, in the background of this picture, one can also clearly see the magnificent rose pergola of the terrace garden, featured in **Fig 34.2**. The sunken garden itself – pictured as it was c.1930 in **Fig 34.3** – must also have been constructed at this time, and still exists today, almost exactly as it was during the early 1920s, when the pictures in Figs 34.1 and 34.2 were taken. Sadly, the pergola no longer exists, although the

Fig 34.3 *The Sunken Garden at 'The Node', with the lakes in the background, c.1930* (Photo from Codicote Local History Society)

Fig 34.4 *The water garden at 'The Node' in 2001*

Fig 34.6 *The rocky bank of one of the lakes at 'The Node', c.1930*
(Photo from Codicote Local History Society)

pathway that ran through it is still there, and one can identify the slabs that mark the locations where each of the pillars once stood.

The pathway leads to the water garden and the rock garden, which were also constructed at this time – i.e., the latter months of 1911[135] – and the water garden remains much as it must have been one hundred years ago. As is evident from **Fig 34.4**, it is still a secluded, peaceful haven that is capable of soothing even the most harassed of minds. The rock garden lies just beyond here, and **Fig 34.5** shows it as it was c.1932. It is built from natural Westmorland stone, and is still in good order, although quite overgrown.

Lord Brocket sold 'The Node' in 1926 to Carl Holmes, a wealthy American who invested lavishly in improving and enhancing the estate even further. His estate agent, Henry Dunsford, recalled how the two large interconnecting lakes beyond the Sunken Garden – shown here in **Fig 34.6**, and in the background of Fig 34.3 – were dug *'during the mid-1920s'*,[136] which indicates that this must have been soon after he took up residence. They were apparently dug *'in order to provide work for the local unemployed'*,[137] and they still exist – very much as they were in those days – but now as part of the grounds of the neighbouring garden centre.

Fig 34.5 *The Rock Garden at 'The Node', c.1932* (Picture provided by Frances Brooks)

Fig 34.7 *The Dell at 'The Node'*, c.*1932* (Picture provided by Frances Brooks)

Two further features for which Carl Holmes was responsible are the Dell and the Japanese garden, which were constructed c.1930-31. The Dell is located just beyond the rock garden, tucked away on the rear boundary of the estate. Unfortunately, it has not been properly maintained for quite some time – the gardening budget being one of the first things to suffer from the economic pressures of recent years. **Fig 34.7** shows what it was like soon after its construction.

If one battles on to the fence bordering the adjoining property, and peers through the undergrowth, one can glimpse an arch folly, shown on the left of **Fig 34.8a**. It was almost certainly put there by James 3, because it is so similar to others known to have been erected by him. It shows up quite clearly in the background of the photograph, **Fig 34.8b**.

Carl Holmes and his wife happened to be extremely interested in 'anything Japanese', and the final garden feature for which they were responsible was the Japanese Garden – in the north west corner of the estate. This was probably built around the same time as the Dell, c.1930, and is one of the gardens about which I was told – as noted in the previous chapter – that a Professor from the Japanese School of Gardening in Tokyo is reputed to have come over to design it, bringing with him a team of Japanese gardeners who worked alongside "local workers".

I was left to guess who these "local workers" might have been. James 4 was in charge of the business at that time, and, in view of their known association with other parts of these gardens, it seems only logical to think that they were probably involved in some way here. This part of the garden is now separately and privately owned, but it still exists – albeit massively overgrown – and some old photographs of it still survive, so one can at least see how it used to be.

One of these is reproduced in **Fig 34.9**, and, although it is not possible to provide a 'guaranteed' caption for it, it does not detract from one's enjoyment of it. There is a crane and two Yoshi Lanterns here, as illustrated in the page from the *Pulham Garden Ornament Catalogue* reproduced in Fig 33.1.

Figs 34.8a and b *The folly at 'The Node'. Right: early photograph, c.1932*
(Photo from Codicote Local History Society)

Fig 34.9 (right) *The Japanese 'rest house' by the pool* (Photo from Codicote Local History Society)

Fig 34.10 (below left) *Stream flowing under a typical 'Pulham bridge' and over cascades into a rocky pool in the Rock Garden* (Photo provided by Frances Brooks)

Fig 34.11 (below right) *The Peach House at 'The Node', designed by Joseph Paxton c.1850, and erected at 'The Node' between 1852 and 1865*

Fig 34.10 shows another 'Pulhamesque' scene at 'The Node', with the stream running under the bridge and over some shallow cascades into the rocky pool below. It is in the area of the rock garden, and the bridge would also date from this period. It appears to be of a much 'rougher' standard of construction than most of the earlier examples shown in this book.

There is one other feature of these gardens for which the Pulhams were probably not responsible. This is a Peach House that dates back to the time of William Reid – i.e. 1849-67 – who commissioned Joseph Paxton to design and build it for him, in what was then his kitchen garden. It is pictured here in **Fig 34.11**, and local legend has it that this is the only Peach House in the world outside Kew Gardens, but I have found no evidence to support this suggestion. In fact, when I queried it with Kew Gardens, I was told that they had no knowledge of a Peach House, and could find no record of such a structure in their archives.

I understand from Mr Dunsford's granddaughter that the glass in the Peach House came from the Great Exhibition of 1851, and that this date is scratched onto one of the panes. This puts the date of construction at 'The Node' between 1852 and 1865, which fits with both Joseph Paxton's life and William Reid's ownership of 'The Node'. It also makes it possible that it could have been constructed by James 2, although the evidence to support that suggestion is probably just as elusive as it is for the one about the Peach House at Kew Gardens.

Carl Holmes lived at 'The Node' until 1938, after which it passed through two or three more private hands before being converted into a state-of-the-art hotel and conference centre in 2000. Uninvited admission is consequently not possible.

Also Noted:
1912 – *'Marl House'*, Bexley, Greater London

- 35 -

RHS GARDEN

WISLEY, NEAR WOKING, SURREY

1911-1912

Fig 35.1 *The rock garden steps alongside water dripping down into small pools,* c.*1912*
(From the *Journal* of the RHS, 1912 – reproduced by kind permission of the RHS)

The Royal Horticultural Society's Garden at Wisley, near Woking, in Surrey, is probably the most famous – and certainly one of the best loved – gardens in the country. Covering 240 acres, it offers a fascinating blend of the beautiful with practical and innovative design, together with illustrations of cultivation techniques that have made it a Mecca for garden lovers everywhere.

George Ferguson Wilson, a rich businessman, scientist, inventor, and keen gardener, purchased the site in 1878, and established 'The Oakwood Experimental Garden' with the express objective of growing 'difficult' plants successfully. The garden soon became renowned for its collection of lilies, gentians, Japanese irises, primulas and water plants, and, despite a number of changes that have taken place since then, it has remained true to his original concept to this day.

On the death of Mr Wilson in 1903, Sir Thomas Hanbury – a wealthy Quaker who had founded the celebrated garden of La Mortola, on the Italian Riviera – bought the estate, and presented it in trust to the RHS.[138] Under their stewardship, the range of gardens was enlarged to incorporate a canal; a rock garden; summer garden; winter garden; a fruit field, glasshouses and an arboretum; alpine gardens, and model vegetable gardens.

James 3 was invited to create the rock garden in 1911, and an item in the *Gardener's Magazine* during that year describes it thus:[139]

'The garden has an area of nearly two acres, and is not less remarkable for the judgement and taste shown in its design and construction than for its large area.

'As tasteful design and utility have been happily combined, the garden will long be regarded as a model of what a rock garden should be, irrespective of its area, and Mr Pulham, who is assisted in the various branches of the business by his sons, may be heartily congratulated on the success achieved.'

Fig 35.2 *The Lower Fall at Wisley,* c.*1920* (Photo reproduced from the *Pulham Garden Catalogue,* c.*1920*)

On 13th August 1912 – i.e. six months after that article appeared – James 4, rather than his father, was invited to read a paper on the Wisley rock and water garden to a meeting of the Society. The paper was published in the *Journal of the Royal Horticultural Society* later that year,[140] and here is a brief excerpt from what he had to say about the decisions that led to his firm's appointment to undertake the project:

'I think I am not giving away any secrets when I say that suggestions for a rock garden were considered by the Council during their earlier occupation of Wisley, but nothing definite was undertaken until the summer of 1910, when it was resolved to invite a few firms to submit plans and schemes for their consideration. Certain necessary conditions were specified, within the limits of which a wide discretion was allowed to the competitors, who were given a fixed sum to work upon . . . One of the conditions laid down required competitors to submit samples of the stone they proposed to use in construction to enable the Council to judge of its suitability.

'After mature consideration, the scheme of Messrs Pulham was selected. The designer of a rock garden should be, on his own lines, as much an architect as he who designs houses. . . . Messrs Pulham kept before them one leading idea – viz, that every rock

garden must have, above all things, a definiteness of plan, and an aim to reproduce with fidelity some particular gesture of Nature. Then, and then only, can success be obtained.

'In preparing their scheme, they fortunately succeeded in obtaining the professional advice and assistance of Mr Edward White, under whom they have constructed many rock and water gardens in the past. Mr White collaborated with them throughout, and advised as to the landscape portion of the scheme, for it was realised that this important work, being for the premier horticultural society, should be not only an example of what a rock garden ought to be, from both educational and picturesque points of view, but one that might rank among the finest in the kingdom. It was therefore decided to confer with a landscape gardener of wide experience, so that no detail, whether from a landscape or rock building point of view, should be overlooked.'

Fortunately, the journal containing the report of J.R. Pulham's presentation also contained a number of photographs, one of which is reproduced here in **Fig 35.1**. James 4 also included a picture of the Wisley gardens in the firm's *Garden Catalogue, c.*1920, and a copy of this is reproduced in **Fig 35.2**.

Fig 35.3 *Looking down over the rocks and stream, 2000*

One notices that James 4 mentioned the name of Edward White – son-in-law of H E Milner – in connection with these gardens. Milner also designed the rock garden at Gatton Park – only about 18 miles from Wisley – and Ardross Castle, in Scotland, at around this time, and the Pulhams were responsible for the construction of both of these. It would therefore be interesting to see a list of all the other rock and water gardens on which they collaborated, since this might help to fill in a few more gaps in one's knowledge of the firm's work during the early part of the 20th Century.

The rock garden at Wisley is constructed from natural stone, and continues a trend that is very noticeable in Pulham gardens from around this time. There is no sign of Pulhamite here, and – in this case at least – this had its advantages, because it made it possible to make some changes later on. Some of the rocks have indeed been moved around at various times over the years, and a new pump has been installed to facilitate the flow of water. The effects of this were described, some fifty years later, in the *Newsletter of the Alpine Garden Society*,[141] when the rock garden, as it was at that time, was described as follows:

'The beauty of the Wisley rock garden is enhanced by its situation on a north-facing hillside away from, and out of sight of, all formal and artificial surroundings. It is built with Sussex sandstone, which allows the inclusion of both lime-loving and lime-hating plants.

'No rock garden is quite complete without some accommodation for moisture-loving plants, and perhaps the most pleasing feature of the Wisley rock garden is the series of pools of various sizes, and at various levels, which are connected by miniature waterfalls. A continuous flow of water was made possible in 1959 by the installation of an electric pump, set near the bridge at the foot of the alpine meadow. Another interesting feature of the rock garden is the small spring of water which rises approximately half way up on the western side, trickles down the slope, and drips happily through a stone cave to fill the small pool below. From there it overflows to the bog garden, and joins the chain of pools which extends along the entire length at the foot of the alpine meadow, bordered by Iris kaempferi, Osmunda regalis, Primulas etc.

'The descent of about sixty-five feet from the highest point of the rock garden to its lowest level is made in easy stages, by means of winding paths and informal flights of stone steps. Such a north-facing aspect might appear to many readers to be a disadvantage, yet it does provide suitable homes for those plants which prefer a cool, shaded position. For example, the red river of Rhododendron forrestii has a shaded ravine to itself, species of Ramonda are placed in deep vertical crevices on the full north of the largest rock faces, and Primula edgeworthii delights in similar situations, leaving hundreds of positions on the more exposed terraces of the rock garden for plants requiring full sun.'

There were further alterations made to the garden in 1984, and Sally Festing, writing in the *Journal of The Garden History Society*[142] in that year, described these as follows:

'During the current reconstruction, virtually the whole [rock garden] will be amended with the exception of the path of the watercourse through the garden and the cave. They are likely to remain much as in the original Pulham construction, and the rock that is being used for reconstruction is Sussex sandstone from the same area that Pulham obtained it.'

It is therefore difficult to look at the Wisley rock garden today and regard it as a 'genuine Pulham masterpiece', because other hands have been at work here since it was first laid out. But never mind that – James 3 (or 4) was the man who started it, and it is still a garden that can be visited by anyone, and gives a great deal of pleasure to the thousands of enthusiasts who visit Wisley each year.

There is a fascinating postscript to this story. In 2009, I received an email from the stepdaughter of James 4's grandson, Michael Goodchild, who now lives in Zambia. I already knew that James 4 only had one daughter, Freda, and that she married a Stanley Goodchild. I also knew that they – or she – later moved to Northern Rhodesia (now Zambia), so I gave up all hope of ever locating them. I did not know that they had a child, Michael, and that Freda moved to Zambia without Stanley, taking Michael with her. Freda died in 1991, and Michael married a lady who already had a daughter named Karen.

I could hardly believe my luck when Karen emailed me, following her discovery of my website at www.pulham.org.uk, and was able to supply these pieces of the Pulham jigsaw. Not only that, she then revealed that Michael had some old family photographs and two silver cups that his grandfather had been awarded almost a century ago. It was even more exciting when Michael offered to donate these items to the Lowewood Museum in Hoddesdon, where they are now in safe custody – less than a mile from the site of the Pulhams' old house and manufactory. One of these cups was presented to James 4 by the RHS in 1913 in commemoration of his work at Wisley. It stands nearly 31cm high, and is pictured here in **Fig 35.4**. (The other one? Well, that wasn't awarded until 1931, so I shall deal with that in the next Chapter.)

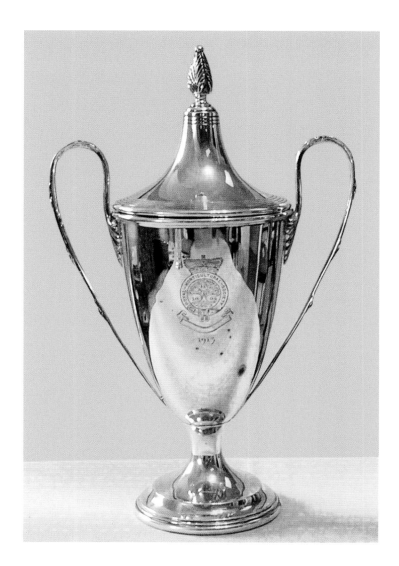

Fig 35.4 *The Wisley Cup, awarded to James 4 by the RHS for the rock garden at Wisley in 1913 (approx. 31cm high)*

- 36 -

THE LONDON EXHIBITIONS
1912-1931

Fig 36.1 *The Japanese Garden at Barrow Hills, Surrey* (*From the* Pulham Garden Catalogue, c.*1920*)

1912: The Chelsea Exhibition

It is known that James 2 loved to exhibit the firm's terracotta wares at the International Exhibitions during the 1850s and '60s, but the firm's commitment to this form of promotion did not stop there. They also created gardens for the Chelsea and Olympia Exhibitions in later years.

As discussed in Chapters 33 and 34, James Pulham and Son – then under the direction of James 3 – were actively involved in the creation of Japanese gardens during the early years of the 20th century. This is confirmed by the Pulham *Garden Catalogue*, c.*1920*, which contains a photograph of one they constructed at Barrow Hills, in Surrey. This site has since been redeveloped, so it is not possible to show any contemporary pictures of it, but **Fig 36.1**

is a reproduction of their catalogue picture, so at least it is possible to see that it came complete with some ubiquitous Okayama lanterns, and with a 'classical' Japanese tea house.

This photograph was also used in an edition of the now defunct *Hoddesdon Journal,* under the title of '*Made by Brittain'*.[143] It tells the story of a Mr George Brittain, about whom it says:

'Mr Brittain, who lived at 7 Bell Lane, Hoddesdon, for many years, was indeed a craftsman of the old order. Employed by Messrs Pulham and Son, of Station Road, Broxbourne, for nearly thirty years, he spent a great deal of his spare time making cabinets, dolls houses, and so on for many of the wealthy Hoddesdon residents of days gone by . . .

Fig 36.2 *Construction of the Japanese tea house at the Pulham manufactory, c.1912, with head carpenter, Mr George Brittain, in the foreground* (Photo reproduced from the *Hoddesdon Journal*, February 1967)

'Mr Brittain's faithful dog used to carefully carry a hot dinner in a basket every day for his master, from his home in Bell Lane to Messrs Pulham's works in Broxbourne. A golden retriever, christened Bill, this faithful dog was bought from a bargee at Ware for a shilling! Bill also accompanied the Hoddesdon Fire Brigade – of which George was a member – to local conflagrations, and waited patiently until the fires were quenched.

'Apprenticed as a builder and joiner to Mr John Alfred Hunt, Mr Brittain travelled to many parts of the world in connection with his work for Pulhams.'

It is almost certainly stretching a point to claim that Mr Brittain travelled to *'many parts of the world'* for Pulhams, although it is very likely that he travelled to many parts of the United Kingdom. Another intriguing clue in this short article is the reference to his apprenticeship to John Alfred Hunt – a local master builder and Joiner – because one of my own family connections is to a John Ricketts – no relation to Fred Rickett, the Pulham rock builder whose diary is discussed in Chapter 44 – another carpenter and joiner who also happened to be apprenticed to Mr Hunt.

A second picture associated with the *Hoddesdon Journal* article shows the tea house under construction in the Pulham joinery. It is reproduced here as **Fig 36.2**, and its caption claimed that the picture was taken in 1912, and that, later that year, the tea house was one of the attractions at the Chelsea Exhibition. The caption in the *Journal*

beneath the catalogue picture (Fig 36.1) stated that it was taken at the Exhibition *'in a special landscape setting'*, but the more likely explanation is that the tea house was actually made for the exhibition, and then moved to Barrow Hills – where that picture was taken – when the exhibition closed.

1923: The Olympia Exhibition

James 4 evidently carried on the family tradition of exhibition displays, as can be seen from the special commemorative postcard reproduced in **Fig 36.3**. It was produced in 1923, when he constructed and planted a special garden in honour of HRH Princess Mary – later to become The Princess Royal, the only daughter of King George V and Queen Mary.

Another promotional card from the same period is shown in **Fig 36.4**, which pictures the firm's 'Mercury Fountain' at Madresfield Court, Worcestershire – see Fig 11.8.

Fig 36.3 *'HRH Princess Mary's Garden' – Pulhams' exhibit at Olympia in 1923* (Photo discovered by Pat Hibberd)

Fig 36.4 (above) *Promotional card*, c.*1920s* (Card discovered by Geoffrey Green)

Figs 36.5a and b (above right, top) *James 3 and James 4*, c.*1919* (Pictures provided by Michael Goodchild)

Fig 36.6 (above right) *The Pulham Rock Garden at the Chelsea Flower Show in 1931, showing James 4 being congratulated by King George V and Queen Mary* (Photo provided by Michael Goodchild)

1931: The Chelsea Exhibition

I also mentioned in the previous chapter that I had been contacted by Michael Goodchild, the grandson of James 4, who now lives in Zambia. He very generously donated two silver cups to the Lowewood Museum that had been awarded to the firm for their work nearly 100 years ago – one of which, 'The Wisley Cup', is pictured in **Fig 35.4**.

He also sent me some family photographs, two of which are reproduced in **Figs 36.5a and b**. They show James 3 and James 4,

and I estimate that they are likely to have been taken *c.*1919. Another is reproduced in **Fig 36.6**, and this was taken at the Chelsea Exhibition in 1931. It shows James 4 talking to King George V and Queen Mary during their visit to the firm's exhibit.

Michael Goodchild's second cup was awarded for this 1931 garden exhibit, and is pictured here in **Fig 36.7**. Standing 19.5cm tall, and measuring 21cm across its handles, it carries the crest of the RHS, and the inscription *'The Great Spring Show at Chelsea 20th, 21st and 22nd May 1931. Awarded to Pulham and Son for their Rock Garden'*.

Fig 36.7 *The 'Chelsea Cup'* (Kindly donated to the Lowewood Museum by Michael Goodchild)

1914: Selfridges Roof Garden

Another 'special assignment' undertaken by Pulhams was the creation of a roof garden at Selfridges department store in Oxford Street, London, in 1914[144] – shown here in **Fig 36.8** – although it has long since ceased to exist. I know nothing about this, apart from the fact that, in his definitive history of the store,[145] Gordon Honeycombe writes:

'The history of the roof garden is not well documented. It seems that, soon after the store opened in March 1909, a Pergola Tea Garden, so called, was established on the roof of the original Selfridge building. It was only open in the summer. . . . . It appears that the Roof Garden, which extended along the full eastern side of the roof, was further developed in June 1911. Apart from a pergola, flower beds, a rock garden and a pond, there was a square observation platform or tower raised 10 feet above the roof. An American Soda Fountain completed the scene. . . In May 1912 part of the roof was set aside for golfers, where they could practice putts and tee shots into a net.'

Fig 36.8 *The roof garden at Selfridges store in Oxford Street, London, c.1915* (Image courtesy of the Selfridges Archive held at The History of Advertising Trust)

- 37 -

LYTHAM ST ANNES
LANCASHIRE
1914-1916

Fig 37.1 *Large waterfall in Promenade Gardens, Lytham St Annes, c.1930s* (Photo provided by Fylde Tourism and Leisure Dept)

The advent of the railways was really beginning to have an effect on people's lives by the latter part of the 19th century. They began to travel by train to spend their leisure time at the seaside, which, in a way, was lucky for James Pulham and Son, because their traditional patrons – i.e. the landed gentry and wealthy business people with their town houses and country estates – were beginning to feel the financial strain. Garden maintenance was very labour intensive, and was one of the first things to suffer from the growing economic pressures caused by the First World War and subsequent depression.

Private garden construction contracts were consequently becoming increasingly scarce, but some relief was available from the local authorities of the popular coastal resorts. They wanted to 'beautify' their amenities in order to attract more visitors, and this was also a way of providing work for local unemployed labour. The first coastal site landscaped by James 3 was the Madeira Walk area of Ramsgate, Kent – discussed in Chapter 21 – and there were actually two further projects in Ramsgate during the 1920s and 1930s. These will be dealt with in a later chapter, but there were one or two others that need to be dealt with first in order to preserve a more or less chronological sequence.

The first is at Lytham St Annes, in Lancashire, where, in February 1914, James Pulham and Son were engaged to build two waterfalls on the new lake in the Promenade Gardens. **Fig 37.1** is a picture of the large waterfall at the top of the lake, taken *c*.1930, and one can see from this how the footpath winds through a tunnel under the waterfall, and that the lake is bordered by a line of natural stones.

St George's Gardens – later to become known as the Ashton Memorial Gardens – were originally laid out in the centre of Lytham in 1874-75. At a Council Meeting on 12th June 1914, James 4 – or possibly James 3 – was invited to submit a proposal for laying out a rock and water garden in the north-east section of these gardens, but the original plans must have been rather ambitious, because he was asked to amend and resubmit them.[146] He did this, and returned to present them to the next meeting of the Parks and Pleasure Grounds Committee just ten days later, on 22nd June 1914. It was resolved that his terms were accepted, and work started on clearing the ground in October 1914.

Many tons of rock were brought in, and arranged to simulate natural geological strata around the irregular shoreline of the lake, fed by a cascade and waterfall at the southern end. Much of the rockwork relating to these features still remains, and the water supply was reconnected during a recent restoration programme. The spoil from the forming of the lake was used to create banking around its perimeter to echo the banking around the nearby Rose Garden.

The work must have been a success because, at further council meetings early in 1915, the firm was invited to lay out and plant both the Rock Garden and the Rose Garden, and to supervise the council workmen in laying out the rest of the Memorial Gardens. While all this was going on, they were also called upon to make some alterations to the waterfall on the South Promenade, for which a further eight tons of stone had to be carted on to the site. Everything seems to have ended on a happy note, because the Meeting on 21st June 1915 resolved that:

'. . . the thanks of the Council be conveyed to Messrs Pulham & Son for the gift of four 'Cirencester Pots' for the corners of the Lily Pond in the Rose Garden.'

On 9th March 1916 the Council also resolved that:

'Mr Pulham's offer to supply, free of cost, a plan for laying out the Sunk Garden near the St George's Square Entrance to the Ashton Gardens be accepted with thanks,' and that 'Mr Pulham's offer to prepare drawings, showing how he proposes to improve the Entrance Lodges to Ashton Gardens, be accepted, on the understanding that the same are prepared free of cost.'

It is therefore quite clear that the Pulhams were responsible for practically the whole of the Ashton Memorial Gardens, and, indeed, the Council also resolved, on 6th July 1916, that:

'. . . the question of forwarding a congratulatory letter to Messrs Pulham, on the admirable way they have laid out the Ashton Gardens, be left in the hands of the Chairman, Vice-Chairman, and Chairman of this [Parks and Pleasure Grounds] Committee.'

Compliments were also made in the local paper, the *Lytham St Annes*

Fig 37.2 *The lake in Ashton Memorial Gardens, Lytham St Annes, c.1930s* (Photo provided by Fylde Tourism and Leisure Dept)

Express which reported:[147]

'The whole design of the Rock and Water Garden is more admired the more it is seen. The name of Mr Stracey, of Messrs Pulham and Son, will ever be associated with this remarkably fine piece of landscape gardening.'

And then, a few months later, they enthused:[148]

'From the Rose Garden a short path leads to the Rock and Water Garden, which is the work of Messrs Pulham and Son, of London. This garden is a reproduction of Nature, and something new in public gardens. It is, in fact, more like a nobleman's private garden than a park. The treatment is free, and great attention has been given to obtain the effect of distance in every vista. About 500 tons of weatherworn rock have been brought in from near Grange, and has been arranged to give the effect of natural strata, gradually sloping towards the sea with outcrops of stone. Plants and shrubs are introduced as if in natural habitats. And the whole conception has been to give age as well as beauty.

'One of the first effects which enraptures the visitor is the waterfall and cascade. The water falls over layers of water-worn rock, a direct fall in the centre, with a cascade on the left side. The water gives the appearance of falling from a "beck", and is received into a winding lake made in a bed of glacier stone. This lake is over 200 feet long, and is bridged by a quaint one-span low bridge, whilst further in the distance is a background of trees and shrubs hiding the boundary walls and houses. Grass glades shelve down to the shores of the lake, which is prettily fringed with irises.'

This very evocative description of the gardens manages to paint a vivid picture, but words are no substitute for the picture itself. The lake, as it appeared *c.*1930, is pictured here in **Fig 37.2**, and the

Fig 37.3 (left) *'Quaint one-span low bridge' over lake in Ashton Memorial Gardens, Lytham St Annes* (Photo by Brian Turner)

Fig 37.4 (below) *Rustic bridge over rocky banks in Ashton Memorial Gardens, Lytham St Annes* (Photo by Brian Turner)

'quaint one-span low bridge' is shown in **Fig 37.3**. It is quite clear that this is a Pulham construction, because it is so similar to others discussed earlier in this book. The reference to *'Mr Stracey, of Messrs Pulham and Son'* is also interesting – could this be the son of J Stracey, one of the team of workers whose names were inscribed on a rock at Madresfield Court in 1879 – Fig 11.7?

Another rustic bridge is shown in **Fig 37.4**, and, although most of the rockwork in these gardens seems to follow the fashion at this time of being in natural stone, it is clear that the rocky banks on which this bridge is placed are of Pulhamite. The Ashton Memorial Gardens are registered as a Grade II listed site in the English Heritage Register of Parks and Gardens of Special Interest in England.

- 38 -

ABBOTS POOL

ABBOTS LEIGH, BRISTOL

1915-1930

Fig 38.1 *The large 'Top Pond' at Abbots Pool, with a small island on 'stilts' in the centre*

Walter Melville Wills, the tobacco magnate from Bristol, was a very loyal patron of James Pulham and Son. As well as engaging them to do a lot of work at his home at Bracken Hill, and his 'holiday house' at Rayne Thatch – discussed in Chapter 31 – he also got them to create a lovely water feature for his hunting lodge at Abbots Pool, in the small village of Abbots Leigh, just over two miles to the west of Bracken Hill.

Abbots Pool is in an area of public woodland of nearly 10 hectares on the southern edge of Abbots Leigh, and is one of about sixty mediaeval fish ponds in the Bristol area, which were always arranged in groups of two or three to cover the complete sequence of breeding, catching, and storing fish for the table. The pools were generally situated within a deer park to help ensure security.[149]

Melville Wills bought Fishpond Wood and the pool when the estate was sold in 1915, and it was probably around this time that he also developed the fish ponds and watercourse through the woods.[150] Having only recently completed the landscaping of his garden at 'Rayne Thatch', it is not surprising that he engaged James 3 to do the work.

He made the 'Top Pond' bigger and deeper – to around 20ft – by raising the level of the dam, and controlled the flow of water into the pool by digging back the spring heads above the pool, culverting the flow, and digging drains in the impermeable rocks. He also added an island on 'stilts' – shown here in the centre of **Fig 38.1** – a boat cave, slipway, and some occasional rocky outcrops around the edge of the pool.

Fig 38.2 *The boat cave by the 'Top Pond' at Abbots Pool, with singed rockwork to the left of the mouth*

The path into the woods rises steeply towards the 'Top Pond', which is still quite well stocked for the enjoyment of the local fishermen. The water flows out of the pond over the dam and cascade situated on its north-west edge. There is a Pulhamite slipway near the north-west corner, and a narrow causeway runs across the dam, where there is a capstan that used to control the flow of water – although this was too rusted up to be serviceable at the time of my visit in 2005.

The rustic boat cave is in the north-east corner of the pond, at the far end of the causeway path, and is pictured here in **Fig 38.2**. This is a typical Pulham structure, with blocks of natural sandstone interspersed with Pulhamite stratification layers. A few embedded 'fossils and shells' are scattered across the surface, and it is generally in quite good condition, apart from some evidence of scorching on the face of the rocks to the left of the cave entrance – obviously caused by fires being lit there at some time.

One can descend from here to the stream that flows along the bottom of the valley below the waterfall – which must be around 15-20ft high – and, like the boat cave, is also constructed from alternating layers of local limestone rock and Pulhamite, this time stratified to simulate a natural geological fault. **Fig 38.3** gives some idea of the scale of this cascade, which descends in three falls to the 'Middle Pond' below.

From here, the stream flows over another small cascade, under a charming little rustic bridge – **Fig 38.4** – and into one of the two lower ponds. It is quite possible that the original three fish ponds consisted of the large 'Top Pond', and these two lower ponds, and

that the 'Middle Pond' was added by Pulhams for Melville Wills in order to split the fall of the water. It is known that they returned to do some more work here in 1930, but it is not clear exactly which sections were done at that particular time.[151]

In an article written for the *Journal of The Garden History Society*,[152] Sally Festing reports that there is also an extended sequence of small trout pools separated by cascades in the Markham Brook, to the West of Abbots Pool. This also belonged to the Wills family, and is likely to have been created by Pulhams, but it is now 'so silted up as to be almost obliterated', that I did not attempt to investigate it.

Walter Melville Wills died in 1941, and the land at Abbots Pool was offered to the local council, but they had no need for it at the time, so they leased most of it to the Forestry Commission – apart from the 'Lower Pond' area, which is still in private hands. The Abbots Leigh Civic Society, with the help of the North Somerset Council Rangers, have worked extremely hard to restore and preserve the area with the help of a Local Heritage Initiative grant. This is another example – like Holly Hill Park, in Fareham, Hampshire, discussed in Chapter 13 – where a tremendous amount of hard work has already been done to help preserve our garden heritage, thanks partly to the interest shown by the local council, and partly to the enthusiastic support and help of a local organisation of 'Friends'.

Also Noted:
1919-20 – Shipton Court, Shipton-under-Wychwood, Oxfordshire
1926-30 – Bristol Homeopathic Hospital, Bristol, Avon
1920-22 – *'Dunira'*, Comrie, Perthshire, Scotland

Fig 38.3 (right) *Looking up at the large cascade from the 'Middle Pond' at Abbots Pool* (Photo by Cesi Jennings)

Fig 38.4 (below) *Small rustic bridge over the 'Middle Stream' at Abbots Pool*

- 39 -

BRACKEN HILL

BRISTOL

1917-1930

Fig 39.1 *Gunnera pond and bridge at the side of Bracken Hill House*

Fig 39.2 *The first rock archway at Bracken Hill*

Walter Melville Wills chose the undeveloped woodland of Nightingale Valley, on the Somerset side of the Clifton Suspension Bridge, as the perfect place in which to make his home, so he built his house there in 1896, and called it Bracken Hill. He was a very keen gardener, with a special appreciation of exotic trees and plants, but, as far as is

known, he did not invite the Pulhams to landscape his gardens here until sometime after they had worked for him at both Rayne Thatch and Abbots Pool.

The rock garden and water garden were constructed between 1923-25,[153] but the work over the whole site was carried out in three or four stages between 1917 and 1930, and Melville Wills was obviously very keen that no expense should be spared to achieve the best possible results. He even went to the trouble of building a small railway extension so that huge blocks of limestone could be brought in from the Cheddar Gorge direct to Bracken Hill by a Foden's steam wagon.

Sally Festing describes Bracken Hill as follows:

> 'Exuberant rockwork around the house, made from alternate layers of natural and Pulham-simulated limestone, constructed into archways, two pools and alpine flower beds. A wall at the back of the garden is still partly covered with Pulhamite – as was once the wooden gate set in its corner and elsewhere – in a gently rolling topography of about two acres, hand-moulded boulders with the characteristic incised central strata lie side by side with natural rock.'

When Walter Melville Wills died in 1941, his son, Captain Douglas Melville Wills, inherited the estate, but he did not want to stay there himself, so he donated it to the University of Bristol in 1947 'for the furtherance of agriculture'.[154] It served as the University's Botanic Garden for more than fifty years, during which time the general framework of the gardens changed little, although Walter Melville Wills would doubtless have been amazed at the number of new species and plant families that were introduced during the University's occupation. (Sadly, the University moved the Botanic Gardens to another site since my visits to Bracken Hill in 2000 and 2001, and the following notes and pictures are consequently a record of what I saw then, rather than of what can be found there today. However, the gardens are listed and still in good order, and the house has been converted into flats.)

There was a beautifully-kept wild flower lawn at the front of the house, and a path led around the left side of the house to the pond and gunnera area that contained many aquatic, insectivorous and marsh

Fig 39.3 *The second rock archway at Bracken Hill*

Fig 39.4 *Meticulous stratification markings in Pulhamite bonding between two natural stones*

plants. Part of this is shown in **Fig 39.1**, and some typical Pulhamite rockwork can be clearly seen masking some of the house wall.

A few steps further on, the path passes through two spectacular rock arches – shown in **Figs 39.2 and 39.3** – and **Fig 39.4** is a close-up picture that shows clearly how the sandstone blocks are 'mortared' together by Pulhamite cement to form a carefully stratified structure. This is a good illustration of the meticulous care and skill with which the sculpting was done, and the arches also demonstrate the degree of engineering ability – as well as geological knowledge – demanded of the rock builder responsible. Both of the arches here are still quite secure after all these intervening years, and would have been part of the first stage of the work done in this garden in 1923-25. I am fairly certain that this was the work of Fred Hitching, my grandfather – who was responsible for the garden at Rayne Thatch – although I can't be quite sure about that. It is known, however, that Fred Rickett was definitely involved.

On then to the fernery, where the cool and moist conditions enabled many native and foreign species to thrive, and just beyond that is the Acid Mound, where the original alkaline soil was replaced with special ericaceous soil to encourage the growth of heathland plants. This led on to the hardy bamboos that provided protection to this area from the cold winter winds, and next, just near the far end of the back of the house, is a 'young' 100-year old Giant Redwood, an Himalayan Cedar, and a Cedar of Lebanon. Past the corner of the house were beds of plants from Australia, Mexico, South Africa and New Zealand, and, beyond these, a rock garden that contained a selection of mountain plants that thrive in the gritty soil.

A corner of this section of the garden is pictured in **Fig 39.5**; as the quality of the Pulhamite workmanship is not nearly as good, it was probably constructed at a later period to the arches.

Fig 39.5 *A rocky exit from the garden at Bracken Hill*

Fig 39.6 *The recently cleared rock garden*

Fig 39.6 shows another separate area of rock garden that was only uncovered just prior to my second visit in 2001. This was possibly laid down at an even later time, because the scattered arrangement of natural stone here is far more economical in style and scale than the other sections of the garden, and more reminiscent of the style prevalent after the First World War.

In the far corner of the property is the 'Formal Lily Pool', which probably dates from around 1919, because there is a picture of it in Pulham's *Garden Catalogue* published *c*.1920 – reproduced here in **Fig 39.7**. **Fig 39.8** was taken at the time of my visit in 2000.

1920: The Death of James Pulham 3

James 3 died at his home in Broxbourne on 31st August 1920, and was buried next to his father's grave in the churchyard of St Augustine's, Broxbourne, just a few yards from the manufactory. His obituary, published in the *Hertfordshire Mercury,*[155] reads:

'On Saturday, we recorded the death of Mr James Pulham, who died at his residence in Station Road, where he has lived well over sixty years. Since the death of his father in 1898, Mr Pulham became head of the well-known business firm, Pulham and Son. He died on the centenary of the firm, which was established in 1820. The deceased was a man of sound principles, much esteemed by his employees, and by a wide circle of friends. Outside his business, until the last year or so, he took an active interest in parochial matters, having been Chairman of the Lighting Inspectors, and subsequently Chairman of the Lighting Committee of the parish. He was a regular attendant and staunch supporter of the Parish Church, and also took an active interest in the Boys' School. During the period he was Head of the firm, the latter received the four Royal Warrants which they now hold.'

The above references raise one or two questions for which I have no definitive answers. For example, his memorial stone – pictured in **Fig 39.10** – states that James 3 lived in *'this Parish'* for *'nearly seventy years'* – a fact confirmed by the obituary article, which translates this into *'well over sixty years.'* As he was 75 at the time of his death, this can only mean that he must have moved away from Broxbourne for six or seven years at some point before returning to Broxbourne, where he died. Perhaps this means that he moved to London – possibly Tottenham, like his father before him – in order to be closer to the London Sales Office.

The obituary also states that he died *'on the centenary of the firm, which was established in 1820'*, but this is an exaggeration, since his grandfather, James 1, was still working in Woodbridge with William Lockwood at that time. 1820 was, however, the year in which James 2 was born, so perhaps that was the cause of the confusion. And then there is the reference to *'four Royal Warrants'* awarded to Pulhams. As has been discussed in earlier chapters,

Fig 39.7 *The 'Formal Lily Pool' at Bracken Hill* (Reproduced from *Pulham's Garden Catalogue*, c.1920)

Fig 39.8 *The lily pool in 2000*

was still a 14-year-old scholar at the time of the Census – later set up the Hardy Plants Nursery at Elsenham – just a few miles north-east of Broxbourne, near Bishops Stortford – where he cultivated rockery plants for the firm's landscape work. After all, why buy them in when you can grow them yourself?

So that leaves Ernest, who was only nine at the time of the Census. According to an article in the *Hoddesdon Journal*,[156] Ernest was the last surviving son, who sought his career in the Merchant Navy, and later became works manager with a firm making motorcycle engines.

In 2005, I met a Mr Fred Pallet – an elderly man from Broxbourne – who told me that he could remember Mr Pulham from when he was a young lad. Fred was well into his nineties at the time, so he would have been talking about the years immediately preceding the First World War, when James 3 was himself in the autumn years of his life. Fred said that he and his friends often used to play in and around a road called Churchfields – which is only a few yards from the manufactory in Station Road, Broxbourne – and he recalled how Mr Pulham often used to stop and chat to them, and give them the occasional penny for sweets. 'He was a lovely old gentleman,' he said.

Fig 39.9 *Portrait of James 3 reproduced from the* Gardener's Magazine *10th February 1912*

there were only two – one in 1895 for their work at Sandringham from HRH The Prince of Wales, and another from him in 1904 for their work at Buckingham Palace, by which time he had become HM King Edward VII.

Fig 39.9 shows a portrait of James 3 that appeared in the *Gardener's Magazine* on 10th February 1912. It is devoted to an appraisal of the firm's work, and mentions that James 3 was '*assisted in the various branches of the business by his sons*'. As shown in the Family Tree in Fig 1.1, these were James 4, Frederick, Sydney, Herbert and Ernest.

Apart from James 4, not a lot is known about them, although the 1891 Census for Broxbourne does shine a little light on the subject. It describes James 4 – who was eighteen at the time, and being trained to take over the firm when his father eventually died – as an '*Earth Modeller and Draughtsman*'; Frederick, at sixteen, as a '*Clerk in a Paper Warehouse*', and Sydney, at fifteen, as an '*Apprentice in Artificial Stone Work*'. This implies that Sydney was also being trained to work in the production area – perhaps as production manager.

One gets the impression that Frederick intended to find his fortune outside the firm, although it is known for certain that Herbert – who

Fig 39.10 *Memorial to James 3 in St Augustine's churchyard, Broxbourne*

- 40 -

'THE LEAS'

ZIGZAG PATH, FOLKESTONE, KENT

1920-1921

Fig 40.1 *On the way to the first turn of the zigzag path on 'The Leas'*

One of the first Pulham sites of which I was ever aware was the zigzag path on 'The Leas', because my grandfather, Fred Hitching, loved to tell us about his time as foreman there when my brother and I were very young. I have since learned that his brother, John, worked with him – perhaps as joint foreman[157] – as did Fred Rickett, about whom there will be more to write in a later chapter.

The Upper Leas gardens at the top of the cliffs at Folkestone, and the Lower Leas gardens in Sandgate Road, along the foot of the cliffs, were created by Lord Radnor in the late 19th century in order to attract Victorian holidaymakers to the town. He also built a water-balance lift in 1885, at a cost of £3,000, to transport promenaders nearly 50m from top to bottom – and vice versa.[158] This lift (still

working at the time of my visit in 2005) was the only survivor of three that once existed along 'The Leas'.

Though successful, the lifts did not cater for people in bath chairs, so the council decided to construct a new path – known as the zigzag path – up (or down) the face of the cliff. Following the successful construction of Pulhamite features in Ramsgate and other seaside towns over the previous few years, the contract was awarded to James Pulham and Son.[159]

Like the majority of Pulham sites constructed around this time, most of the unskilled work was carried out by local unemployed men, working under the supervision of one – or possibly three, in this case

Fig 40.2 *Looking up and down from the second turn, showing iron handrails that have replaced the original wooden ones*

– of the Pulham 'rock builders'. This was a large 'Pulhamite' job, involving a tremendous amount of earth-moving, cement mixing and carrying, which meant that it consequently provided employment for a number of men who had returned from the First World War, but for whom very few regular jobs were available. It was also hoped that the provision of a new attraction might encourage more visitors to the town.

Work began on the path in June 1920, and was completed in June 1921, at what is believed to have been a cost of £8,649.[160] The council collected some statistics on Saturday 20th August 1921 which showed that 2,639 pedestrians and 37 perambulators descended the path, and 2,324 pedestrians and 19 perambulators came up it, so presumably the lift was quite busy that day.

Despite this good early start, the path attracted some adverse publicity in its early days, and Pulhams were called back to replace and make good losses of plants from between the rockeries. They did this for the sake of goodwill, but pointed out that at least some of the damage had been caused by vandalism, and the council agreed to the additional planting of rhododendrons, pines, hollies and barberries at a total cost approaching £1,000.

I visited Folkestone once in 1962, and walked up the zigzag path because I knew of my grandfather's involvement with it, but this was long before I began to get seriously interested in the history of the Pulhams and their work. Once I started to get involved with this research, I decided to go back and study the path in greater detail.

There can be no denying that Folkestone is not now the holiday resort that it was in Edwardian days. The port, from which steamers started sailing to France in 1844, is now closed – a victim of the competition introduced by the opening of the Channel Tunnel, through which many people pass, but never get off to eat, sleep or shop in Folkestone.

This is what Sally Festing wrote in 1988 about Pulham's work at Folkestone:[161]

> 'The work covers a substantial vertical area about seventy-five metres across and, roughly, perhaps fifty metres high either side of what is known locally as the zigzag path. The lie of the strata is prominently depicted by means of a slight overhang and incised lines, the whole embellished with steps, seats, plant pockets, low walls, tunnels, arches and caves. To the west of the path there are smaller outcrops to effect a natural gradation, and a small octagonal-topped sundial pedestal on a scalloped base.'

I didn't see the sundial pedestal, but I certainly saw the zigzag path. Having walked up it in 1962, I decided to walk down it in 2005 – having already established that the lift was working in preparation for my return journey.

Fig 40.1 was taken along the top section of the path, and **Fig 40.2**, was taken from the second turn. Moving down towards the third turn, and looking back at the rockwork above, it is obvious that it is beginning to suffer from the effects of time and the sea air.

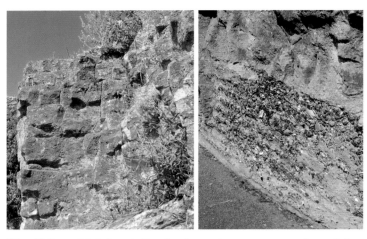

Figs 40.3a and b (above) *Erosion becoming apparent on the rock face (left), and shells embedded into the core of the rock face (right) between the second and third turns*

Fig 40.4 (below) *Archway and weathered rock face on the way to the fourth turn*

The left-hand picture in **Fig 40.3** shows a quite serious area of erosion, where the surface cement has worn away. This could be quite an extensive and expensive restoration project, but surely well worthwhile. The picture on the right, taken at ground level, is a good example of one of Pulham's favourite signatures. He often used to insert shells and odd pieces of ceramic into the surface cement to simulate evidence of the pre-historic existence of sea life in the strata, and what better place to do so than on the coast.

Around the third turn, and down the next stretch, there is a rustic Pulhamite archway (**Fig 40.4**), and here one can see – if one looks out for it – another Pulham trademark. It is the outline of a face – shown in the left-hand picture of **Fig 40.5** – and legend has it that this is a caricature of the foreman, who was supposed to have been a miserable old character, but I don't believe it, because the foreman would have been my grandfather, and he was anything but a miserable old character. The face doesn't look like him, either . . . A number of 'Pulham faces' have already been pointed out in earlier chapters. My own feeling is that the 'rock builders' occasionally got somewhat bored with sculpting natural rock simulations, and

introduced one or two humorous variations by cutting the outline of a human or animal face into the surface of their work. These were usually in quite out-of-the-way places, where people could walk past many times without even noticing them. My host at Folkestone agreed with this, and admitted that there were other examples along the path – one of which was only a few yards away, and is shown here in the right-hand picture in Fig 40.5. He was always spotting something new whenever he walked up or down the path – a lot depending on the angle or direction of the sun at the time, and the way the shadows fell.

Apart from the small archway near the bottom of the fourth stretch of the path, the walk from the top to the fourth turn is completely in the open, but things change at the fifth turn, which is the final one before reaching the lower level. There is a massive tunnel here that appears to have been hewn out of the very side of the cliff face, but, in reality, is completely man made. It is quite an awe-inspiring construction, and **Fig 40.6** shows the view one gets when walking down the path.

A few years ago, a small landslip caused some damage to the pathway leading down from this point, and a flight of steps was put in to replace the damaged stretch of path, but this made it impassable for anyone needing wheels to proceed on their way, so a new, steeper, slope was added in its place.

Pulhams thoughtfully incorporated a long seat-high ridge around the curve of this turn, and I imagine that it has served as a welcome point of rest for many visitors since then. I wondered if the council still suffered from incidents of nuisance or vandalism along the path, and was told that this had been a slight problem a few years ago, but the council had recently installed some gentle LED lighting at this point and in the lower entrance cave, and this had resulted in a significant increase in usage. By the time of my visit in 2005, this path was well used, and consequently much safer and more popular than it had been previously.

The path opens out at the bottom onto a natural grassed amphitheatre where visitors and locals can enjoy the occasional performance or concert. The new subdued lighting in the cave also helps to make it an ideal vantage point on such occasions.

This is in stark contrast to the early days, when the Undercliff and Lower Sandgate Road area were never particularly well cared for. A Mr E H Woodall describes the area, in a letter in *The Garden* journal,[162] as:

' . . . a wilderness of asphalted paths, with here and there a garish patch of wild mustard or a flourishing colony of nettles.

'It is not possible to exaggerate the poverty, the misery and neglect of the so-called gardens . . . Never did I see so many

Figs 40.5a and b *The Foreman's Happy Face underneath the archway near the fourth turn, and another face on the way to the fifth turn*

half-dead trees and shrubs . . . I think the Men of Kent should rise up in arms and demand that one of the principal passenger ports of England should show a more attractive face to its many visitors . . . Let it be no longer deserving the name of the Land of Neglect.'

Thankfully, those days are over.

Fig 40.6 *Fifth turn down the path*

Fig 40.7 *The author at the foot of the zigzag path*

During my visit, I was asked to pose for a photograph, standing in front of the path – *'It would be nice to have a shot of you standing in front of your grandfather's work'* – and the result is shown in **Fig 40.7**, with the signpost pointing in the direction of the cave entrance. The scope, slope and scale of the path can be seen winding up the cliff face in the background.

The council are now making serious efforts to regenerate interest and activities along the lower promenade, and exciting times could hopefully lie ahead. The structure has now been listed by the Department of Culture, Media and Sport, and has group value with the listed Leas Cliff Hall.

I returned to the top in the funicular railway that was still one of Folkestone's most famous landmarks. It is called a 'water balance lift' because it is operated by water that is pumped into a tank in the top car, which is linked to the bottom one by a cable so that, when the brakes are released, the combined weight of water and people pulls the top car down, and the bottom one up.

Fig 40.8 *The group of workmen who laid out the zigzag path on 'The Leas', at Folkestone, in 1921. Mr J R Pulham is fourth from left in the back row, and Fred Hitching is sixth from left* (Photo reproduced by permission of Folkestone Library)

In Conclusion

It would not be possible to close this chapter without referring to one of those incredible pieces of luck that I have had since starting my research into the work of James Pulham and Son. Knowing that my grandfather was in charge of the work at Folkestone, one of the first things I did was contact the people at the local library to ask if they might have any pictures taken at the time the work was done.

A few days later, I received a copy of a picture published in the *Folkestone Herald* in 1973.[163] It was one of those 'fifty years ago today' pictures, and showed a group of workmen above a caption that read:

> 'A group of workmen who laid out Folkestone's zigzag path, which was completed in 1921. Standing fourth left is Mr J R Pulham, of Margate, responsible for the design and construction of the path.'

That picture is reproduced here as **Fig 40.8**, and shows James 4, in his sporty cap and moustache, the fourth from the left in the back row. The person who really attracted my attention, however, was the man standing two away to his left – i.e. to the right of him in the picture. It is my grandfather, Fred Hitching, and the man standing between them might well have been his younger brother, John, although I am unable to confirm this. I know that they both worked on this scheme together, because his grand niece tells me that he often used to talk about his work on the 'helter skelter' at Folkestone.

In conclusion, there are a couple of small things that I would question about the item in the *Folkestone Herald*. As the item was published in 1973, it seems a little strange to have celebrated something that was originally constructed in 1921, and the second thing is that James 4 lived in the firm's manufactory in Broxbourne, Hertfordshire, and not in Margate. My great-uncle, John Hitching, did live in Margate, however, so at least they got the initial right.

Also Noted:
1922-23 – Cliff Walk, North Shore, Blackpool, Lancashire
1929-33 – Exbury Gardens, Southampton, Hampshire (possible)

- 41 -

RAMSGATE

KENT

1923-1936

Fig 41.1 *The West Cliff Chine rockwork under construction, 1925* (Photo provided by Jenifer White)

1925-26: The West Cliff Chine – 'The Second Stage'

Some thirty years after completing the rockwork and waterfall along the sides of Madeira Walk, in the centre of Ramsgate – discussed in Chapter 21 – James Pulham and Son were commissioned to 'beautify' the West Cliff Chine, which lies about a mile or so to the west of the town centre, along Royal Parade, St Augustine's Road and Royal Esplanade.

The picture in **Fig 41.1** was taken when the construction was still in progress *c*.1925, and **Fig 41.2** is of the plaque that commemorates the opening of the promenade and gardens by HRH The Prince of Wales – later to become King Edward VIII – on 24th November 1926. As can be seen from **Fig 41.3**, the pathway is now quite overgrown, and the area is little used, apart from by some of the local people; many visitors to the town don't even know about it. It is nevertheless a listed conservation area, and the local authority has

Fig 41.2 *Plaque to commemorate the opening of the West Cliff Chine on 24 November 1926* (Photo by Terry Wheeler)

its restoration and renovation in mind. The question is what to do about it, and how to stimulate the public's awareness of it without attracting the wrong sort of attention.

Despite their overgrown state, the rocks and pathways seem to be in quite good order, and there is little doubt that, given the right care and continuing attention, it could once again become a pleasant walkway to the Western Undercliff. I can't pretend that the 'cliff work' through which the winding path passes is among Pulham's most imaginative pieces of work, but it is certainly a very good use of the space available, and it would be a tragedy to let it degenerate beyond the point of redemption.

1923-36: Winterstoke Chine, East Cliff – 'The Third Stage'

At the other end of the town are the Winterstoke Gardens on the East Cliff, created by Dame Janet Stancomb-Wills during the early 1920s. Dame Janet was the adopted daughter of her uncle, William Henry Wills, who founded and became chairman of the Imperial Tobacco Co – an amalgamation of W D and H O Wills with a number of other tobacco companies – in Bristol in 1901.[164] She changed her name to Stancomb-Wills in 1893.

Fig 41.3 *The West Cliff Chine Archway, 2005*

William and his family were listed as living in Clifton, Bristol, in the 1871 Census, but the 1891 Census showed them as living near the East Cliff in Ramsgate – presumably after he had retired from the Imperial Tobacco empire. He was knighted, elevated to Baron Winterstoke of Blagdon in 1906, and died in 1911. Dame Janet inherited much of his fortune, and became an extremely generous local benefactress – being particularly interested in art, and educational and social matters.

She laid out the Winterstoke Gardens near her home, and presented them to the Corporation in 1920. They included lawns along the cliff top – with fountains and plenty of seating space for the benefit of local residents and holidaymakers – and a Memorial Colonnade, all of which were opened to the public when she became the first female Mayor of Ramsgate in 1923-24. **Fig 41.4** shows the Colonnade as it was at that time, although it is now in a rather dilapidated state of repair. Plans are in hand to regenerate regular use of the area.

If one studies the entrance garden to the Colonnade in Fig 41.4, one can see a length of Pulhamite rockwork along the far edge – a feature that is mirrored on the opposite side, and extends around the corners onto the promenade. There is even a good chance that Pulhams might have constructed the entire colonnade and surrounding gardens.

No documentary evidence is available to substantiate this, but it would not be surprising, because Dame Janet would have been no stranger to the Pulhams' work. Apart from the extensive feature along the sides of Madeira Walk – which was built soon after the Wills family came to live in Ramsgate – her cousin, Walter Melville Wills, had also engaged them on a number of occasions since 1909. Their work at Bracken Hill, 'Rayne Thatch' and Abbots Pool, around the old family home at Clifton, in Bristol, are discussed in earlier chapters, and the dates lead one to speculate as to whether Melville Wills might initially have got his inspiration for these commissions from the work that Pulhams did along Madeira Walk.

James 4 would have supervised the construction of the Memorial Colonnade and Gardens in the early 1920s – some five or six years before they were brought back to build the rock features in the West Cliff Chine. According to the *Isle of Thanet Gazette*,[165] they then came back again in 1935 to assist with the conversion of the rocky foreshore and rugged cliff below the Winterstoke Gardens into a:

> '. . .beautiful promenade that is sure to attain popularity among the town's holiday multitudes.'

The opening of the Winterstoke Undercliff and rock gardens was almost the last major project on which the Pulhams are known to have worked, and it extended Ramsgate's cliff walks by over a quarter of a mile.

Fig 41.4 *Winterstoke Memorial Colonnade c.1925, with Pulhamite rockwork in background* (Photo provided by Terry Wheeler)

Fig 41.5 *Construction of the Winterstoke Cliff Path under way* (Photo provided by Jenifer White)

The *Isle of Thanet* reporter recounts how the foundations of the undercliff wall were laid, and how the wall was then constructed. The cliff face was literally 'reshaped' by cutting away eight thousand tons of chalk – which was then used to form the foundations for the promenade – and reinforcing the base with a wall of blocks made from the reddish-hued Maidstone sand. By comparison with the Madeira Walk project some forty years earlier (discussed in Chapter 21) this one took one year to complete, at a total cost of £23,000.

Fig 41.5 is a reproduction of another old picture, which shows the work in progress on the Winterstoke Cliff Path, with the low wall of blocks along the promenade at the base of the cliff. The basic concept of this path is similar to that of the zigzag path on 'The Leas' at Folkestone – discussed in the previous chapter – except that the slope of the cliff face here does not allow for such a winding path to be constructed. There is only room for one corner, half way up,

Fig 41.6 *Steps leading down the Winterstoke Cliff Path at Ramsgate, 2005* (Photo by Terry Wheeler)

making the path rather steep. Originally, a number of seats offered rest along the way for the weary climber. **Fig 41.6** shows the view from the top of the path.

The then Mayor, Alderman H. Stead, opened the new gardens on 10th July 1936, and the *Isle of Thanet Gazette* reported:

'Walking along the undercliff from the direction of the bathing pool, the resident or the holidaymaker rounds a bend, and is suddenly struck by the view of a great mass of rockery towering above him like a miniature Cheddar Gorge.

'This rockery – Ramsgate's eastern chine – is much more ambitious than the one leading down to the western undercliff, and Mr J W Hitching [my grandfather's younger brother], the man who was responsible for its construction, claims it to be the largest of its kind on the coast – and he should know, for the firm with whom he is connected are the recognised experts for this type of work all over the country. He it was who directed the construction of Madeira Walk, the Winterstoke Gardens and the western chine.

'From the undercliff to the Winterstoke Gardens, there is a walk of about two hundred yards – an untiring climb up steps, made of cement specially treated to avoid unwelcome glare. If the feet should grow tired during the journey, walkers have the choice of nine alcoves in which they can repose on comfortable teak seats.

'So ingeniously has the rock been formed by expert workers, that it is difficult to convince oneself that it is artificial. In reality, it consists of roughcast blocks faced with cement. Of course, the rocks are bare as yet, but they will look a blaze of colour when planted out this year.'

The Mayor cut the red, white and blue tape with a pair of golden scissors presented to him by a director of the Holborn Construction Co. – who were responsible for the construction of the undercliff promenade, and reshaping of the cliff face – and then proposed a vote of thanks that was seconded by James 4. He mentioned that Mr J W Hitching, who was in charge of that part of the scheme, was a resident of Ramsgate, and recalled past improvements in the town with which his firm had been associated. He foresaw the time when, with the means of transport becoming ever more rapid, the town would attract still greater throngs of visitors.

The Mayor then led the civic party down to the undercliff, where he unveiled a tablet commemorating the opening ceremony (**Fig 41.7**), after which they all adjourned for tea at the Winterstoke Gardens, and enjoyed a programme of music played by the Band of the Royal Air Force, from their local base at Manston.

I have to take issue with one part of this report, because, at the time of the Madeira Walk project in 1894, John Hitching would have been only 23 years of age. There is certainly a possibility that he may have worked on it in a more junior capacity, but if a Hitching really was in charge, then it is much more likely to have been my great-grandfather, William. I shall never know the answer to that, however.

Ramsgate Council have commissioned a number of surveys relating to the conservation of the Pulham work around their town over the past few years, and found it to be in need of some restoration. Thankfully, following the debacle of the so-called 'restoration' attempt at Battersea Park during the 1980s – discussed in Chapter 6 – they decided to engage a geological consultant to advise on the composition of the Pulhamite, and to establish a properly controlled programme of restoration before risking any further damage to what currently exists.

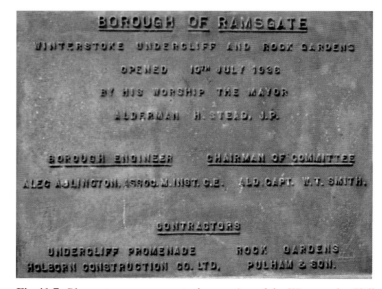

Fig 41.7 *Plaque to commemorate the opening of the Winterstoke Cliff Path and Rock Garden at Ramsgate* (Photo by Terry Wheeler)

- 42 -

STOKE POGES MEMORIAL GARDENS
BUCKINGHAMSHIRE
1934-1936

Fig 42.1 *The central pool in the sunken parterre Garden*

The historic parkland of Stoke Park, Stoke Poges, was laid out during the 1750s by 'Capability' Brown, and later improved by Repton, who added the imposing three-arched bridge over the lake in front of the mansion. On the south side of the park lay St Giles Church, made famous by Thomas Gray in his *'Elegy Written in a Country Churchyard'*.[166]

Much of the area survived until the early 1900s, when part was sold off to form a golf club, and more was taken for housing development. When another twenty acres of land to the south side of St Giles Church came under threat of development in the early 1930s, Sir Noel Mobbs, the then Lord of the Manor of Stoke Poges, decided to acquire it 'in order to preserve the tranquil and rural

setting of the church'. He wanted to leave the land as a memorial garden, to be a 'living memorial to the dead and of solace to the bereaved', and intended for:

> '. . . the repose of the ashes of cremated persons . . . designed and maintained in a fashion for which there is no building, structures or monuments of any kind likely to remind one of a cemetery.'[167]

The gardens were designed by Edward White, and completed on 1st November 1937. The main feature is a colonnaded central parterre garden, reached by a central path leading from the Church Cottage. Secondary paths extend at right angles from this, linking with the

Fig 42.2 *The colonnade and sunken parterre*

circuitous paths around the perimeter, where woodland areas lead naturally into the surrounding parkland. There is also an avenue along the eastern boundary, bordering the lake and Stoke Park.

All the evidence indicates that White commissioned James 4 to construct these gardens to his plans – not only had the firm of Milner Sons and White worked with the Pulhams on several sites in the past, there are a number of features here that are clearly 'Pulhamesque' in style. The passage of time and the effects of severe weather took their inevitable toll over the years, but English Heritage registered them as Grade II listed, and, in 2001, the Heritage Lottery Fund contributed half of their £1 million restoration costs. As a result, not only are they the only known example of a memorial garden in this country, they are one of the few gardens of this period that still survives unchanged, and are an important example of the work of a foremost British landscape architect of the early 20th century.

I only became aware of them in 2009, but it was a significant discovery because it provided me with positive verification that Pulhams were indeed still active during the mid-1930s. It was an extremely wet day at the time of my visit, but this was more than compensated for by the fact that I was introduced to Len Harris, a nonagenarian who actually worked on the construction of the gardens when he was only in his late teens. He recalled that he

worked under the supervision of a Mr Cox Senior – whose name I had not heard before – and that the general method of operation was absolutely typical of this firm, in that the 'supervisor from Head Office' was responsible for the recruitment and supervision of local men to do the heavy work.

Fig 42.1 is a picture of the small central pool and fountain in the centre of the sunken parterre garden, from which a series of paths radiate out to a colonnaded pergola that totally encircles the garden – **Fig 42.2** – which shows a remarkable similarity to the other Pulham pergolas illustrated in this book. Just inside this boundary runs a small rill in which there are installed a number of miniature fountains.

There is another very large fountain in an adjacent part of the gardens, and this is shown in **Fig 42.3**. Once again, the clarity of style plainly indicates that it is likely to have come from the Broxbourne manufactory.

There is even more evidence around the boundary of the formal gardens, and bordering the lake in Stoke Park. This takes the form of a charming, winding rocky stream, complete with a small cascade and a typical 'Pulhamesque' stretch, with rocky banks, steps and stepping stones, as can be seen in **Fig 42.4**.

Fig 42.3 (right) *The main pool and fountain*

Fig 42.4 (below) *The stream, stepping stones, path and steps in the rock garden*

Looking across the lake in Stoke Park (**Fig 42.5**), one can see the Repton bridge in the foreground, with Stoke Park Mansion behind, and finally in this section, **Fig 42.6** shows me with Len Harris on the right. We are looking back to the 1930s from the back of a buggy on a very wet, but otherwise most enjoyable day.

Fig 42.5 (above) *Stoke Park Mansion and the Repton Bridge*

Fig 42.6 (left) *Looking back to the 1930s with Len Harris, one of the original construction team (Photo by Bernard Linsell)*

- 43 -

END OF THE LINE

1935-1957

Fig 43.1 *The house and manufactory built by James 2 in Station Road, Broxbourne, just before its demolition in May 1967. The drive on the left leads down, under the archway, to the workshops* (Photo by Bishop Marshall, provided by David Dent)

To the best of my knowledge, the Winterstoke Gardens at Ramsgate and the Memorial Gardens at Stoke Poges were probably the last major landscaping projects undertaken by James Pulham and Son. That is not to say that they did nothing else, or that they ceased their production of quality terracotta wares – it's just that, if they did, I have not heard of them.

As far as I am aware, the business continued to decline until it was finally forced to close altogether at some time around the start of the Second World War in 1939. Someone – whose name I don't know, but who used to live in a house that overlooked the manufactory during this period – told me that these were desperate times for the firm, and that, in the end, they were reduced to manufacturing 'common or garden flower pots'. What a sad end for a firm that had earned itself such an enviable reputation throughout its existence . . .

And what a burden for James 4 to realise that he would be unable to

pass on the heritage left to him by his father, grandfather and great-grandfather. Not that it was really any fault of his, because the structure and balance of society had changed dramatically since the beginning of the century, and the general economic situation in which he now found himself was no longer capable of supporting a manually intensive business such as this.

He had also come to the end of the line as far as the continuation of the company name was concerned. As noted in Chapter 35, he had one daughter, Freda, who moved to Zambia (as it is now), and all the company records were deliberately destroyed when it finally went out of business. All my efforts to trace other members of the family came to nothing, although, incredibly, I have been contacted by some of them as a direct result of them discovering my website at www.pulham.org.uk. One of them, Chris Pulham, was able to provide some details of the family tree, and Freda's son, Michael Goodchild, very generously handed on some photographs, and the two silver cups that have already been discussed.

Fig 43.2 *The remains of the Pulham manufactory, just prior to its demolition in May 1967. The house has already been removed* (Photo by Bishop Marshall, provided by David Dent)

1957: Death of James Pulham 4

James 4 died on 20th April 1957 at the General Hospital in Edgware, North London as a result of an accident. The following obituary appeared in the *British Fern Gazetteer*: [168]

'It was distressing news that J R Pulham died on 20th April 1957, as a result of an accident. He was 84 years old.

Pulham's services to the [Fern] Society were such that they should not pass without record . . . Pulham was an Associate of the Institute of Landscape Architects; he had inherited the well-known firm of Pulham and Son; and among other work with which he had been concerned was the massive Rock Garden at Wisley. He had been Secretary of the Alpine Garden Society for many years, and Secretary of the Horticultural Club. He was also the Secretary of the British Fern Society between 1948-50.'

His address was given as 24 Ashcombe Gardens, Edgware, which obviously means that he moved away from the old family home in Station Road, Broxbourne, some time before that. I do not know exactly when that was, but I understand that, towards the end of its life, the house in Broxbourne was divided into flats.

1966-86: Demolition and Commemoration

Pulham House and the remains of the adjoining manufactory were eventually demolished in 1967 to make way for more flats near the railway station – a sad end to a fascinating piece of Hoddesdon and Broxbourne's industrial heritage. **Fig 43.1** is a picture of the near-derelict house, taken not long before its demise, with the drive leading down to the workshops visible on the left. **Fig 43.2** is an aerial picture that was taken after the house was razed to the ground, but while the manufactory behind it – which can be clearly seen in the centre of the picture – was still standing.

Fig 43.3 *The Pulham puddling wheel* (Photo by Bishop Marshall, provided by David Dent)[169]

Fig 43.4 *The plaque commemorating the restoration of the wheel and kiln by Broxbourne Borough Council in 1986*

The good news is that someone somewhere realised what was going on just before it was too late, and managed to persuade the developers to preserve the puddling – or grinding – wheel and part of one of the six kilns as a memorial to the firm and its contribution to local history. The remains of the puddling wheel are shown in **Fig 43.3**, with the workshops in the background – the 'work-yard' side of the archway leading to the drive that runs up the side of the house can be seen in the centre

The clay and other coarse granulate ingredients of the terracotta ornaments were spread in the circular trough that ran around inside the outer rim of the base of the puddling wheel, and one can quite easily imagine a couple of plough horses being harnessed to these massive *'edge-runner'* wheels, and walking constantly round and round while the materials were ground down to a fine powder.

In an article in the *Journal of The Garden History Society*,[170] Sally Festing records that this powder was then carried by a miniature railway to the workshops, where it was moulded into tiles, ornaments and sculptures prior to being baked in the coal-fired kilns that worked continually for twenty-four hours per day.

The final act took place almost twenty years after the buildings were demolished – by which time the token remnants had become almost completely overgrown. Plans were being drawn up for the construction of flats on the area where the wheel and kiln were 'rediscovered', and, in early 1986, the Broxbourne Borough Council decided to preserve them properly.[171] The area was restored and railed off, and a memorial plaque erected (**Fig 43.4**) at a total cost of £8,000.[172]

It was opened officially at the end of August of that year, and can be found by leaving Broxbourne railway station; turning right into Station Road; over the New River bridge, and down a narrow pathway a few yards along on the right, beside the second block of flats. The plaque reads:

> 'The brick kiln & puddling wheel are the remains of a terracotta works built in the late 1840s by James Pulham. The wheel was horse driven & used to grind claystone which was then moulded & baked in the kiln to make terracotta. This was used to decorate buildings & gardens throughout Britain. The works closed in 1945 & were restored by Broxbourne Borough Council in 1986.'

The only thing I would argue about there is the closing date given of 1945. I don't know the true answer to that, but have based my own assumptions of 1939-40 on other reports that I have read. This is because I can't really imagine what – or how much – the firm is likely to have done during the actual war years. But that is relatively immaterial – the really important and interesting thing is what they did during the previous one hundred years, and I hope that my research into the subject, and this resulting book, has managed to throw some light on the subject. If the results prove as interesting and satisfying to the reader as they have been to me throughout the whole of this project, then my efforts will all have been worthwhile . . .

On a Personal Note

I don't know exactly when my grandfather, Frederick Hitching, retired, but I imagine it must have been sometime around his 65th birthday, in 1932, because I am almost certain that he was not involved with his younger brother John on the Ramsgate project in 1935-36. However, I do know that he worked on one or two private rock-building jobs up to the summer of 1939, when he was 72.

Fig 43.5   *Fred Hitching at work on a private assignment, c.1939*

Fig 43.6   *Fred Hitching and friends, including myself (at the age of 11) on the left, and my brother, Fred, on the right*

Fig 43.8   *John William Hitching, a Pulham rock builder* (Photo supplied by Sue Davies)

I have also made a number of references to Fred's younger brother, John, throughout the latter chapters of this book. John was also a Pulham rock builder, although I knew very little about him until I was contacted – again via my website – by Sue Davies, the great-grandniece of John's wife, Florence. She is the source of some of the information to which I have been able to make occasional references, and she also sent me a photograph of John, which is reproduced in **Fig 43.8**. I have to say that I was amazed to see the strong family resemblance when I first looked at it.

One of these was for a local businessman, during which time the photographs shown in **Figs 43.5** and **43.6** were taken. The first is a picture of him in his customary white apron and hat preparing to do some rockwork there, and Fig 43.6 includes me, aged 11, and my brother, Fred. **Fig 43.7** shows Fred standing proudly in his own garden, which he created when he was well into his eighties.

Fig 43.7   *Fred with the rockery he built in his own garden in Hoddesdon during the 1950s, when he was well into his 80s. He made the Pulhamite bird bath, and the supports were moulded from a piece from the back of an old chair.*

- 44 -

THE POWER OF THE INTERNET

2005-2011

A number of incredible coincidences have happened during the course of this project, almost entirely as a result of people discovering my website at www.pulham.org.uk. Some were actually connected to the Pulham family – like Chris Pulham and Ian Denney, for instance. Chris was kind enough to send me a copy of the Pulham family tree that he had compiled, and upon which Fig 1.1 is based, and Ian – directly descended from Obadiah Pulham – sent me the scans of Obadiah's Apprentice Certificate (Fig 2.32), and of a painting that he did while working in Naples – reproduced in Fig 2.33. I would have known nothing about any of these if it had not been for the website.

As noted in Chapter 3, following an article that I had written for a magazine, a professional terracotta restorer contacted me with information about a Pulham fountain that he had recently restored, and – again, thanks to the internet – I was able to trace it to the Bellagio Hotel Casino in Las Vegas, and a lady who works in the Las Vegas Virtual Library very generously took a camera along, and took some photographs for me. One of them is reproduced in Fig 3.30.

Over the years, I have received messages from all over the UK – and some from overseas – from a number of people asking for information or identification of features for which they have supplied photographs, and I am very happy to say that, in a few cases, my verification has helped to lead to the successful application for a Heritage Lottery Restoration grant. Several others have passed on information to me, or asked if I knew whether or not some rockwork that they had just discovered had been Pulhams' work. In view of the fact that no official company records remain of work they did after 1877, some of these questions have led to completely new and interesting lines of enquiry and research.

One recent example is Mark Gibson, who telephoned me during September 2010. He purchased the Craigengillan estate in Dalmellington, Ayrshire in 2000, and told me:

> '. . . everything was crumbling, and the gardens overtaken by the jungle. This year, we began to unearth an amazing rock garden and a series of six ponds connected by waterfalls. The rocks are . . . beautifully positioned at an angle to resemble natural rock. Some are nine tenths buried, again to look natural.'

He knew that, between 1901-05, the property was owned by Charlotte McAdam, who had the gardens completely redesigned, landscaped and planted. Mark and his wife, Fi, began carefully uncovering the rocks, ponds and cascades at the beginning of 2010. The more they discovered, the more they marvelled at the inspiration and artistry of whoever had created the garden. Unfortunately, the McAdams – who had lived at Craigengillan since the 1580s – had left no written records or plans, so it seemed unlikely that they would ever know the identity of the guiding hand.

Then, in July of 2010, they were invited to a garden party at Buckingham Palace. Exploring beyond the lake, they came across the rock garden, and noticed that it bore an uncanny resemblance to that at Craigengillan. With their excellent records, the Palace was able to confirm that theirs was the work of Pulham & Son in 1903-04.

This meant very little to Mark, so he checked the internet, found my website, and decided to contact me. I had never heard of Craigengillan, so he sent me some photographs of some of the rocks, and I was happy to confirm that they were indeed genuine, which consequently meant that another, hitherto unknown site could be added to the database, and we also had a date range to ascribe to it.

Diary of a Rock Builder by Fred Rickett

About two weeks after that, I received another telephone call, this time from Lorna Milligan, who told me that her father, Fred Rickett, was a Pulham rock builder – just like my grandfather, Fred Hitching. The name of Fred Rickett was not unknown to me, because he was one of the team of Pulham workmen whose names had been written on the back of an old envelope, and hidden away inside the frame of a garden seat at Blakesley Hall in 1908, as noted in Chapter 23, and pictured in Fig 23.8.

Lorna had been given my contact details, and wanted to know if I was interested in knowing about a diary that her father used to keep, in which he recorded the dates and locations of all the Pulham jobs on which he worked. Interested? Of course I was interested! This was potentially an extremely valuable document, and would obviously help to fill a number of gaps in our knowledge of Pulhams'

Fig 44.1 (right) *Two pages from Fred Rickett's Diary, 9th November 1909 to 6th November 1910*

Fig 44.2 (right, below) *Two pages from Fred Rickett's Diary, 26th June 1914 to 19th July 1919*

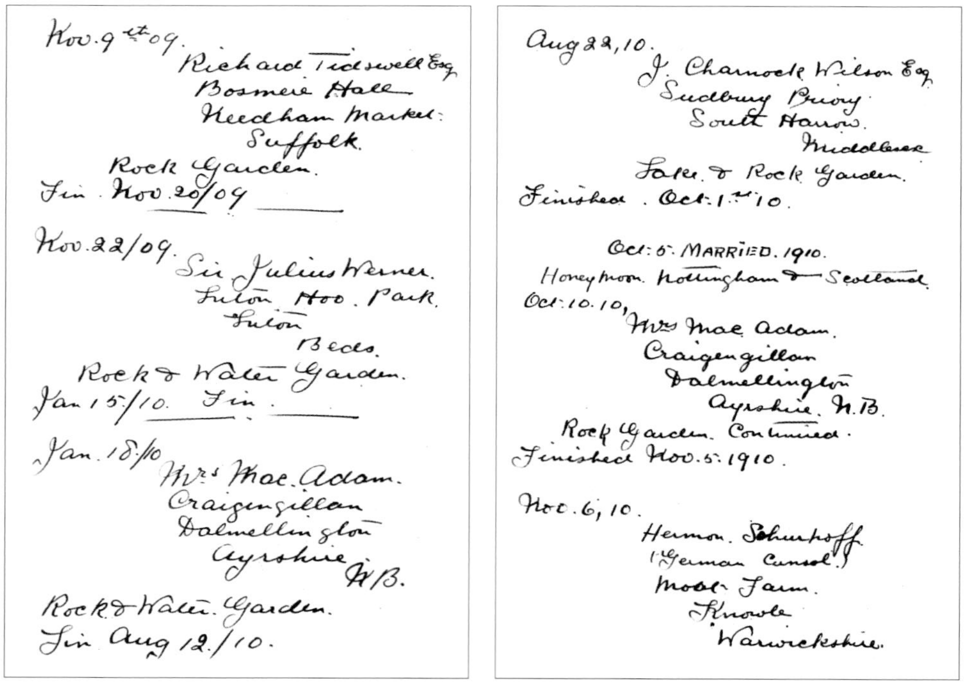

Nov. 9th 09.
Richard Tidswell Esq
Bosmere Hall
Needham Market:
Suffolk.
Rock Garden.
Fin. Nov. 20/09

Nov. 22/09.
Sir Julius Werner.
Luton Hoo. Park.
Luton
Beds.
Rock & Water Garden.
Jan 15/10. Fin.

Jan. 18/10
Mrs Mac. Adam.
Craigengillan
Dalmellington
Ayrshire N.B.
Rock & Water Garden.
Fin Aug 12./10.

Aug 22, 10.
J. Charnock Wilson Esq
Sudbury Priory
South Harrow
Middlesex
Lake & Rock Garden.
Finished. Oct. 1st 10.

Oct. 5. MARRIED. 1910.
Honeymoon. Nottingham & Scotland
Oct. 10. 10,
Mrs Mac Adam.
Craigengillan
Dalmellington
Ayrshire. N.B.
Rock Garden. Continued.
Finished Nov. 5. 1910.

Nov. 6, 10.
Herman Schunhoff
(German Consul.)
Moat Farm.
Knowle
Warwickshire.

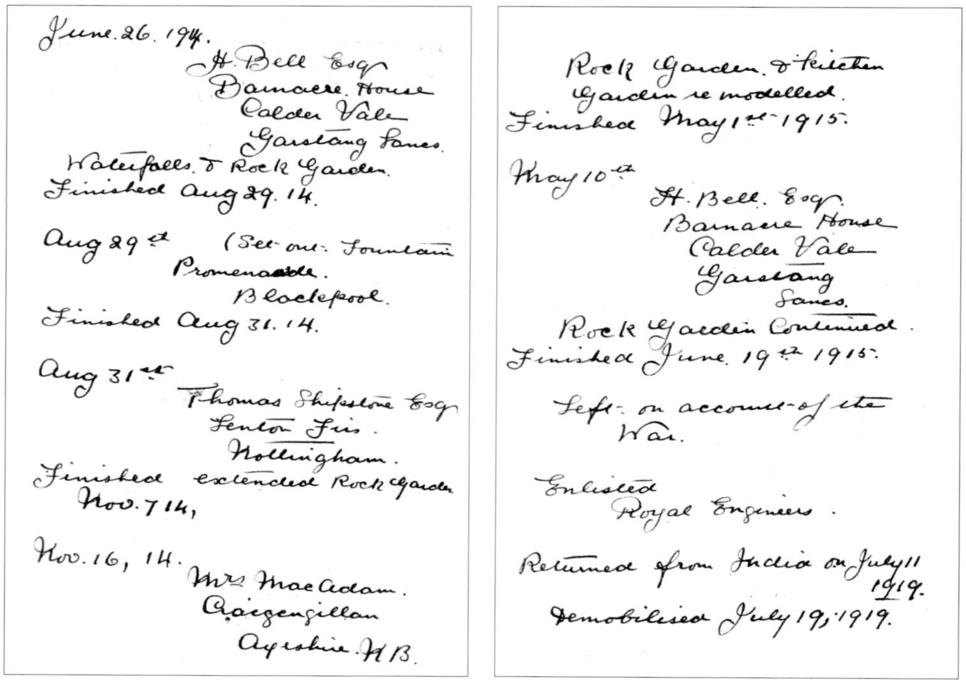

June. 26. 1914.
H. Bell Esq
Barnacre House
Calder Vale
Garstang Lancs.
Waterfalls & Rock Garden.
Finished Aug 29. 14.

Aug 29th (Set out Fountain
Promenade.
Blackpool.
Finished Aug 31. 14.

Aug 31st
Thomas Shipstone Esq
Lenton Firs.
Nottingham.
Finished extended Rock Garden
Nov. 7 14,

Nov. 16, 14.
Mrs Mac Adam.
Craigengillan
Ayrshire N.B.

Rock Garden & Kitchen
Garden re modelled.
Finished May 1st 1915.

May 10th
H. Bell. Esq.
Barnacre House
Calder Vale
Garstang
Lancs.
Rock Garden Continued.
Finished June. 19th 1915.

Left on account of the
War.

Enlisted
Royal Engineers.

Returned from India on July 11
1919.
Demobilised July 19, 1919.

work after 1877, as well as provide a lot of new information. She was reluctant to send it to me – or even let a photocopy shop handle it – because it was too precious to her to let out of her sight, so I took my portable scanner, and spent a most enjoyable day with her.

This is not the place to reproduce all the pages from her father's *Diary of a Rock Builder*, although occasional references to it have been made in the footnotes to some of the later chapters in this book. It should be noted here that Fred's diary only contains details of the jobs on which he was personally involved. There were other rock builders out there, some of whom, like my grandfather, were working on other sites, and it is also possible that Fred was not present on a site throughout the whole of the time it was in progress. It is still a fascinating and precious addition to our archive, because it enables us to ascribe actual dates to the work done on some sites that had previously had to be estimated, as well as identifying others that had hitherto been unknown.

The diary only provides the briefest of notes about who, where, when and what was involved with Fred's work, but it nevertheless provides a fascinating insight into the life and character of the man. For instance, he was born on 24th January 1885, and the first entry in his diary is dated 28th October 1898, when he was only 13! He records that he worked at Friar Park, Henley-on-Thames – discussed in Chapter 24 – until 1st May 1901, constructing:

> 'Caves, dry and water, waterfalls, lake and Matterhorn, including Ice Cave and Glacier.'

He returned there for two months in 1902, and for another three months in 1906 to make 'alterations to Matterhorn', which helps to illustrate what a perfectionist Sir Frank Crisp was. Another site on which Fred worked is described in Chapter 25 – namely that of Francis Baring-Gould at Merrow Grange. He worked there from July 1902 to February 1903, helping to construct 'rockwork and fernery'.

He worked for a couple of weeks for Mark Fenwick at Abbotswood – Chapter 26 – although this was obviously only to make some minor alterations to a job that I believe was mainly done in 1901, and he worked from 23rd September to 24th December 1903 on the 'rock formation' for King Edward VII at Buckingham Palace (Chapter 30). This means that he must then have worked here alongside my grandfather, Fred Hitching, with whom he must also have worked at 'Rayne Thatch', the Bristol home of Walter Melville Wills (Chapter 31). He was there between January and April 1909, building the 'Swimming bath and bungalow, waterfalls etc'.

While working on the second stage of the project at Blakesley Hall – Chapter 23 – between 29th May 1907 and 3rd June 1908, he met Lucy Jane Hedges, a personal maid to Mrs Bartholomew. They fell in love, and began a courtship that often had to be conducted over long distances.

And then came two fascinating pieces of information. It turns out that, between 18th January and 12th August 1910, Fred was constructing a 'Rock and Water Garden' for none other than Mrs McAdam, at Craigengillan, Dalmellington, Ayrshire – the very place now owned by Mark Gibson, mentioned above, so it is now possible to pin down at least part of that work to a specific date. Was this a coincidence or not?

Two pages from Fred's diary are reproduced here in **Fig 44.1**, and, if one compares the handwriting with that on the 'envelope in the bottle' at Blakesley Hall – Fig 23.8 – it is almost certain that Fred was the writer of that, too. The Craigengillan entry can be found at the foot of the first page – but the second page is even more interesting. Fred then moved on to help build 'Lakes and Rock Garden' for J Charnock Wilson, Sudbury Priory, in South Harrow, Middlesex, where he stayed until 1st October but the next two lines tell a completely different story. He records, in the simplest possible detail, that, between 5th to 9th October, he:

'Married and Honeymoon, Nottingham and Scotland'.

And where was he on the 10th October, after a five-day honeymoon? Back at work on Mrs McAdam's rock garden at Craigengillan, where he stayed until 5th November. For the benefit of those who like to have a little more detail about this sort of thing, Fred's daughter, Lorna, tells me that they got married at Lucy's local Parish Church at Adstone, near Towcester, Northamptonshire.

It transpired that, when I had absorbed all this information, and passed it on to Mark Gibson, it happened to be exactly one hundred years to the week after Fred was actually constructing his gardens. He could hardly believe it, and it was a most exciting moment for us both.

The next page of the diary – not shown here – records Fred's work on the 'Rock and Water Garden' at RHS Wisley (Chapter 35), followed by the 'Rock and Water' at 'The Node' at Codicote (Chapter 34). He also spent a week erecting the pergola at Warren House in March 1912 (Chapter 32), and a month in January 1914 building the 'Bridge with Kentish Ragstone' at Ewell Court House (Chapter 18).

A number of small projects followed, and then, from 16th November 1914 until 1st May 1915, he spent another six months working for Mrs McAdam at Craigengillan, remodelling the rock garden and

Fig 44.3 *Fred Rickett with his wife, Lucy Jane (far right), and their three daughters, Freda, Gladys and Lorna, in 1935*

kitchen garden. By then, of course, the First World War was well under way, and the two pages of his diary reproduced in **Fig 44.2** include another touching masterpiece of understatement. Immediately following an entry that records him working at Barnacre House, in Garstang, Lancashire between 10th May and 19th June 1915, he simply notes that he:

'Left on account of the War. Enlisted Royal Engineers.'

The next line is dated 11th July 1919, when he 'Returned from India', to be demobilised on 19th July. He celebrated with two weeks' holiday before he 'Commenced again for Pulham and Son' on 6th August, and went to build a rock garden for Lord Treowen, at Llanover, Abergavenny, in Monmouthshire.

Between June 1920 and June 1921, Fred was working alongside the two Hitching brothers on the zigzag path on 'The Leas', Folkestone – Chapter 40 – after which a high proportion of his jobs appear to have been on various projects in and around Bristol for Walter Melville Wills. In fact, the final entry in his diary, dated 13th March 1930, marks the beginning of some work at Abbots Pool – Chapter 38 – and there is no date to indicate when it finished.

Lorna, tells me that this was the time when he left the employment of James Pulham and Son to set up a landscaping business of his own in Bristol, in which he spent the major part of his time on more projects for the Wills family. She was also able to let me see a family photo taken on the occasion of Fred's Silver Wedding anniversary in 1935 – reproduced here as **Fig 44.3** – which shows Fred and Lucy Jane with their three daughters, Freda, Gladys and Lorna. Fred died in 1965, aged 79.

Fig 44.4 *Your author, Claude Hitching, Val Christman, Cllr Lyn White, Mayor of Broxbourne, and Jack Sexton, at the handover ceremony of the 'Lowewood Pots' at Lowewood Museum*

A Final Twist

In 2009 I was just about to mark the tenth anniversary of the start of this project, which seemed to be a good point at which to end it. It wouldn't matter how long I kept going, it was already evident that, whenever I decided to call it a day, something new would come along that could potentially lead to a new avenue of research. But, sooner or later, things had to be called to a halt. So I polished up my notes, got to *'The End of the Line'*, saved and closed the final file, and turned off my computer. A celebratory cup of tea seemed to be in order.

But before I could take my first sip, the phone rang. It was a call from a lady named Valerie Christman, who asked if I might be able to help her with some information about her family tree. She knew hardly anything about her family history, and when she asked her father if they had any famous ancestors, he could only think of one possible contender. He seemed to recall that there might once have been a builder or someone with the rather strange name of Michael Angelo Pulham, so she checked on the internet and was amazed to find it on my website – so she decided to get in touch.

Thanks to Chris Pulham, I have quite a lot of information about the members of the 'James branch' of the Pulham family, so I checked this out, and we were able to confirm all the relevant family links. Val's father's name is Jack Sexton, and it turned out that his grandfather, John Sexton, was married to Clara Pulham – daughter of Michael Angelo – who is shown on the section of the Pulham family tree reproduced in Fig 3.26.

Even after ten years researching the lives and work of this remarkable family, I had never yet been able to locate or speak to a member of the actual 'James branch', and here I was, talking to the 3-times-great-granddaughter of James 1, who had chosen to phone me, completely out of the blue, within five minutes of my closing the final file! It was time to turn the computer on once more.

Yet another coincidence was about to be revealed. It turned out that Val is an incredibly enthusiastic amateur geologist who 'loves her rocks', as well as being a professional landscape gardener and garden designer! She and her brother, John, work with her father, Jack Sexton, who runs his own garden landscaping business, and specialises in the construction of rock gardens, pergolas, water features, boathouses etc. Bearing in mind that, before our conversation took place, none of them knew anything about their true family history, one can only speculate about how their interest and involvement in gardening must be rooted in their genes.

It was also quite obvious that we were going to have plenty of things to talk about, and one of the first things we did together was attend the 'handover ceremony' of Michael Angelo's 'Lowewood Pots' – pictured in Fig 3.28 – at the Lowewood Museum in Broxbourne. A picture of our group is shown in **Fig 44.4**, with Jack holding a pot that was actually designed by his great-grandfather.

The name of Jack's firm is Class Gardens, and **Figs 44.5 and 44.6** show two small rock gardens that he built for designer David Stevens. F.W. Woolworth commissioned them to construct gardens for exhibition at the Chelsea Flower Show in 1986 and 1987 – and **Fig 44.7** is a picture of the Gold Medal they were awarded for each one.

Figs 44.7a and b *Gold Medal awards to
F. W. Woolworth at the 1986 and 1987
Chelsea Flower Shows for gardens designed
by David Stevens in association with Jack Sexton,
and constructed by Class Gardens*

Fig 44.5 *Award–winning garden at the 1986 Chelsea Flower Show, designed by David Stevens in association with Jack Sexton, and constructed by Class Gardens for F. W. Woolworth*

Fig 44.6 *Award–winning garden at the 1987 Chelsea Flower Show, designed by David Stevens in association with Jack Sexton, and constructed by Class Gardens for F. W. Woolworth*

Fig 44.8 *Class Gardens' 'Victorian Cottage' exhibit at the Chelsea Show 2010*

Fig 44.9 *Valerie Christman being introduced to HM Queen Elizabeth II by Peter Seabrook, gardening editor of the* Sun, *at the Chelsea Show in 2010* (Photo reproduced by permission of Arthur Edwards / The Sun)

Nearly 25 years on from this, they are still exhibiting at Chelsea. In 2010, they were commissioned by the *Sun* newspaper to construct a small cottage garden that might have been tended by an elderly Victorian couple celebrating their Golden Wedding anniversary. It was designed by Valerie who – inspired by her newly-discovered interest in all things related to the Pulham family – recreated the front of her great-grandmother's cottage. That picture is shown in Fig 3.27, and her version of it is pictured in **Fig 44.8.**

Her garden won a Silver Gilt award, and Valerie also had the honour of being introduced to The Queen by Peter Seabrook, gardening editor of the *Sun*, as can be seen in **Fig 44.9**. She was absolutely thrilled by the occasion, and what a fitting comparison this provides with Fig 36.6, which shows James 4 – her second cousin twice removed – talking to King George V and Queen Mary at the Chelsea Show in 1931.

Closing the Circle

And, once again, that would have been the point at which this story ended, had it not been for one more episode that took place just after I had handed the manuscript over to my publisher. Strictly speaking, it should therefore come under the heading of 'author's corrections', but they very generously agreed to overlook that technicality, and add it in.

Readers will know that the Antique Collectors Club are located on the outskirts of Woodbridge – the very place at which this story begins. As noted in Chapter 1, James 1 was born in Woodbridge in 1793, and William Lockwood 2 – whose father took James and Obadiah Pulham's into apprenticeship – wrote a series of *Reminiscences of Woodbridge in Olden Times*, a copy of which still resides in the Woodbridge library. The first half of these chronicles is devoted almost exclusively to extolling the Pulhams' incredible artistic talents as stone modellers.

He also provides a very positive clue about where they lived when he describes them as members of:

> '. . . a numerous family, born of poor parents, near the West end of the Thoro'fare, in that part of Woodbridge since called Cumberland Street.'

A further clue was provided by Chris Pulham, who discovered during his researches that their father, William Pulham, was a shoemaker by trade.

Cumberland Street still exists, as do also a lot of its old houses and cottages, so my meeting with ACC in Woodbridge provided a golden opportunity to check whether the Pulhams' old house might still exist. Val was just as keen as I was to find the house in which her great-grandmother's grandfather was born, so we set off together on our own special voyage of discovery.

The 'West End of Cumberland Street' runs into the Ipswich Road, near a large garden centre, just opposite which is the Cherry Tree public house, pictured in **Fig 44.10**. This dates back to the 17th century, and must consequently have stood there when the Pulham family lived nearby. This was an obvious place to go for lunch, and to contemplate how many times the family members may have visited for refreshment two hundred years previously. In view of the fact that it is thought they might have been a Quaker family, it is possible that they never visited at all, although Quakers do not forbid the drinking of alcohol outside the Meeting House, so we were content to imagine that they had indeed frequented the bar in which we sat.

After lunch, we set off to explore Cumberland Street itself, in which we found quite a varied selection of houses. Some were large, and some were not, although they were all in very good order, and most

Fig 44.10 (right) *The Cherry Tree, near Cumberland Street, Woodbridge*

Fig 44.11 (below) *Valerie Christman standing by the house in Woodbridge in which her great-grandmother's grandfather, James 1, was born in 1793*

had obviously been renovated over recent years. Bearing William Lockwood's directions in mind, we concentrated our attention on the West end of the street – or what in those days used to be called the 'poorer' end.

Somehow, we seemed to gravitate intuitively towards a row of cottages that had two passageways through from the street to the back at the left-hand end. The one beside the narrow passage seemed to fit the criteria we had, but there was nobody at home when we knocked on the door. I consequently later wrote to the owner, who was kind enough to phone and confirm that, to the best of their knowledge, their house had indeed once been a cobbler's shop, where customers used to go through the side passage, and hand their shoes through a small window at the back. The small courtyard – reached through the larger passage – apparently used to be a market garden.

So our intuition had served us well – the ring had been closed; the circle completed. **Fig 44.11** shows Val standing in the entrance to the passageway through which her ancestors must have passed many times, many years before. Apparently, the present row of four

cottages had been converted a few years ago from a row of six, so one can only speculate as to how cramped it must have been to raise a family of nine children in one of them in those days.

It is hardly surprising that her recent accumulation of knowledge about her ancestral roots has inspired Val to do everything she can to maintain the gardening tradition that she has inherited. Bearing in mind that her father, Jack, is now rather reluctantly approaching the point of retirement, she is looking forward to setting up her own business of consultancy, garden design, construction and restoration – including, wherever possible, the preservation and restoration of some of the Pulham gardens. This would not involve her doing everything herself, because she has a very good circle of contacts with the relevant expertise to handle most of the practical and physical work that would be involved. She would concentrate instead on the aspects of consultancy and survey work, with a view to co-ordinating and managing the resulting work with associated firms of specialist craftsmen – something for which she is eminently qualified.

The Pulham Legacy lives on. . .

ENDNOTES

1   English Heritage is very interested in the restoration and preservation of Pulhamite features in parks and public gardens; in 2008 it published *Durability Guaranteed: Pulhamite Rockwork – Its Conservation and Repair*. The organisation is also producing an essential reference work for conservators entitled English Heritage Practical Building Conservation, Mortars, Renders and Plasters by Alison Henry and John Stewart (Farnham Ashgate Publishing, 2012).

2   *Reminiscences of Woodbridge in Olden Times* by William Lockwood 2, published privately, 1889

3   *Mrs Coade's Stone*, by Alison Kelly, Self Publishing Association, 1990 (Vine House Distribution)

4   *Dickensian Inns and Taverns*, pp.129-130, by B W Matz, Cecil Palmer, London, 1922

5   *The Old Inns of Old England* by Charles G Harper, Chapman & Hall, 1906

6   *Martin Chuzzlewit* by Charles Dickens, ch. 25, published 1844

7   http://www.maps.lbhf.gov.uk (maps; sculptures)

8   *Thomas Smith 1798-1875, An Architect of Note* by John Corfield, published by the Hertford and Ware Local History Society

9   Research into the history of Benington undertaken by Harry Bott, the previous owner of Benington Lordship, whose great-grandfather, Mr A Bott, purchased the Lordship in 1906

10 *Picturesque Ferneries and Rock Garden Scenery* – a promotional booklet written and published by James 2, *c*.1877

11 *The Cement Industry 1796-1914 – A History* by A J Francis, published by David & Charles, 1977

12 *Journal 1* of the magazine of the Hertford and Ware Local History Society in 1998

13 *Thomas Smith 1798-1875, An Architect of Note* by John Corfield, published by the Hertford and Ware Local History Society

14 *The Cement Industry 1796-1914 – A History* by A J Francis, published by David & Charles, 1977

15 Letter to Major A J Francis from C H Curtis, Hertfordshire County Bibliographical Officer, 25th April 1973

16 Article by J A Hunt in *East Herts Archaeological Society Transactions* - Vol 2, Part 1, 1902

17 *In My Grandfather's Time* by Metford Warner – unpublished reminiscences, 1926

18 Letter written by Mr C H Curtis - the Hertfordshire County Bibliographical Officer - to Major A J Francis, author of *The Cement Industry in England 1796-1914*, to which several references were made in the previous chapter

19 *Hoddesdon's Past in Pictures*, by David Dent, published by The Rockingham Press, 1992

20 'On Cements, Artificial Stone and Plastic Compositions' by James Pulham 2, *The Builder*, 5th April 1845

21 Letter concerning terracotta in *The Builder,* dated 23rd January 1847

22 *The Cement Industry 1796-1914 – A History* by A J Francis, published by David & Charles, 1977

23 *Thomas Smith 1798-1875, An Architect of Note* by John Corfield, published by the Hertford and Ware Local History Society

24 *Thomas Smith 1798-1875, An Architect of Note* by John Corfield, published by the Hertford and Ware Local History Society

25 *The Buildings of England – Bedfordshire, Huntingdonshire and Peterborough* by Sir Nikolaus Pevsner, Penguin Books, 1968

26 *Broxbourne Past and Present*, by R G Hoare, 1897

27 *Hoddesdon – Tales of a Hertfordshire Town* by E W Paddick, 1971, published by Hoddesdon Urban District Concil

28 *Reminiscences of Woodbridge in Olden Times* by William Lockwood 2, published privately 1889

29 *Thomas Smith 1798-1875, An Architect of Note* by John Corfield, published by the Hertford and Ware Local History Society

30 *Hertford Mercury* dated 18th January 1862

31 *Mrs Coade's Stone* by Alison Kelly, Self Publishing Association (Vine House Distribution), 1990

32 *Antique Garden Ornament* by John Davis, Antique Collectors' Club, 1991

33 *Garden Ornament Catalogue* published by Pulham & Son, *c*.1925

34 *The Jurist 1849* – p.448 London Gazette Section, October 30th

35 *The Art Journal: Illustrated Catalogue of the International Exhibition* 1862

36 'The Terracotta Works of James Pulham, Broxbourne', *Art Journal* pp.25-27 (sometime in 1859)

37 'Great Credit upon the Ingenuity and Taste of Mr Pulham' by Sally Festing, *Journal of The Garden History Society,* (Vol 16/1), 1988

38 *The Victoria and Albert Museum: the history of its building* by John Physick. London V & A, Phaidon, 1982, (pp.148-150)

39 'In Search of Pulham's Fountains', by the Author, in the *Journal of The Garden History Society Newsletter* (Spring 2003) and the *Fountain Society's Newsletter* of February 2004

40 Article by an anonymous writer in *Country Life Illustrated*, published on 1st April, *c*.1899

41 *Picturesque Ferneries and Rock Garden Scenery*, a promotional booklet written and published by James 2 *c*.1877

42 *Highnam Memoranda* by Ernest Gambier Parry, *c*.1902

43 The Dunorlan sale brochure of 1871, a copy of which is held by the Tunbridge Wells Museum and Art Gallery

44 *Picturesque Ferneries and Rock Garden Scenery*, a promotional booklet written and published by James 2 *c*.1877

45 Tunbridge Wells Council website at www.tunbridgewells.gov.uk/fodp/history.htm

46 *The Dunorlan Story* by James Akehurst, published by the Friends of Dunorlan Park, 2005

47 Item by 'W.H.' in *The Gardeners' Chronicle*, 22 October 1881

48 John Davis's description of the Hebe Fountain in *Antique Garden Ornament* – published by the Antique Collectors' Club, 1991

49 *Kent and Sussex Courier*, interview by Mary Harris, September 2004

50 Article by Mr J Robson in *The Journal of Horticulture and Cottage Gardener,* 29 November 1864

51 *Battersea Park* from http://www.wandsworth.gov.uk/batterseapark/bphistory.htm

52 *Garden Visit and Travel Guide – Battersea Park* from http://www.gardenvisit.com/g/bat4.htm

53 *Picturesque Ferneries and Rock Garden Scenery*, a promotional booklet written and published by James 2 *c*.1877

54 *The Garden* magazine dated 15th March 1873

55 *The Gardener's Magazine* dated 24th October 1874

56 'Pulham Has Done His Work Well' by Sally Festing, *Journal of The Garden History Society*, (Vol 12/2), 1984

57 'We Must Have Our Noble Cliff' by Brent Elliott, *Country Life* 5th January 1984

58 *Battersea Park Cascades Feasibility Study* – preliminary report for Wandsworth Borough Council, by Derek Lovejoy & Partners, July 1987

59 *The Gardens of Audley End* by Michael Sutherill MSC, published by English Heritage, 1995

60 *Picturesque Ferneries and Rock Garden Scenery*, a promotional booklet written and published by James 2 *c*.1877

61 *The Victorian Flower Garden* by Jennifer Davies, BBC Books, 1991

62 'Pulham Has Done His Work Well' by Sally Festing, *Journal of The Garden History Society,* (Vol 12/2), 1984

63 Correspondence with Scilla Latham, historic gardens consultant

64 Historical notes provided by Christine Stevens, curator at the Museum of Welsh Life, St Fagans

65 The original bridge here was a simple flat, wooden bridge, and its current replacement was built by museum craftsmen during the 1960s

66 The eventual bridge at 'B' was very much simpler than that indicated in the original plan

67 *Picturesque Ferneries and Rock Garden Scenery*, a promotional booklet written and published by James 2 *c*.1877

68 History notes from *The Swiss Garden*, the official guide leaflet designed and produced by the Department of Environment and Economic Development, Bedfordshire County Council

69 *The History of Shuttleworth*, from http://www.shuttleworth.org/collection/background.htm

70 *Shuttleworth, Old Warden Park*, official historic notes to Old Warden House

71 *Picturesque Ferneries and Rock Garden Scenery*, a promotional booklet written and published by James 2 *c*.1877

72 *Journal of Horticulture and Cottage Gardener*, dated 29th July 1880

73 *Picturesque Ferneries and Rock Garden Scenery*, a promotional booklet written and published by James Pulham 2 *c*.1877

74 Official visitors' guide to *Madresfield Court Gardens*

75 'Pulham Has Done his Work Well' by Sally Festing, *Journal of The Garden History Society*, (Vol 12/2), 1984

76 *The Victorian Flower Garden* by Jennifer Davies, BBC Books, 1991

77 'Lord Rothschild's Rock Garden' by Anna Pavord, *Independent*, 7 November 1992

78 'Baron Ferdinand de Rothschild' by Sophieke Piebenga, Spring 2005, for the Rothschild Research Forum

79 www.waddesdon.org.uk

80 *Waddesdon Manor – The Heritage of a Rothschild House* by Michael Hall, published by Harry N Abrams Inc., 2002

81 Correspondence with D Redwood, chairman of Friends of Holly Hill Woodland Park

82 Historical notes based on the official guide to *Sheffield Park Garden*, published by The National Trust, 1994

83 Notes from a collection of research papers written by Mr A Newnham, a Sheffield Park volunteer

84 'Milton Mount Park, Crawley – Originally Known as Worth Park' by Claire Denman, for the *Sussex Gardens Trust Newsletter*, No. 30, Autumn 2004

85 'Worth Park, Sussex', *Country Life*, 30th September 1899

86 Joe Linger's Internet Orchid Web Page http://linger.dyndns.org/opic.html?UID=116

87 *Gardeners' Chronicle*, 30th April 1910

88 *Gardeners' Chronicle*, 29th August 1891

89 'Historical notes on Ross Hall, Glasgow', based on the *Historical Background* booklet published by BMI Ross Hall Hospital

90 A collection of *Letters of Mr Lachlan Cowan – written during his journey round the world to his uncle, James Cowan Esq, of Ross Hall* discovered by Catriona Morrison, a project assistant who recently worked on the Cart River Valleys Project

91 Notes by local historian, Ron Emslie, on http://www.derek.phillips.ukonline.co.uk/ech&bridges.htm

92 Carol Hill, local historian

93 Kelly's Directory of Suffolk

94 'A Theme on Which to Fondly Dwell' by Sally Festing, *Journal of The Garden History Society,* (Vol 25/2), 1997

95 CADW Welsh Historic Monuments – Register of Parks and Gardens in Wales PGW (Gt) 19

    Thomas Mawson is also commonly known as 'Thomas H. Mawson' or 'Thomas Hayton Mawson', although, for the sake of consistency, he will be referred to simply as 'Thomas Mawson' throughout this book. Anyone interested in learning more about this fascinating man could do no better than read *Thomas Mawson – Life, gardens and landscapes* by Janet Waymark (Frances Lincoln Ltd., 2009).

96 Report in *Thanet Extra*, 2nd December 1988

97 Contract issued to James Pulham and Son by the mayor, aldermen and burgesses of the Borough of Ramsgate on 5th April 1894

98 'Great Credit upon the Ingenuity and Taste of Mr Pulham' by Sally Festing, *Journal of The Garden History Society*, (Vol 16/1), 1988

99 *South Wales and Monmouthshire at the Opening of the Twentieth Century* by J Austin Jenkins

100 *Dewstow – Impressions and Recollections of Childhood* by William C Winter (published by W.C. Winter), 1987

101 'Buried Treasure' by Stephen Anderton, *Saga Magazine,* August 2005

102 'Digging Deep' by Anne Wareham, *Garden Magazine,* January 2006

103 *Blakesley Hall – Landscape Appraisal Report* prepared by Ian Lyne and Associates in association with Roger Coy Partnership for Mr and Mrs P Burt, February 1999

104 *Gardeners' Chronicle*, 1898

105 *Hertfordshire Mercury*, 20th August 1898

106 *Who Was Sir Frank Crisp?* – Geocities.com website

107 *Country Life,* 13th June 1903

108 'No Stone Unturned' by Penelope Dawson-Brown – *Country Life*, February 2005

109 *Diary of a Rock Builder 1898-1930* by Fred Rickett – Chapter 44

110 *The Garden Book* published by Phaidon Press Ltd, 2000 – contributed to by a collection of authors

111 *The Gardens of Merrow Grange* by Pat Hibberd – written for the Merrow Historical Society, 2003

112 'Cliffs, Glades and Grottos at Merrow Grange' by Sally Festing, *Journal of The Garden History Society*, (Vol 11/2), 1983

113 *Diary of a Rock Builder 1898-1930* by Fred Rickett – Chapter 44

114 *Country Houses of Gloucestershire Vol III (1830-2000)* by Nicholas Kingsley & Michael Hill, Phillimore, 2001

115 *Country Life*, 22nd February 1913

116 *Diary of a Rock Builder 1898-1930* by Fred Rickett – Chapter 44

117 *The Garden Makers* by George Plumptre, Parkgate Books, 1993

118 *Country Life*, 4th July 1903

119 www.batsford-arboretum.co.uk

120 *The History of Danesfield House*, company brochure and website

121 *Danesfield House*, http://en.wikipedia.org/wiki/Danesfield_House

122 http://www.roger-moore.com/pinep.htm

123 *Pinewood Studios – An Overview* by Pinewood historian, Morris Bright (brightsideproductions@supanet.com)

124 *The Garden at Buckingham Palace* by Jane Brown, Royal Collection Publications, 2004

125 *Bristol Evening Post*, 21 April 1977 – writer unknown

126 http://www.warrenhouse.com/history.php

127 http://www.warrenhouse.com/history.php

128 'Veitch's Water Garden' by Graham Pattison, *The Garden* August 1989

129 *The Garden*, August 1989 (pp 395-398)

130 *Picturesque Ferneries and Rock Garden Scenery*, a promotional booklet written and published by James 2 *c*.1877

131 *The Japanese-style Garden in the British Isles, 1850-1950*, by Jill Y Raggett, University of York Dept of Archaeology, 2002

132 *Diary of a Rock Builder 1898-1930* by Fred Rickett – Chapter 44

133 *Shell-BP News*, December 1972, when 'The Node' was owned by Shell-BP – article by Geoffrey Baines, Manager, Group Training Centre

134 'A Splendid Record', *The Gardener's Magazine* dated 10th February 1912

135 *Diary of a Rock Builder 1898-1930* by Fred Rickett – Chapter 44

136 Based on e-mail correspondence with Frances Brooks, Mr Dunsford's granddaughter

137 'What a Rich American and a Japanese Lady gave to "The Node" ' by Geoffrey Baines, Manager, Group Training Centre, Shell-BP, *Shell-BP News*, December 1972

138 http://www.rhs.org.uk/whatson/gardens/wisley/wisleyhistory.asp

139 'A Splendid Record', *The Gardener's Magazine* dated 10th February 1912

140 'The Wisley Rock and Water Garden' by J R Pulham FRHS – copy of a paper presented to the RHS on 13 August 1912 – *Journal of the Royal Horticultural Society,* Volume 38, Part 2, 1912, pp.225-233

141 *Newsletter of the Alpine Garden Society*, Vol 29, 1961, by Francis Hanger, VMH, the then curator of the RHS Garden Wisley

142 'Pulham Has Done His Work Well' by Sally Festing, *Journal of The Garden History Society*, (Vol 12/2), 1984

143 *Hoddesdon Journal*, dated February 1967

144 *Diary of a Rock Builder 1898-1930* by Fred Rickett – Chapter 44

145 *Selfridges, Seventy-Five Years: The Story of the Store 1909-84* by Gordon Honeycombe, 1984

146 Personal research into Minutes of meetings held by St Annes on the Sea UDC undertaken by Arnold Sumner, Ashton Gardens History Society

147 *Lytham St Annes Express*, 4th February 1916

148 *Lytham St Annes Express*, 16th June 1916

149 *Abbots Pool Woodland - Draft Management Plan* - North Somerset Council, 2002

150 *Abbots Leigh – A Village History* by William Evans, Abbots Leigh Civic Society, 2002

151 *Diary of a Rock Builder 1898-1930* by Fred Rickett – Chapter 44

152 'Pulham Has Done His Work Well' by Sally Festing, *Journal of The Garden History Society*, (Vol 12/2), 1984

153 *Diary of a Rock Builder 1898-1930* by Fred Rickett – Chapter 44

154 'Bristol University's Botanic Garden' by Lyn Morgan – *Gloucestershire and Avon Life*, July 1980

155 *Hertfordshire Mercury*, 11th September 1920

156 'Story of a House' by R.G. Freeman, *The Hoddesdon Journal* dated April 1966

157 *Diary of a Rock Builder 1898-1930* by Fred Rickett – Chapter 44

158 Various internet websites

159 Schedule published by Department of Culture, Media and Sport, 10th October 2000

160 Paragraphs 2.26 and 2.27 from a DCMS report dated 10th October 2000

161 'Great Credit upon the Ingenuity and Taste of Mr Pulham' by Sally Festing, *Journal of The Garden History Society*, (Vol 16/1), 1988

162 *The Garden Journal*, 8th July 1922

163 *Folkestone Herald*, 15th September 1973

164 http://members.cox.net/ghgraham/janetstancombwills/html (Check Janet Stancomb-Wills on a Google search)

165 *The Isle of Thanet Gazette*, dated 14th July 1936

166 http://www.stoke-poges.com/village/buildings.shtml#spark

167 South Bucks District Council Website

168 *British Fern Gazetteer*, 1958 (pp.203-204)

169 The photographs in Figs 43.1, 43.2 and 43.3 were taken by Bishop Marshall, and are reproduced by permission of David Dent. Figs 43.1 and 43.3 are included in his book *Broxbourne and Wormley's Past in Pictures*, Rockingham Press 1995

170 'Great Credit upon the Ingenuity and Taste of Mr Pulham' by Sally Festing, *Journal of The Garden History Society*, (Vol 16/1), 1988

171 *Cheshunt and Waltham Telegraph*, 13 February 1986

172 *Cheshunt and Waltham Telegraph*, 3 September 1986

CHRONOLOGICAL GAZETTEER OF PULHAM SITES

This section contains a chronological listing of all currently known Pulham sites, although it is not likely to be totally comprehensive. As has been stated several times throughout this book, all the firm's records were destroyed when they finally went out of business at the outbreak of the Second World War *c*.1939. The only 'official' details that remain of the work they carried out come from a promotional booklet written and published by James 2 *c*.1877, in which he included a list of 'satisfied clients'. But even that is not totally comprehensive, since it only related to the firm's landscaping activities, and not to the sites on which its ornamental terracotta pieces were installed.

The key to the sources from which the following information has been drawn is therefore as follows:

P = *Picturesque Ferneries and Rock Garden Scenery*, written and published by James 2 *c*.1877.

E = *Durability Guaranteed: Pulhamite Rockwork – Its Conservation and Repair*, published by English Heritage, 2008.

R = *Fred Rickett's Diary*. This is a journal kept by Pulham rock builder, Fred Rickett, of all the jobs on which he worked between 1898 and 1930. It provides valuable additional information, but only lists the jobs on which he was personally involved, and there were obviously several other teams at work at the same time.

H = Claude Hitching. These sites are either those that I have seen for myself, or been told about by friends and visitors to my website.

The dates shown in the 'Date' column are sometimes approximate, being based on the best available information. They will therefore appear as '*c*.1870' or '1870s' etc. The firm often returned to a site to carry out additional work, and, where this is known, the dates will be shown as a range (e.g. '1835-38'). This does not mean that they were there continuously between those dates – only that they made more than one visit during that period.

It should also be borne in mind that many of the sites listed here are no longer viable. Some have been totally redeveloped, and some have become so overgrown and derelict that people are probably no longer aware of what they used to be like in their heyday. Fortunately, however, there are many sites that have survived the tests of time, and are still lovingly maintained by their owners, or in the process of restoration by teams of hard-working local enthusiasts. Several of these are discussed in this book, and are marked in bold print in the following list. It is also almost certain that – perhaps partly as a result of this book – other sites will be recognised or re-discovered, in which case the updating of this list will be an extremely pleasurable task.

James 1 (1793-1838) and Obadiah (1803-80)

Source	Date	Patron	Work Description
H	*c.*1806	William Lockwood, **The Castle**, Woodbridge, Suffolk	See Chapter 1
H	1825	**'The Black Bull'**, outside the Ravenscourt Arms, King Street, Ravenscourt Park, Hammersmith, London	See Chapter 1
H	1826	William Stuart, **Tempsford Hall**, Tempsford, Bedfordshire	See Chapter 1
H	1828-31	St James' Church, Silsoe, Bedfordshire	Built complete church.
H	1830s	**'Pulham Faces'**, Duncan Terrace and Highbury Terrace, Islington, London	See Chapter 2
H	1832-33	Hertford County Hospital, Hertford, Hertfordshire	Designed by Thomas Smith. It is very possible that Obadiah and James 2 were responsible for at least the ornamental stonework.
H	1834	Thomas Smith, **'Smith's Folly'**, North Road House, Hertford, Hertfordshire	See Chapter 1
P/E	1835-38	George Proctor, **Benington Lordship**, Benington, Hertfordshire	See Chapter 1
H	1836	Hoddesdon Clock Tower, Hoddesdon, Hertfordshire	Designed by Thomas Smith, and possibly built by James 2 under the direction of Obadiah.
H	1852-56	Sir Thomas Robinson Woolfield, **Villa Ste Ursule**, Cannes, France	See Chapter 2
H	1857-59	Sir Thomas Robinson Woolfield, **Christ Church**, Cannes, France	See Chapter 2
H	1857-59	Sir Thomas Robinson Woolfield, Villa Victoria, Cannes, France	Designed by Thomas Smith, and built adjacent to Christ Church, with Obadiah as the Clerk of Works.
H	1859-62	Anglican Community of Nice, **Church of the Holy Trinity**, Nice, France	See Chapter 2
H	1860	Sir Thomas Robinson Woolfield, Villa du Parc, Cannes, France	Designed by Thomas Smith, this is a small villa built in a corner of the land on which Thomas Woolfield built the Villa Ste Ursule. Obadiah was Clerk of Works.
H	1862-65	English Community of Naples, **Christ Church**, Naples, Italy	See Chapter 2
H	1865-66	Anglican Community of Stuttgart, **St Catherine's Church**, Stuttgart, Germany	See Chapter 2

James 2 (1838-65)

Source	Date	Patron	Work Description
P	1842-62	J. Warner Esq, **Woodlands**, Hoddesdon, Hertfordshire	See Chapter 2
E/H	1845-48	William Robert Baker Esq, Bayfordbury, Hertford	Alpine rock garden in natural and artificial stone (very nearly demolished) and circular pool with fountain, which has now been replaced. Rocky path and open-topped grotto in Pinetum recently part-recovered. EH Registered Park and Garden, open to the public. Pumps by Green and Carter.
E/H	1845	**Pulham's Manufactory**, Station Road, Broxbourne, Hertfordshire	See Chapter 3
H	1845	**Church of St Mary Redcliffe**, Bristol, Avon	See Chapter 2
P/E	1847-62	T. Gambier Parry, **Highnam Court**, Highnam, Gloucestershire	See Chapter 4
P/E	1848	F. Sterry Esq, Coombe House, Croydon, Surrey	Rocky pool or water cave enclosing tank for watering garden.
P/H	1851	Great Exhibition, Crystal Palace, London	Exhibition of terracotta wares.
P/E	1851-64	Oak Lodge, Kensington, London	Waterfall, cliffs, fernery. Designed by Robert Marnock.
P/E	1852-56	E.W. Cooke Esq. 'The Ferns', Kensington, London	Fernery, rocky banks in Tufa.
H	1853	Conrad William Finzel, Clevedon Hall, Bristol, Avon	Copy of Pulhams' Hebe fountain that won a medal at the Great Crystal Palace Exhibition of 1851. The original is still working in Dunorlan Park, Tunbridge Wells.
P/E/H	1854-60	Sir D. Salomons Bart, Southborough (now Broomhill), Tunbridge Wells, Kent	Rocky pass, banks, cliff, fernery. The pass and banks still exist in good condition, but not accessible to the public.
H	1855	**Cemetery Chapel**, Ware, Hertfordshire	See Chapter 2
H	1855-57	**St Augustine's Church**, Broxbourne, Hertfordshire	See Chapter 2
P/E	1856	J.P. Gasiot Esq, Clapham Common, London	Fernery with dropping well.
P/E	1856-57	Mrs Walker, Southgate House, Southgate, London	Cave, rocky pond, cliffs for fernery, rocking stone.
P/E/H	1858	J. Levick Esq, Ponsbourne Manor, Newgate Street, Hertfordshire	'Rocky Pond, Fernery.' Fernery built on internal wall of Ponsbourne Manor, but later removed to Enfield. No longer exists. Rocky stream still survives.
P/E/H	1859	W.J. Blake Esq, Danesbury Park, Welwyn, Hertfordshire	'Cave, Dropping Well, Pass for ferns and other rock plants in old chalk pit but in artificial stone'. One of Pulhams' earliest ferneries, but now in a very dilapidated state. Designed by Anthony Parsons.
P/E/H	1859-60	Marquis of Westminster, Fonthill Abbey, Fonthill Gifford, Tisbury, Wiltshire	'Waterfalls in a rocky stream, pond, island, rocky pass and cliff.' Surviving rockwork is inaccessible, and in a dangerous state. Everything very overgrown, but still exists. Pumps by Green and Carter.

James 2 (1838-65) cont.

Source	Date	Patron	Work Description
P/E/H	1859-68	J. Noble Esq., Berry Hill, Taplow, Buckinghamshire	'Waterfalls, Ford across lake, Cliffs and cave to hide Gas Works.' Most of the rockwork has now deteriorated beyond recognition, but there are the remains of a large sunken fernery with a central fountain; a 'Berry Hill Fountain' is listed in the firm's *Garden Ornament Catalogue*. EH Registered Park and Garden. Designed by Robert Marnock.
P/E	1860	F. Wilson Esq, Tunbridge Wells, Kent	Fernery, cliff to bank.
E	1860s	James Pulham 2, 'The Orchard', High Cross, Tottenham, London	Fernery and alpinery.
P/E	1861	F. Berger Esq, Lower Clapton, London	Fernery.
P/H	1862	**International Exhibition**, Kew Gardens, Richmond, Surrey	See Chapter 3
H	1862	International Exhibition, **'The Kew Fountain'**, Kew Gardens, Richmond, Surrey	See Chapter 3
P/E/H	1862-63	W. Duckworth, Orchardleigh Park, Lullington, Somerset	Waterfalls in rocky stream, cliffs, bank, rocky island and pond. No longer viable.
P/E/H	1862-64	H. Reed Esq, **Dunorlan Park**, Tunbridge Wells, Kent	See Chapter 5
P/E/H	1862-67	His Grace the Duke of Portland, Welbeck Abbey, Worksop, Nottinghamshire	'Subterranean Passage, Dropping Well, Drinking Fountain'. Pulham is known to have constructed the lining for a tunnel, and it is quite possible that he also worked on many other features, including the Riding House and subterranean ballroom. EH Registered Park and Gardens.
P/E	1863	S.H. Mountain, Norland House, East Dulwich, London	Fernery.
P/E/H	1863-70	Alderman Stone, 'The Hoo', Sydenham Hill Wood, London	'Rocky Stream, Ruins etc'. The 'stream' is now a rocky pathway; around half the 'ruined archway' folly still remains.
P/E	1864-65	F. Wright, Osmaston Hall, Derby, Derbyshire	Fernery. Designed by Edward Milner.
P/E/H	1864-65	Preston Corporation, Miller Park / New Park, Preston, Lancashire	'Waterfall, Cliffs, Rocky Pond, Drinking Fountain - naturalistic.' The rockwork features still exist in good condition, and there is a 'Preston Vase' listed in the Pulham catalogue. Some replicas still remain. EH Registered Park and Gardens. Designed by Edward Milner.
P/E/H	1864-71	Lt Col R. Loyd Lindsay and Lady Overstone, Lockinge House, Wantage, Oxfordshire	'Waterfalls, Rocky Stream, Cliffs for alpines and ferns'. Small but pleasant example of Pulham's 'naturalistic' artistry; on a private estate with no public access.

James Pulham and Son – James 2 and James 3 (1865-98)

Source	Date	Patron	Work Description
H	1865	**Pulham Manufactory**, Station Road, Broxbourne, Hertfordshire	Change of business name to James Pulham and Son. See Chapter 3
P/E	1865	J. de Paricinni Esq, Datchet, Berkshire	Small fernery.
P/E	1865	J. Fielding, Forest Hill, London	Fernery against house.
P/E	1865	Colin Campbell Esq, Woodseat, Uttoxeter, Staffordshire	Fernery.
P/E	1865-66	Sir F. Goldsmid Bart, MP, Rendcomb Park, Cirencester, Gloucestershire	'Waterfalls, Lake, Island in local stone'. Pumps by Green and Carter.
P/E	1865-66	Miss Pipe, Clapham Park, London	'Fernery, Dropping Well'. A Clapham Terminal is listed in the firm's *Garden Ornament Catalogue*, but could relate either to this or another site in Clapham.
P/E/H	1865-70	Coles Child Esq, Palace Gardens (now Civic Centre), Bromley, Kent	'Waterfalls and Ferneries'. Now the Town Hall and Civic Centre, the gardens only contain a very small sample of Pulham's work, in the form of some rockwork near the old well along the edge of the lake.
P/E	1865-70	HM Commissioners of Works and Royal Parks, **Battersea Park**, London	See Chapter 6
P/E/H	1865-92	R. Hanbury, Poles Park, Ware, Hertfordshire (now Hanbury Manor Hotel)	'Conservatory, Fernery, Dropping Well'. Also rose garden with fountain, and kitchen garden. EH Registered Park and Gardens.
P/E/H	1865-97	Preston Corporation, Moor Park, Preston, Lancashire	'Rocks for bridges to rest on, Drinking fountain, Rocky tunnel and roadway.' These features still survive in good condition. EH Registered Park and Gardens. Designed by Edward Milner.
P/E	1866	J. Stewart, West Wickham, Kent	Fernery.
P/E	1866	Henry Chaplin Esq., Blankney Hall, Lincoln, Lincolnshire	'Cave, Rocky Pass for ferns and other Rock Plants'.
P/E	1866	T. Hicks, Streatham, London	Fernery.
P/E/H	1866	R.C. Hanbury Esq. MP, Bedwell Park, Essendon, Hertfordshire	'Fernery, Cliffs to hide wall of Walled Garden, Root House for ferns, rock plants and shrubs'. Still in good condition. Not open to the public.
P/E	1866-67	S.J. Anderson Jun. Esq, Ankerwycke House, Wraysbury, Berkshire	Fernery.
P/E	1866-67	John Platt Esq. MP, Bryn-y-Neuadd, Llanfairfechan, Conwy, Wales	'Waterfalls, Fernery, Ponds'. EH Registered Park and Garden.
P/E	1866-67	Marquis of Hastings, Donington Park, Castle Donington, Leicestershire	'Cave for Eagles, Waterfalls, Rocky Stream, Pond'.
P/E	1866-67	Sir Fowell and Lady E. Buxton, Cromer, Norfolk	'Conservatory, Fernery, Dropping Well. Seat and Flower Stand'. There is also a Cromer Sundial' listed in the firm's *Garden Ornament Catalogue*.

James Pulham and Son – James 2 and James 3 (1865-98)

Source	Date	Patron	Work Description
P/E	1866-73	J. Kitchin, Dunsdale, Yorkshire	'Rocky Stream, Waterfalls, Boat House, Lakes and ponds concreted'. Water features no longer exist. Follies remain but derelict.
P/E/H	1866-75	Preston Corporation, Avenham Park, Preston, Lancashire	'Waterfall, Cave etc'. Adjoins Miller Park (with which it is jointly graded). Pumps by Green and Carter. EH Registered Park and Garden. Designed by Edward Milner.
P/E	1867	J. Green Esq, Chislehurst, Greater London	'Rocky entrance to Gateway'.
P/E	1867	J. Wigan Esq, Winchmore Hill, Greater London	'Fernery and Rocky Banks'.
P/E	1867	James Platt Esq. MP, Oldham, Greater Manchester	Fernery.
P/E	1867	J. Batten, Bickley, Kent	Fernery.
P/E	1867	Edward Milner, Dulwich Wood Park, London	Fernery. Designed by Edward Milner.
P/E	1867	Miss Watkins, Dulwich, London	Fernery.
E	1867	Commissioned by V & A Museum, **Mulready Memorial**, Kensal Green Cemetery, London	See Chapter 3
P/E	1867-68	Lord Braybrooke, **Audley End**, Saffron Walden, Essex	See Chapter 7
H	1867-68	**V & A Museum**, Exhibition Road, South Kensington, London	See Chapter 3
P/E/H	1867-69	George Jones, Rosherville Gardens, Gravesend, Kent	'Cavern with Dropping Well for Drinking Fountain'.
E	1867-1880s	J.L. Moilliet, Abberley Hall, Abberley, Worcestershire	'Watercourse and cascades on hillside, to pool'. Recently uncovered and hopefully due for restoration Registered Park and Garden.
P/E	1868	Mrs Ingram, Mount Felix, Walton-on-Thames, Surrey	'Cave and Dropping Well, Fernery'.
P/E	1868	H.F. Barclay Esq, Woodford, Essex	'House for Ferns and Orchids, rich-coloured Ornamental Leaf Plants, with Dropping Well, in which a variety of plants are flourishing about the rock, with Orchid.' A very ornate 'Barclay Vase' is listed in the firm's *Garden Ornament Catalogue*.
E	1868	J.H. Cox Esq, Uxbridge, Greater London	'Rocky Cliff, Dropping Well, and Alpinery, to hide a Gardener's Cottage, and forming fernery and Alpinery'.
P/E	1868	W.C. Morland Esq, Lamberhurst Court Lodge, Lamberhurst, Kent	Fernery.
P/E	1868	Lt Col Thomas Birchall, Ribbleton Hall, Preston, Lancashire	Fernery etc.
P/E	1868	J. Dugdale Esq, Wroxall Abbey, Wroxall, Warwickshire	Fernery.

James Pulham and Son – James 2 and James 3 (1865-98)

Source	Date	Patron	Work Description
P/E	1868-69	R. Prescott Decie Esq, Brockleton Court, Worcestershire	'Hardy Fernery and pathway between Rocks'.
P/E/H	1868-74	J.W. Pease Esq. MP, Hutton Hall, Guisbrough, North Yorkshire	'Waterfalls in Mountain Stream, Exotic Fernery, Rocky Stream through Pleasure Grounds. In natural stone.' The old Hutton Hall no longer exists, and no trace of Pulham's work remains visible.
P/E	1868-1902	J. Lamplough and J. Chamberlain, Highbury Hall, Birmingham, West Midlands	'Small Fernery and Rock Garden'. EH Registered Park and Garden.
P/E	1868-1905	HRH The Prince of Wales (later HM King Edward VII), **Sandringham**, Norfolk	See Chapter 8
P/E/H	1869	H. Pease Esq, Pierremont Park, Darlington, Co Durham	'Boathouse in the rock, Fernery, Dropping Well'. The house has since been converted into flats. The magnificent 'Pierremont Fountain' – listed in the firm's *Garden Ornament Catalogue* – has since been moved to South Park, and recently restored with the help of a Heritage Lottery Grant.
P/E	1869	H.D. Davies Esq, Isleworth, Greater London	Fernery.
E	1869	J. Piggot Esq, Isleworth, Greater London	'Rocky cliff to hide wash house of neighbouring property'.
E	1869	S. Mendel Esq, Manley Hall, Greater Manchester	'Rocky Lake, Pathway, Cliff, Boat House'.
P/E	1869	Capt. Henry Platt, Gorddinog, Conwy, Wales	'Waterfalls, Rock Bridge, as if natural, Lake and Streams'.
P/E	1869	H. Moser Esq, Forest Hill, London	'Rockwork for Ferns and Camellias'.
E	1869	W. Nicholson, Herne Hill, London	'Hardy Fernery and Dropping Well supplied from Fountain'.
P/E	1869	E.W. Allen Esq, Peckham, London	Fernery.
P/E	1869	W.J. Mace Esq, Sydenham, London	Fernery with dropping well.
P/E	1869	H. Gover, Sydenham, London	Fernery.
P/E	1869	F. Peek, Sydenham, London	Fernery.
P/E	1869	Mrs. Johnson, Blundeston Lodge, Blundeston, Suffolk	Fernery.
E	1869	Lt Col Dubath, Chichester, West Sussex	Fernery and aviary.
P/E	1869-70	G.J. Morris Esq, Liverpool, Merseyside	'Rocky Road and Drive, Rocks for Bridge to rest upon and to hide buildings'.
P/E	1869-71	H. Bessemer, Bessemer House, Denmark Hill, London	'Bridge on Rocks, Waterfalls, large Fernery entirely built of Rock, forming Cliff outside, a Moorish Temple in the Rock, a Boat-house entirely in Rock, Lake and Ponds concreted, also Rocky Island and Streams'.

James Pulham and Son – James 2 and James 3 (1865-98)

Source	Date	Patron	Work Description
P/E	1869-72	T.H. Ismay Esq, 13 Beach Lawn, Waterloo, Sefton, Lancashire	'Fernery with stream from Dropping Well, Aquarium in rocky recess, Aviary, Cliff with Alpines and Ferns'. EH Registered Park and Garden.
E	1870	H. Hoare Esq, Staplehurst Hall, Staplehurst, Kent	'Rocks on margin of lake for Alpine and other Rock Plants'.
P/E/H	1870	T. Miller Esq, Singleton Hall, Singleton, Lancashire	'Cave, Dropping Well' Feature still exists, but is overgrown. On private property.
P/E	1870	J. Thorpe Esq, Leicester, Leicestershire	'Fernery, Dropping Well'.
P/E	1870	Capt. Whitmore, Gumley Hall, Gumley, Leicestershire	'Fernery, Rocks formed to support slippery bank of lake'.
P/E	1870	E. Brook Esq, Caen Wood Towers (now Athlone House), Fitzroy Park, Highgate, London	'Fern-clad Ravine, Dropping Well, Waterfall, Stream'. Designed by Edward Milner.
P/E/H	1870	Buxton Corporation, Pavilion Gardens, Buxton, Derbyshire	'Waterfalls, Rock, Banks'. EH Registered Park and Gardens. Designed by Edward Milner.
P/E	1870	R. Leigh Esq, Barham Court, Canterbury, Kent	'Dropping Well, Rocky Pool'.
P/E	1870	Lattimer Clark Esq, Sydenham Hill, London	'Cliff to support a bank, Cave for Seat, Dropping Well, Rocky Footpath'. Overgrown with Alpines, but remains of the rocky bank and 'cave for seat' can still be seen along the bank in Crescent Wood Road.
P/E	1870	G. West Esq, Alscot Park, Stratford-upon-Avon, Warwickshire	'Interior and Exterior Temperate Ferneries made of Rock'.
P/E	1870	F. Osley Esq, Birmingham, West Midlands	'Inside Fernery with Dropping Well'.
P/E	1870-71	S.J. Russel Esq, Handsworth, Birmingham, West Midlands	'Two Interior Ferneries of different temperatures'.
P/E	c.1870	J.B. Blythe Esq, Woolhampton Hall, Berkshire	'Rocky Recess'.
P/E	1870s	J.R. Ormsby Gore Esq. MP, Brogyntyn Hall, Oswestry, Shropshire	'Waterfalls, the principal one flows over a broad high rock, under which you can walk behind the water, as at the falls of the Geisbach etc'. Site now redeveloped. Pumps by Green and Carter. EH Registered Park and Garden.
E	1870s	Earl de Grey, Studley Royal, North Yorkshire	Pulhams' Terracotta vases.
E	1870s	Wortley Hall, Sheffield, Yorkshire	Pulhams' Terracotta.
P/E	c.1870s	Mason, Beckenham, Greater London	Fernery.
P/E	c.1870s	J. Corbett, Droitwich, Worcestershire	'Waterfall, Fernery'.
P/E	c.1870s	Thomas Collin Esq, Roydon Hall, Yalding, Kent	Fernery with dropping well etc.

James Pulham and Son – James 2 and James 3 (1865-98)

Source	Date	Patron	Work Description
P/E	*c*.1870s	J. Clayton Esq, Lincoln, Lincolnshire	Natural rock for fernery and alpinery.
P/E	*c*.1870s	J. Morris, Crouch Hill, London	Small fernery.
P/E	*c*.1870s	J.G. Barclay Esq, Knotts Green House, Leyton, London	'Cliff for plants to grow on'.
P/E	*c*.1870s	F. Mather, Berwick-on-Tweed, Northumberland	Fernery.
P/E	*c*.1870s	J. Wilkinson Esq, Accrington, Lancashire	Fernery.
H	1870s	Sir Isaac Holden, Oakworth House, Holden Park, Oakworth, West Yorkshire	Large artificial rockwork feature, with grotto, hermit's cave, summerhouse etc. Thought to be by Pulham, but not yet confirmed.
P/E	1871	J. Burbridge, Champion Hill, London	Fernery.
E	1871	P. Crowley Esq, Croydon, Greater London	'Fernery, Dropping Well'.
P/E/H	1871	Robert Barclay, High Leigh, Hoddesdon, Hertfordshire	'Pulhamite rockwork, cave, grotto, cascade, pathway across water'. May have been used as a 'show ground' to illustrate examples of the firm's work. Still exists, but in poor order.
P/E	1871	A.J. Hamel Esq, Leicester, Leicestershire	'Small Fernery, Dropping Well'.
P/E	1871	J.A. Jackson Esq, Thurnby Court, Thurnby, Leicestershire	'Rocky Banks for Ferns, Alpines and Shrubs'.
P/E	1871	J.C. Im Thurn, Champion Hill, London	'Pond concreted and Rockified, Rocky Stream, Waterfalls, Boat House formed in Bank. All in Rock'.
P/E	1871	Aston, Gipsy Hill, Norwood, London	'Dropping Well etc in Garden for ferns and alpines to grow about'.
E	1871	C. Jacomb Esq, Springfield Park, Upper Clapton, London	'Fernery, Dropping Well etc' EH Registered Park and Gardens.
P/E	1871	C.H. Fison Esq, Thetford, Norfolk	Fernery.
P/E/H	1871	G.L. Gower, Esq, Titsey Place, Oxted, Surrey	'Waterfalls, Rocks, Bridge in Stone and Artificial Stone'. EH Registered Park and Gardens.
P/E/H	1871-1906	T. Higgs, Highland Gardens, New Barnet, Greater London	'Rocky Bank forming cliff, with Dropping Well. For Ferns, Alpines and Shrubs'. A small but attractive example of Pulham's work – including an archway near a rocky bank – that is tucked well away from he road. FR Diary: '1906 – Rock and water garden for Mr Braithwaite'.
P/E	1872	Mrs Sinnock, Hailsham, East Sussex	Alpinery, fernery.
P/E/H	1872	J. Newman Esq, Buckfield Keep, Leominster, Herefordshire	'Fernery of Rock, Corridor, Dropping Well with streamlet from it. Path over to look down on works'. Still in quite good condition. A 'Newman Vase' is listed in the firm's *Garden Ornament Catalogue*.

James Pulham and Son – James 2 and James 3 (1865-98)

Source	Date	Patron	Work Description
P/E	1872	J. Stafford Esq, Leicester, Leicestershire	Fernery.
P/E	1872	A. Turner Esq, Leicester, Leicestershire	Interior fernery.
P/E	1872	F.F. Buffen Esq, Hendon, London	'Banks supported with Rocks for Alpines and Plants'.
P/E	1872	G.F. Neame Esq, Grange Road, Upper Norwood, London	'Rocky Banks for Ferns and Alpines'.
P/E	1872	J. Dunville Esq, Norbiton, Surrey	Alpinery etc. A 'Norbiton Seat' is listed in the firm's *Garden Ornament Catalogue*.
P/E	1872	H. Lee Esq, Worcester, Worcestershire	'Fernery, Alpinery, and Waterfall'.
P/E	1872-73	J. Johnson Esq, Kenyon Hall, Kenyon, Lancashire	Large fernery.
P/E	1872-73	W.O. Foster Esq. MP, Apley Park, Bridgnorth, Shropshire	'Rock Cliffs to support banks for Alpines'. Designed by Edward Milner. There is a 'Bridgnorth Balustrade' listed in the firm's catalogue.
P/E	1872-74	J. Booth Esq, Nottingham, Nottinghamshire	Fernery.
P/E/H	1872-75	Brighton Corporation, Great Aquarium (now Sea Life Centre), Brighton, East Sussex	'Fernery, Cliff, Waterfalls, Sea Lion's Den, Fairy Cave, Rocky Stream, Aquarium Tanks'. Fernery now demolished, but rockwork in display tanks and balustrading still exist. A 'Brighton Vase' and 'Brighton Sundial' is listed in the firm's *Garden Ornament Catalogue* – none of these remain. Open all year round.
E	1872-76	Lady Mary Windsor-Clive, **St Fagans Castle**, Cathays Park, Cardiff	See Chapter 9
P/E	1873	J.P. Chatto, Torquay, Devon	Fernery.
E	1873	J. Temple, Esq, Leyswood House, Withyham, East Sussex	Large fernery.
P/E	1873	H. Austin, Beckenham, Greater London	
E	1873	E.N. Buxton Esq, Woodford, Essex	'Rocky Dell for Fernery and Alpines'.
P/E	1873	J. McArthur, Esq. MP, Brixton, London	Dropping well etc.
P/E	1873	Mrs Burroughes, Burlingham Hall, Acle, Norfolk	Fernery etc.
P/E	1873	Rt. Hon. Earl of Stradbrooke, Henham Hall, Henham, Suffolk	'Fairy Cave' – now totally demolished to make way for a new development.
P/E	1873	Thos. Anderson Esq, Waverley Abbey, Farnham, Surrey	Not known.
P/E	1873	J. Fielden Esq, Nutfield Priory, Reigate, Surrey	'Noble Cliff of Rock to support high and falling banks and trees. For Ferns, Heaths and Alpines'.

James Pulham and Son – James 2 and James 3 (1865-98)

Source	Date	Patron	Work Description
P/E/H	1873-74	S. Scott, Sundridge Park, Bromley, Kent	'Chasm, Fernery, Alpinery, Cliff'. Good condition. Now a private Management Centre. EH Registered Park and Gardens.
H	1873-74	? Streatham, London	'Artificial ruin of Castle Gateway, Tower for Summer Retreat and View, Fernery'.
P/E/H	1873-75	H. Ainsworth, Smithills Hall, Bolton, Lancashire	'Waterfall, Rocky Stream with Bridge across'. Still in quite good condition. EH Registered Park and Gardens.
P/E	1873-75	E.W. Whinfield, Severn Grange, Worcester, Worcestershire	Balustrade.
P/E/H	1873-80	J. Leaf Esq, Park Hill, Streatham, London	'Fernery and Artificial Ruin of Castle gateway and Tower for summer retreat and view'. Fernery (since demolished), sunken walkway, grottoes, bridge and lake, conservatory (now demolished) etc. EH Folly listed. Registered Park and Gardens.
P/E	1874	Mrs Crossfield, Warrington, Cheshire	Fernery.
P/E	1874	F. Wright, The Hayes, Swanwick, Derbyshire	
P/E	1874	A. Manser Esq, Hoddesdon, Hertfordshire	Fernery.
P/E	1874	H. Snow Esq, Leicester, Leicestershire	Fernery.
P/E	1874	L.J. Baker, Haydon Hall, Ruislip, Middlesex	Fernery.
P/E	1874-75	Rt Hon Lord Carysfort, Glenart Castle, Arklow, Co Wicklow, Eire	'Boat House, Waterfall, Fernery, Island on Lake, Vases'.
P/E/H	1874-75	R.S. Holford, Westonbirt House, Tetbury, Gloucestershire	'Fernery, Alpinery, Lake concreted'. The fernery and alpinery are no longer there, although the lake remains. There is also rockery and dropping well in a 'dingle' – or wooded dell. Everything in good condition. A 'Westonbirt Vase' is listed in the firm's *Garden Ornament Catalogue*, and the pumps are by Green and Carter. Westonbirt is now a school. Open NGS Day – see website for details. EH Registered Park and Gardens.
P/E	1874-75	Manchester Corporation, Manchester Aquarium, Greater Manchester	'Rocks to tanks'. There is a 'Manchester Tazza' listed in the firm's catalogue.
P/E	1874-75	F. Crowley Esq, Alton, Hampshire	Fernery.
P/E	1874-75	J. Ridgway Esq, Goudhurst, Kent	Fernery.
P/E	1874-75	Dr Barry, Sydenham Hill, London	Dropping well.
P/E	1874-75	Rt. Hon. Earl of Durham, Berwick-upon-Tweed, Northumberland	Fernery.

James Pulham and Son – James 2 and James 3 (1865-98)

Source	Date	Patron	Work Description
P/E/H	1874-75	Baron Lionel de Rothschild, Gunnersbury Park, Hounslow, London	'Rocks to Boat House, Bridge, Lake and design for building on the lake (not executed)'. Boathouse and rockwork is on the edge of the Potomac Lake, which lies in a corner of Gunnersbury Park. It is privately owned, and not open to the public. There are some other odd remnants of Pulhams' work – such as a basement fernery and a folly – in other parts of the park, however. EH Registered Park and Garden.
E/H	1875	Mark Philips Esq, Welcombe Hall, Stratford-upon-Avon, Warwickshire	Welsh Stone rockwork at head of lake – 20-30ft high – with a cascade. Planted with ferns and rock plants. Designed by William A. Nesfield.
P/E	1875	Mrs Hewitly, Hampton Court House, Hampton, Greater London	Fernery in conservatory.
P/E	1875	H.A. Brassey Esq. MP, Preston Hall, Aylesford, Maidstone, Kent	Waterfall, stream, fernery.
P/E	1875	J. Pratt Esq, Ryston Hall, Downham Market, Norfolk	Fernery. There is a 'Ryston Vase' listed in the firm's *Garden Ornament Catalogue*.
P/E	1875	Mrs Bradshaw, Leek, Staffordshire	Fernery.
P/E	1876	T.H. Brassey, Normanhurst Court, Battle, East Sussex	Unspecified terracotta.
E	1876	Joseph Shuttleworth, **Swiss Garden**, Old Warden, Bedfordshire	See Chapter 10
E	1876	Major Way, Wick Hall, Brighton, East Sussex	Rocky cliff to hide a wall.
P/E	1876	F. Durham, Wall Hall / Aldenham Abbey, Aldenham, Hertfordshire	Fernery.
P/E	1876	Sir Thomas Hare, Downham, Bromley, Kent	Fernery.
P/E	1876	J. Kleinwort, Brixton, London	Fernery.
P/E	1876	J. Patchet Esq, Nottingham, Nottinghamshire	Fernery.
P/E	1876-79	Rt Hon Earl of Beauchamp, **Madresfield Court**, Malvern, Worcestershire	See Chapter 11
H	1877-80	Lord Ardilaun, St Stephen's Green, Dublin, Eire	'Waterfall and Rockwork to lake edge and as an outcrop'. Natural stone and Pulhamite. Still in quite good condition, but some parts may soon be subject to redevelopment.
H	1878	Wigan Corporation, Mesnes Park, Wigan, Lancashire	'Waterfall and cascade, Rocky Bank and Chasm'. Recently rediscovered and restored by the Friends of Mesnes Park, and subject to further restoration. Pumps by Green and Carter. Designed by John McClean.

James Pulham and Son – James 2 and James 3 (1865-98)

Source	Date	Patron	Work Description
H	1878-98	James Harvey Insole, Insole Court, Llandaff, Cardiff	The gardens at Insole Court were laid out in two stages – the first during the 1850s, and later at the turn of the 1880s. Pulhams were not involved in the first stage, but Pulhams constructed a new carriageway, a formal balustraded garden with fountain, and a large natural rock garden and grotto.
E/H	1879-85	John Walter III, Bearwood College, Wokingham, Berkshire	'Rock Garden, Cascade, Stream'. Very overgrown, but still in good condition – special 'tilting rock' feature. Pumps by Green and Carter. EH Registered Park and Garden. Designed by James Tegg.
H	1880	William J.P. Parker, Ware Park, Hertford, Hertfordshire	'Rock garden, with small lake, pool, summer house, small chapel and rock arch etc'. Also walled kitchen garden, with glasshouses etc. Still there, but in urgent need of restoration.
H	1880	Albert Brassey, Heythrop Park, Chipping Norton, Oxfordshire	'Double-entrance "Whale Cave", pool and rocky paths etc, and a walled garden with fountain.' Still in very good condition. Pumps by Green and Carter.
H	1880s	Henry John Simonds, The Old Rectory (later Caversham Court), Caversham, Berkshire	'Fernery with rockwork and cascades etc'.
H	1880s	Henry Harris, Steventon Manor, Basingstoke, Hampshire	'Rocky bank, grotto and fernery'. Unconfirmed, but almost certainly genuine.
H	1880s	Henry Boickow, Marton Hall, Stewart Park, Middlesborough, North Yorkshire	'Rock banks to lake and rock outcrops'. Based on information received.
E	1880s	D.T. Fish, Hardwick House, Whitchurch, Oxfordshire	Fern dell in grounds – made out of old chalk pit. Could be Pulham work.
H	1880s	Eyres Family, Dumbleton Hall, Evesham, Worcestershire	'Lake with boat cave, footbridge and rocky banks etc'.
H	1880s	Bourne Family, Southwood House (now Holbrook Centre for Autism), Holbrook, Derbyshire	Grotto thought to be by Pulhams.
E	c1880s	Lord Ardilaun, St Anne's Clontarf, Dublin, Eire	Lord Ardilaun's principal seat. Pulhams did some work here at about the same time as they did the work at St Stephen's Green.
E	1881-92	Baron Ferdinand de Rothschild, **Waddesdon Manor**, Waddesdon, Buckinghamshire	See Chapter 12
E	1881-92	Quentin Hogg, **Holly Hill Park**, Fareham, Hampshire	See Chapter 13
H	1882	Lloyd Baxendale, Greenham Lodge, Greenham, Berkshire	Unconfirmed information regarding artificial lake and cascade etc. There is a small 'Baxendale Pot' listed in the firm's *Garden Ornament Catalogue*.

James Pulham and Son – James 2 and James 3 (1865-98)

Source	Date	Patron	Work Description
E	1882-85	Henry Holroyd (3rd Earl of Sheffield), **Sheffield Park**, Uckfield, East Sussex	See Chapter 14
H	1883	Alfred Rothschild, Halton House, Aylesbury, Buckinghamshire	Initially owned by Alfred Rothschild, the house incorporated a Winter Garden (or fernery) that was probably constructed by Pulhams. This no longer exists, as the house is now the home of the RAF Officers' Mess. There are, however, the remains of an artificial stream, pool and cascade – and probably a fountain – that is definitely their work.
E/H	1884	Winterbourne, Teignmouth, Devon	'Rock Garden, Waterfalls, Caves with Stalactites, bridges etc'. Declared 'unsafe', and redeveloped.
E	1885-86	Sir Francis Abraham Montefiore, **Worth Park** (later Milton Mount College),Crawley, West Sussex	See Chapter 15
H	1886-93	Herbert Leon, Bletchley Park, Bletchley, Buckinghamshire	Balustraded terrace, with sunken pleasure gardens and small rock garden, and occasional small rock outcrops. Mostly destroyed during redevelopment in 1938, and only 'reconstructed' scraps of Pulhamite and a small section of balustrading now remain.
E/H	1887	T.H. Bryant, Juniper Hill, Mickleham, Surrey	Used to be the home of a wonderful Pulham fernery, but time has taken its toll. Private property, its present owner is doing his utmost to restore it to its former glory.
H	1887	Sultan Abdulhamit, Sale Pavilion, Yildiz Palace, Istanbul, Turkey	This is just a suggestion. The Sultan built the Sale Palace to house important foreign visitors, and had his gardens designed in the Victorian English style. They include a tufa-built grotto and fernery that could easily have been by Pulhams, although no record exists to say they ever worked in Turkey. Perhaps there is a possibility that the contractor was the same person who constructed the gardens at Gisselfeld, in Denmark.
H	1887-89	George Villies, The Dell, Piggotts Manor, (now Bhaktivedanta Manor), Letchmore Heath, Hertfordshire	Small but interesting rock garden in Dell setting. Now being restored as a Memorial Garden for Beatle George Harrison by the International Society for Krishna Consciousness, who renamed the property 'Bhaktivedanta Manor' after the Society's founder. There is a 'Piggotts Manor Sundial' listed in the firm's *Garden Ornament Catalogue*.
E	1888-1913	Baron Schroder, **The Dell**, Englefield Green, Surrey	See Chapter 16
E	1890-91	James Cowan, **Ross Hall Park**, Crookston, Glasgow, Scotland	See Chapter 17

James Pulham and Son – James 2 and James 3 (1865-98)

Source	Date	Patron	Work Description
E	*c.*1890s	Earl de la Warr, Buckhurst Park, Withyham, East Sussex	Early 19th c. cascade by Lewis Kennedy. Rock Garden (late 19th c.) below the dam of the lake. FR Diary: 1911 – 'Repair bridge damaged by floods'. 1912 – 'Repairing buttress and general repairs'. Pumps by Green and Carter. EH Registered Park and Garden.
E	*c.*1890s	Osborne House, Isle of Wight	Pulham's terracotta.
E	*c.*1890s	Bolitho, Hannaford Manor, Widecombe-in-the-Moor, Devon	Pulham terracotta statue of 'Father Time' in terracotta no longer exists. Designed by Thomas Mawson.
E/H	1891	George Palmer, The Acacias, Reading, Berkshire	Conservatory with fernery, cliffs, pools etc. One of the best surviving examples of a Pulham fernery, which used to be part of Reading University, and still exists.
H	1891	Robert Carew, Carpenders Park, Watford, Hertfordshire	Carpenders Park is now the local cemetery. There is a small, comparatively un-maintained section of Pulhamite rockwork and waterfall along the rocky stream that bounds the site.
E/H	1891-94	Count Danneskiold Samso, Manor House, Gisselfeld, Denmark	Artificial lake, waterfall, grotto, subway / tunnel and bridge in the landscaped park on the edge of the Manor House gardens. Almost certainly constructed under the supervision of James Pulham. Designed by H.E. Milner.
E H	1892-97	Henry Hucks Gibbs, (Lord Aldenham), Aldenham House (now Haberdashers' Aske's School), Elstree, Hertfordshire	Lake, rocky stream, cascades, bridges etc. Still in very good condition. Now the Haberdashers Aske's School for Boys. Designed by Henry Hucks Gibbs. Not open to the public.
R	1892-1914	John Henry Bridges, **Ewell Court House**, Ewell, Surrey	See Chapter 18
E	1892-1900s	Sir William Cuthbert Quilter, **Bawdsey Manor**, Bawdsey, Suffolk	See Chapter 19
E/H	1893	John Rolls, The Hendre, Monmouth, Monmouthshire	Rock and water feature in the grounds of 'The Hendre', which are now in a very poor state of repair. Site of the present Hendre Golf Club, and admission is to Club Members Only. EH Registered Park and Garden. Designed by H.E. Milner.
E	1893	Newport Corporation, **Belle Vue Park**, Newport, Wales	See Chapter 20
H	1894-95	John Lawson Johnston, Kingswood House, Dulwich, London	Supporting wall of the 'Kingswood Balustrade' still remains, but the balustrading itself has now been replaced by railings, and the old pond and island is now a lawn and flowerbed. A 'Kingswood Terminal' is also listed in the firm's *Garden Ornament Catalogue*.

James Pulham and Son – James 2 and James 3 (1865-98)

Source	Date	Patron	Work Description
E/H	1894-98	Stoke-on-Trent Corporation, Burslem Park, Stoke-on-Trent, Staffordshire	Rockwork of Pulham stone with cascade topped by a Japanese tea house – maintained to a good standard. EH Registered Park and Garden Designed by Thomas Mawson.
E/H	1894-98	Stoke-on-Trent Corporation, Hanley Park, Stoke-on-Trent, Staffordshire	Municipal Park in Stoke-on-Trent designed by Thomas Mawson with Pulhamite rockwork. EH Registered Park and Garden.
E	1894	Ramsgate Corporation, **Madeira Walk**, Ramsgate, Kent	See Chapter 21
E/H	1895-99	Royal Parks, St James's Park, London	Rockwork to lake edge and Cormorant and Pelican islands. EH Registered Park and Gardens.
E/R	1895-1908	Charles W. Bartholomew, **Blakesley Hall**, Blakesley, Northamptonshire	See Chapter 23
E	1895-1912	Henry Oakley, **Dewstow House**, Caerwent, Monmouthshire, Wales	See Chapter 22
E/H	1896-97	William John Evelyn, Wotton House, Dorking, Surrey	Revetting (lining) of stream around house, large grotto, bridges and cascade in stream, greenhouse and ferneries, ornamental wall along South Terrace. Pulhams possibly also responsible for the restoration of main fountain and temple. EH Registered Park and Gardens.
H	1896	Lord Bulwer-Lytton, Knebworth House, Knebworth, Hertfordshire	Repairs and replacement of balustrading.
E	1897	? Beechy Lees, Rochester, Kent	Sally Festing 1997.

James Pulham and Son – James 3 and James 4 (1898-1920)

Source	Date	Patron	Work Description
H	1898	3rd Marquis of Bute, Mount Stuart, Isle of Bute, Scotland	Water features etc in the gardens of Mount Stuart, which became seriously neglected, but most has now been restored and replanted. Designed by Thomas Mawson.
E/R/H	1898-1906	Major W.J. Joicey, Sunningdale Park, Sunningdale, Berkshire	Pulhams enlarged ornamental lake, and created areas of rockwork – with cascades etc. – between that and the house. Still in good condition.
R	1898-1912	Sir Frank Crisp, **Friar Park**, Henley-on-Thames, Oxfordshire	See Chapter 24
H	1899	Arthur Lloyd, Coombe Wood, Croydon, Surrey	Rocky stream and waterfall feeding pond. The features have thankfully largely been restored.

James Pulham and Son – James 3 and James 4 (1898-1920) cont.

Source	Date	Patron	Work Description
H	1900s-1920s	J.H. Dugdale, Rowney Priory, Ware, Hertfordshire	Small lake and rocky stream with cascades running down to river. Still in fair condition. Also rose garden and kitchen garden that were probably by Pulham.
E	1900s	Major Foster, Southend, Essex	Rocky recess for ferns. Conservatory arrangement. There is a 'Southend Tazza' listed in the firm's *Garden Ornament Catalogue*.
E/H	1900s	Edward Buxton, Knighton Wood, Woodford, Essex	Rocky dell for fernery and alpines.
E	1900	Revd. J. Harman, Enfield, Greater London	Rocks forming screen for path behind.
E	1900s	R. Peill Esq, Hayes, Greater London	Small interior fernery and a small exterior fernery to hide out-buildings.
H	1900s	Frederick Henry Norman, Moor Place, Much Hadham, Hertfordshire	Small Pulhamite formation around banks of lake, and curved pergola that might possibly have been constructed by Pulhams. Pulhams' terracotta.
H	1900s	Mrs Mary Croft, The Priory, Ware, Hertfordshire	Small rock feature around the Priory.
E	*c.*1900s	Marquis of Anglesey, Beaudesert, Staffordshire	Lake, watercourse, series of waterfalls. Fragmented, eroded & very overgrown. Series of ponds & stepped waterfall (now dry) are evident near the ruins.
E	1900s	Felixstowe Council, Cliff Gardens and Town Hall Garden, Felixstowe, Suffolk	EH Register of Parks and Gardens 2003, but there is some doubt about it being by Pulham.
H	1900s	Crawley Borough Council, Goffs Park, Crawley, West Sussex	Small rock feature and banks around pond.
E	1900s	Lady Grenall, Mount Coote, Limerick, Eire	Rock garden – foreman's attitude complimented.
E	1900s	E. Hopkins, Elm Bank, Arkley, Barnet, Greater London	Rock garden – 'Very satisfactory job by foreman and workmen' (Testimonial in firm's *Garden Catalogue*).
E	1900s	Sir Edward Pearson, Brickendonbury, Hertford, Hertfordshire	Pulhamite rockwork at end of moat, with cascade (now dry). Completely overgrown and inaccessible.
E	1900s	? The Grove, Craven Arms, Shropshire	
E	1900s	? Kingswood Lodge, Egham, Surrey	
H	1900s	Ware College, Ware, Hertfordshire	Artificial pool with rocky banks / small cascade. Now redeveloped.
E	1900s	Lt Col S.H. Gwyther, Astley House, Shrewsbury, Shropshire	Rock Garden. 'Foreman and workmen set excellent example to others'. (Testimonial in the firm's *Garden Catalogue*).

James Pulham and Son – James 3 and James 4 (1898-1920) cont.

Source	Date	Patron	Work Description
E/H	c.1900	Edmund Loder, 'Leonardslee', Lower Beeding, Horsham, West Sussex	The rock garden at Leonardslee, near Horsham, West Sussex, was until recently maintained in excellent condition. The property has now changed hands, and is no longer open to the public. Pumps by Green and Carter. EH Registered Park and Garden.
R/H	1900-01	Lord Bethel, Bushey House, Bushey, Hertfordshire	Quite small, but very pleasant rock formation consisting of a rock-lined stream, low bridge, and small cascade into a lake. Now a nursing home for the elderly and not open to the public. Quite good condition, but pump out of order. FR Diary: 1901 – 'Overflow to lake'.
H	1901-03	Robert William Hudson, **Danesfield House**, Medmenham, Buckinghamshire	See Chapter 28
H	1901-05	Charles Dyson-Perrins, Davenham, Malvern, Worcestershire	Once the home of Charles Dyson-Perrins – of Lea and Perrins' Worcestershire sauce fame – the main house of 'Davenham' is now a nursing home. There is a fernery in what is now an adjoining garden, and a tufa-coated tunnel that runs under the road that now splits the two parts. Good condition; privately owned.
R	1901-20	Mark Fenwick, **Abbotswood**, Stow-on-the-Wold, Gloucestershire	See Chapter 26
H	1901	Lt Col John MacRae-Gilstrap, 'Ballimore Gardens', Otter Ferry, Argyllshire, Scotland	Water feature in the stream. Sadly, the gardens have almost completely been lost through time and neglect. Designed by Thomas Mawson.
R	1901	Capt. Harvey, Hullsborough Hall, Guilsborough, Northamptonshire	FR Diary: May - June 1901. Fountain.
E/H	1901	(? 1873 - J. Findlay), Scottish National Exhibition in 1901, Kelvingrove Park, Glasgow, Scotland	Rockwork feature in the park, still survives in good condition.
E/H	c.1901	H.E.M. Davies, Cavenham Park, Cavenham, Suffolk	Garden designed by H.E. Milner including fern dell and rock garden. Possibly by Pulhams but no reference found.
R	1901	Clarke Stevenson Esq, Brook House, Ardingly, West Sussex	FR Diary: 1901. 'Rock and Alpine Garden'.
E	1902-05	Lt Col Grant Morden, **Heatherden Hall**, Iver Heath, Buckinghamshire	See Chapter 29
E/R	1902-07	Francis Baring-Gould, **Merrow Grange**, Guildford, Surrey	See Chapter 25
R	1902	Mr Cruddas, Oakham Lodge, Sneyd Park, Bristol, Avon	FR Diary: 1902. 'Balustrade and fountain etc'.
R	1902	Mr Preston, West Lodge, Cookham, Buckinghamshire	FR Diary: 1902 'Fountain'.

James Pulham and Son – James 3 and James 4 (1898-1920) cont.

Source	Date	Patron	Work Description
E	1902	Lord Redesdale, **Batsford Park**, Moreton-in-Marsh, Gloucestershire	See Chapter 27
R	1902	Herbert Park, Withnell Fold, Chorley, Lancashire	FR Diary: 1902 'Conservatory'.
E/H	1902	Lord Dewar, Homestall (later Stoke Brunswick School), East Grinstead, West Sussex	Charming mixture of the formal and 'naturalistic' styles, and were all probably constructed by Pulhams. There is a lily pond and summer house etc in the formal garden, and a rock garden, stream and ponds, with occasional outcrops of Pulhamite in the outlying areas. Apart from the rock garden, which is now derelict, everything is in excellent condition. Not open to the public. (Testimonial in Pulham's *Garden Catalogue)*.
R	1902	William Astor Esq, Hever Castle, Hever, Kent	FR Diary: 1902 – 'Glen, stone bridge and falls'.
E/R	1903-04	HM King Edward VII, **Buckingham Palace**, London	See Chapter 30
R/H	1903	William Lethridge, Wood, South Tawton, Devon	Waterfall and rocky stream. FR Diary: 1902-03 – 'Falls, watercourses and sluices'. Designed by Thomas Mawson.
H	1903	William Lever (Lord Leverhulme), Lever Park, Rivington, Lancashire	Bridge and cascades. Designed by Thomas Mawson.
E/H	1903	Sir Daniel Ford-Goddard, Oak Hill, Ipswich, Suffolk	Picture in Pulhams' *Garden Catalogue* of their rock garden at Oak Hill, but little remains today, despite it being an EH listed rockwork.
R	1904-08	John Stuart Esq, Stonehurst, Ardingly, West Sussex	FR Diary: 1904-05: 'Lakes, waterfalls, filter beds, landscape etc. Improvements and alterations. 1908 – 'Extensions and improvements'. Designed by Thomas Mawson.
E/R	1904	HM King Edward VII, Frogmore Gardens, Windsor Castle, Windsor, Berkshire	Pulham's Terracotta and rockery. No longer there. FR Diary: 1904 – 'Alpine walls'.
E	1904	Richard Bennett Esq, Thornby Hall, Thornby, Northamptonshire	Rock and water garden, lake, terrace balustrade. There is also a 'Thornby Seat' listed in the firm's *Garden Ornament Catalogue*, but Thornby Hall is now a special school for young children, and none of the features remain. FR Diary: 1904 – 'Rock garden, stream and waterfalls'.
E/R/H	1905-13	London Zoological Society, London Zoo, Regent's Park, London	Pulhamite rock features were built in the Sea Lion Pool, Monkey Enclosure and Polar Bear Enclosure, but were later removed during further alterations. EH Registered Park and Garden. FR Diary: 1913 – 'Alteration'.
R	1905	Mr Vickery, Leigholme, Leigholme Avenue, Streatham, London	FR Diary: 1905-06 – 'Conservatory'.

James Pulham and Son – James 3 and James 4 (1898-1920) cont.

Source	Date	Patron	Work Description
E/H	1906-07	Belper Corporation, River Gardens, Belper, Derbyshire	Rockwork along the banks of the river and around the boat house and bandstand . Erected the fountain. EH Registered Park and Gardens. There is a 'Belper Urn Terminal' listed in the firm's *Garden Ornament Catalogue*.
E/R	1906-07	Mr Mullins, Barrow Hills, Long Cross, Virginia Water, Surrey	FR Diary: 1906-07 – 'Formal and rock and water garden'. 1907 – 'Low wall round carriage sweep'. Since redeveloped.
R/H	1906	R.L. Gunther, Park Wood, Englefield Green, Surrey	FR Diary: 1906 – 'Waterfall, outlet to lake'.
H	1907	Richard Dalton, Park House, Cotham Park, Bristol, Avon	Conservatory and fernery grotto around corner of house. Well maintained and carries all the signs of Pulhams' handiwork.
R	1907	Royal Agricultural Show, Lincoln, Lincolnshire	FR Diary: 1907 – 'Laid out garden to King Edward's Bungalow'.
R	1907	Balkan States, Earls Court Exhibition, London	FR Diary: 1907.
R	1907	Lord Berkeley, Foxcombe, Oxford, Oxfordshire	FR Diary: 1907 – 'Rock steps'.
H	1908	Sunken Garden, Kensington Palace, London	A number of 'Hyde Park Pots'– illustrated in the firm's *Garden Ornament Catalogue* – were provided for the sunken garden at Kensington Palace.
E/R	1908-10	Walter Melville Wills, **Rayne Thatch**, Bristol, Avon	See Chapter 31
E/R	1908-12	Gen. Sir Arthur Paget, **Warren House**, Kingston upon Thames, Surrey	See Chapter 32
E/R/H	1909-10	Sir Julius Wernher, Luton Hoo, Luton, Bedfordshire	The fountain on the lower back terrace is by Pulham, but the sundial and balustraded wall is not certain. The rock garden is mainly built from natural stone, with Pulhamite mortar. Good condition. There is a 'Luton Tub' listed in the firm's catalogue. EH Registered Park and Gardens. FR Diary: 1909-10 – 'Rock and water garden'.
R	1909	W.J. Chrystal, Auchendennan House, Arden, Argyll and Bute, Scotland	FR Diary: 1909 – 'Stream and waterfalls'.
R	1909	Thomas H. Walker, Crosbie Towers, Troon, Ayrshire Scotland	FR Diary: 1909 – 'Rock and water garden'.
R	1909	Mr Moore, Drake Court, Blackheath, London	FR Diary: 1909 – 'Fixed Vase'.
E/H	1909	Charles Dyson-Perrins, Ardross Castle, Alness, Ross-shire, Scotland	Fine balustraded terrace, fountain and other sculptural features constructed by Pulham. Still in excellent condition. Privately owned. EH Inventory garden and landscape. Designed by Edward White.
R	1909	Richard Tidewell, Bosmere Hall, Needham Market, Suffolk	FR Diary: 1909 – 'Rock garden'.

James Pulham and Son – James 3 and James 4 (1898-1920) cont.

Source	Date	Patron	Work Description
R	1909	Mrs Dowling, The Nunnery, Rusper, West Sussex	FR Diary: 1909 – 'Rock garden'.
E	1910	Walter Melville Wills, Markham Brook, Abbots Leigh, Somerset	Series of small trout pools separated by cascades. Now derelict.
E/H	1910-12	Jeremiah Colman, Gatton Park, Reigate, Surrey	Unstratified rock garden, with pools etc, and a Japanese garden at a far corner of the grounds. Designed by H.E. Milner.
R	1910-13	J. Charnock Wilson, Sudbury Priory, Harrow-on-the-Hill, Middlesex	FR Diary: 1910 – 'Lake and rock garden'. 1914 – 'Small restoration'.
R/H	1910-15	Mrs McAdam, Craigengillan, Dalmellington, Ayrshire, Scotland	FR Diary: 1910 - Rock and water garden. 1914-15 – 'Rock garden, and Kitchen Garden remodelled'. There is a 'Dalmellington Sundial' listed in the firm's *Garden Ornament Catalogue*.
E/H	1910	Sir Robert Harvey Bateson, Langley Park, Colnbrook, Buckinghamshire	EH Registered Park and Garden. There is a 'Langley Vase' listed in the firm's *Garden Ornament Catalogue*. Designed by Edward White.
E	c.1910s	1st Baron of Aberconway, Bodnant, Tal-y-Cafn, Nr Colwyn Bay, Conwy, Wales	EH Registered Park and Garden – open to the public.
E	c.1910s	? Henley Hall, Tasley, Shropshire	Rock and water garden, with series of pools with Pulhamite rockwork. EH Registered Park and Garden.
R	1910	Herman Schurhoff (German Consul), Moat Farm, Knowle, Warwickshire	FR Diary: 1910-11 – '3-span bridge, rock outcrops and balustrade'.
E/R	1911-12	**RHS Garden Wisley**, Woking, Surrey	See Chapter 35
H	1911-15	Sir Arthur Paget, **The Watergardens**, Kingston upon Thames, Surrey	See Chapter 33
E/R	1911-32	Charles Nall-Cain (1st Lord Brocket), **The Node**, Codicote, Welwyn, Hertfordshire	See Chapter 34
R	1911	F.W. Wignall Esq, The Rookery, Tattenhall, Cheshire	FR Diary: 1911 – 'Small rock and alpine garden'.
R	1911	Mr Tozer, Catford Bridge, London	FR Diary: 1911 – 'Small rock garden'.
R	1911	Dudley Cary Wright, The Red House, Westcott, Dorking, Surrey	FR Diary: 1911 – 'Rock Garden'.
R	1911	The Hon. Claude Portman, Goldicote Hall, Stratford-upon-Avon, Warwickshire	FR Diary: 1911 – 'Pergola'.
R	1912-13	E. Hesketh, Beechcroft, Eltham, Kent	FR Diary: 1912-13 – 'Rock and water garden and engine house'.
R	1912	Mr Thomas, The Downe, Elstree, Hertfordshire	FR Diary: 1912 – 'Pergola'.
R	1912	R. Harrison, Kings Walden Bury, Hitchin, Hertfordshire	FR Diary: 1912 – 'Rock and water garden'.

James Pulham and Son – James 3 and James 4 (1898-1920) cont.

Source	Date	Patron	Work Description
E/H	1912	Sir Robert Rogers, Marl House, Bexley, Kent	Water garden and rock garden by Pulham - illustrated in the firm's *Garden Catalogue, c.*1920. Site has been completely redeveloped. (Testimonial in the firm's *Garden Catalogue, c.*1920).
H	1912	Preston Corporation, Haslam Park, Preston, Lancashire	Artificial lake and double waterfall. Designed by Thomas Mawson.
R	1912	Ideal Home Exhibition, Olympia, London	FR Diary: 1912.
E/R	1901-1912	Stafford-Charles (1901) and K. D'Arcy (1912), Stanmore Hall, Stanmore, Harrow, London	Rock and water garden, waterfalls, pools. FR Diary: 1901 – (for Stafford-Charles) – 'Formal Rose Garden'. 1912 - (for K. D'Arcy) – 'Rock and Water Garden'.
R	1912	The Earl of Shrewsbury, Variad, Goring-on-Thames, Oxfordshire	FR Diary: 1912 – 'Rock Garden'.
R	1912	Mr Garland, Moreton Hall, Moreton Morrell, Warwickshire	FR Diary: 1912 – 'Rock formation'. There is a 'Moreton Vase' in the firm's *Garden Ornament Catalogue*.
R	1913-14	Hogg, West House, Pinner, Middlesex	FR Diary: 1913 – 'Lake job'.
R	1913	Charles Keyser, Aldermaston Court, Reading, Berkshire	FR Diary: 1913 – 'Rock and water garden'.
R	1913	K. Edgecombe, Aldenham Grange, Letchmore Heath, Hertfordshire	FR Diary: 1913 – 'Lake and rock outcrops'.
R	1913	Ideal Home Exhibition, Olympia, London	FR Diary: 1913.
R	1913	Mrs A.J. Bryans, Manor House, Woodmansterne, Chipstead, Surrey	FR Diary: 1913 – 'Repairs'.
R	1913	G.A. Touche, Bloomfield, Westcott, Dorking, Surrey	FR Diary: 1913 – 'Japanese Teahouse and rock garden'. There is a 'Westcott Vase' listed in the firm's *Garden Ornament Catalogue*.
R	1913	Bilney, W A, Ronneby, Oaklands Chase, Walton-on-Thames, Surrey	FR Diary: 1913 – 'Paving etc - Take particulars for Teahouse'.
E/R	1914-16	Lytham Corporation, Promenade Gardens and Ashton Gardens, **Lytham St Annes**, Lancashire	See Chapter 37
R/H	1914-23	H. Bell, Barnacre House, Calder Vales (now Sullam Hall), Garstang, Lancashire	FR Diary: 1914-15 – ''Waterfalls and rock garden. Rock garden continued'. 1923 – 'Little extension'.
R	1914	O'Connell, Widbury Hill, Ware, Hertfordshire	FR Diary: 1914 – 'Small rock and Alpine garden'.
R	1914	Brown, Penchullee, Bromley, Kent	FR Diary: 1914.
R	1914	RHS, Chelsea Flower Show, London	FR Diary: 1914.
R	1914	**Selfridges Roof Garden**, Oxford Street, London	FR Diary: 1914 – 'Roof garden'. See Chapter 36

James Pulham and Son – James 3 and James 4 (1898-1920) cont.

Source	Date	Patron	Work Description
R/H	1914	Thomas Shipstone, Lenton Firs, Nottingham, Nottinghamshire	Rocky bank etc. Wildly overgrown, but site recently cleared, and some rather damaged Pulham remnants remain. There is a 'Nottingham Vase' listed in the firm's *Garden Ornament Catalogue,* but it is not know whether it was associated with Lenton Firs. FR Diary: 1914 – 'Finished extended rock garden'.
E/R	1915-30	Walter Melville Wills, **Abbots Pool**, Bristol, Avon	See Chapter 38
E/R	1917-30	Walter Melville Wills, **Bracken Hill**, Bristol, Avon	See Chapter 39
E/H	1919-20	John Graeme Thomson, Shipton Court, Shipton-under-Wychwood, Oxfordshire	Tiered formal garden, with lily pool and (what used to be) a swimming pool. Now converted into flats. Still in good condition. EH Registered Park and Gardens.
R	1919-22	Lord Treowen, Llanover, Abergavenny, Monmouthshire	FR Diary: 1919 – 'Rock garden'. 1922 – 'Rock and Water garden'.
R	1919	Cecil Brinton, Yew Tree House, Belbroughton, Worcestershire	FR Diary: 1919 – 'Started large waterfall – postponed owing to railway strike'.
R	1919	Fred Ambler, Lynfield, Chellow Dene, Bradford, Yorkshire	FR Diary: 1919-20 – 'Rock and water garden, sunken rose garden etc'.

James Pulham and Son – James 4 (1920-57)

Source	Date	Patron	Work Description
E/R	1920-21	Folkestone Corporation, **The Leas**, Folkestone, Kent	See Chapter 40
H	*c.*1920s?	? Rosehill, Hillside Lane, Great Amwell, Ware	Plunge Pool, possibly by Pulham, but not confirmed.
E/H	1920-22	William G. Macbeth, Dunira, Comrie, Perthshire, Scotland	Terraces, rose garden, rill, half-moon wall-fountain and pool, but hardly anything remains today. EH Inventory Garden and Landscape. (Testimonial in the firm's *Garden Catalogue.*) Designed by Thomas Mawson.
R	1921	J. Louis Rick, The Manor, Northwood, Middlesex	FR Diary: 1921-22 – 'Terrace, rose garden and pergola'.
E/R/H	1922-23	Blackpool Corporation, Seafront, Blackpool, Lancashire	Installed fountain in seafront promenade gardens, and also engaged to 'rockify' the cliffs of the coastal cliff park, along the north shore of Blackpool. FR Diary: 1914 – 'Set out fountain. Cliff walk along the North Cliffs'. 1922-23 – 'Constructing cliffs'.
E	1923-36	Ramsgate Corporation, St Lawrence and West Cliff (West Chine), and Winterstoke Gardens, **Ramsgate**, Kent	See Chapter 41
H	1923	RHS Flower Show, Olympia, London	Constructed a special garden in honour of HRH Princess Mary – later to become The Princess Royal.

James Pulham and Son – James 4 (1920-57) cont.

Source	Date	Patron	Work Description
E/R/H	1926-30	Walter Melville Wills, Bristol Homeopathic Hospital, Bristol, Avon	FR Diary: 1925-26 – 'Memorial Garden. Terraces of Cotswold Stone, lily pool, rose garden, rock garden and tennis court'. 1926-27 – 'Cotham House extension, rock and landscape also. Garden House in the rose garden – stone'. 1930 – 'Repair to stone paths due to severe frosts'.
R	1928	L.G. Howe, Waltham House, Chelmsford, Essex	FR Diary: 1928 – 'Formal and rock and water garden, lily pool'. Built old piers and walls for pair iron gates.
R	1928	H. Rumsey, Pendeen, Upper Moulsham, Chelmsford, Essex	FR Diary: 1928 – 'Formal pool, fountain and rose garden'.
R	1928	F. Howard Webb, 48 Queens Road, Hertford, Hertfordshire	FR Diary: 1928-29 – 'Sunken garden with formal pool, fountain, lawns, terrace walls and rectangular paving, trellis works. Dial garden and general landscape and planting. Rock garden'.
H	1929-33	Lionel Nathan de Rothschild, Exbury Gardens, Southampton, Hampshire	There is a large natural rock garden here, and a Lower Pond, both of which are very Pulhamesque in style. I have no proof that they actually created these gardens, but my feelings are very strong about this.
R/H	1929-30	H.L. Storey, Burton Hill House, Malmesbury, Wiltshire	FR Diary: 1929-30 – 'Stream, lake, stone and rustic bridges. Waterfalls, rose garden, herbaceous walk 100 yards x 10 ft stone path, 600 yards of natural fencing. Tree planting'. There is a 'Storey Pot' listed in the firm's *Garden Ornament Catalogue*.
H	1930s	Hoddesdon Urban District Council, 'Spinning Wheel', Hoddesdon, Hertfordshire	Small rock and water feature along the front of the new swimming pool.
H	1930s	Henri Deterding, Buckhurst Park, Ascot, Berkshire	Balustraded terrace and fountain.
H	1931	RHS Chelsea Flower Show, London	See Chapter 36
H	1934-36	Sir Noel Mobbs, **Stoke Poges Memorial Gardens**, Stoke Poges, Buckinghamshire	See Chapter 42
H	1935-57	Demise of James Pulham and Son, and demolition of Manufactory, Station Road, Broxbourne, Hertfordshire	See Chapter 43

Dates Unknown

Source	Date	Patron	Work Description
E	Unknown	John Smyth, Ashton Court, Bristol, Avon	Registered Park and Garden (Sally Festing 1997).
E	Unknown	Baron Ferdinand de Rothschild, The Pavilion, Eythrope, Buckinghamshire	Small Pulhamite arch. Pavilion designed by George Devey between 1876-79. Part of Waddesdon Estate.
E	Unknown	Marine Park, South Shields, Co Durham	
E	Unknown	J.H. Ismay, Iwerne Minster (now Clayesmore School), Blandford Forum, Dorset	(Sally Festing 1997). Designed by Edward Milner.
E	Unknown	Talacre, Flintshire, Wales	
E	Unknown	Chauncy, Ardeley Bury, Stevenage, Hertfordshire	
E	Unknown	Colesdane, Harrietsham, Kent	
P/E	Unknown	W.O. Hammond, Esq, St Alban's Court, Nonington, Kent	Rocks arranged for alpine plants.
E	Unknown	Allerton Priory, Allerton, Lancashire	
E	Unknown	Southport Corporation, Aquarium, Southport, Lancashire	Pulhams' terracotta.
E	Unknown	Sir Bache Cunard, Hallaton Hall, Hallaton, Leicestershire	Fernery.
P/E	Unknown	E. Robinson Esq, Dulwich, London	Hardy fernery and dropping well.
E	Unknown	London County Council, Botanic Gardens, Regent's Park, London	Pulhams' terracotta.
E	Unknown	London County Council, Royal Summer and Winter Gardens, Westminster, London	Pulhams' terracotta.
P/E	Unknown	N.C. Tuley Esq, Wimbledon Park, Merton, London	Hardy fernery.
E	Unknown	Bushy House, Teddington, Middlesex	EH Registered Park and Garden. (Sally Festing 1997)
E	Unknown	Colney House, Norwich, Norfolk	(Sally Festing 1997).
E	Unknown	Clifton Family, Clifton Hall Gardens, Clifton, Nottinghamshire	Rocky Recess, Stairway, balustrading and Pulham sculptures. EH Registered Park and Garden. There is a 'Nottingham Vase' listed in the firm's *Garden Ornament Catalogue*.
E	Unknown	National Trust, Polesden Lacey, Great Bookham, Dorking, Surrey	
E	Unknown	Scarborough Corporation, Aquarium, Scarborough, Yorkshire	Pulham's Terracotta - there is a 'Scarborough Tub' listed in the firm's *Garden Ornament Catalogue*.

ACKNOWLEDGEMENTS

INTRODUCTION

English Heritage: Jenifer White (Senior Landscape Advisor, Conservation Dept); Camilla Beresford (Researcher); Simon Swann, (Architectural Conservator and co-author of the Pulhamite Conservation leaflet).

Institute of Historical Research at the University of London, who kindly made a small contribution to my research costs under their annual 'Scouloudi Award' for research scheme.

CHAPTER 1

Pulham Family Members: Chris Pulham, Ian Denney and Michael Goodchild, descendants of the Pulham family, all of whom have made valuable contributions to my research.

Sue Davies, grand-niece of John William Hitching.

Woodbridge, Suffolk: Stewart Salmond (local historian); Chris Pulham (member of the Pulham family); Bob Nerrett, Curator of the Woodbridge Library Archives; Vicky Stott, Words and Images Librarian, Victoria and Albert Museum; Mrs Wendy Blake (local Woodbridge historian); Patricia Shepherd (Suffolk County Gardens Trust).

Benington Lordship, Hertfordshire: Nora Corfield; Sarah Bott.

Thunder Hall, Ware, Hertfordshire: Alec Cole; Harald Hakansson; Bonnie West (Hertford Records Office).

CHAPTER 2

London: Diana Clements (geologist and local historian); John Woodcock.

Rawdon House, Hoddesdon, Hertfordshire: Simon Foden.

'Woodlands' Hoddesdon, Hertfordshire: Neil Robbins (Heritage and Education Officer of the Borough of Broxbourne, and Curator of Lowewood Museum); Anthony Warner; Nigel de Rivaz**.**

St Thomas' Church, West Hyde, Hertfordshire: Canon Alan Horsley.

St Mary Redcliffe, Bristol, Avon: Revd James Wilson; John Pickard.

Kilnwick Percy, Pocklington, Yorkshire: Members of the Madhyamaka Buddhist Centre.

St Augustine's Church, Broxbourne, Hertfordshire: Geoffrey Green.

Europe: Mme Cainard (Directrice des Archives Municipales de Cannes); Father Ken Letts (British Chaplain in Nice); Jidot Kiraly, Sven Vik, Cannes.

CHAPTER 3

Broxbourne Manufactory, Hertfordshire: (Alexandra / Paris Vase) Elenora Johnson; Peter Fidler (Chilstone Garden Ornaments).

V & A Museum, London: Vicky Stott; Kiri Ross-Jones.

Las Vegas Library, USA: Susan Williams (Virtual Reference Section).

CHAPTER 4

Highnam Court, Gloucestershire: Roger Head; Tom Fenton.

CHAPTER 5

Dunorlan Park, Tunbridge Wells, Kent: Jeff Kempster (Parks Manager); Marian Williams (Strategy and Projects Officer); Richard Gosling; The Friends of Dunorlan Park; Tony Ewins (Head Gardener).

CHAPTER 6

Battersea Park, Wandsworth, London: Jerry Birtles (Assistant Park Manager).

CHAPTER 7

Audley End, Essex: Steve Elstub; Martin Duncan (Head Gardeners).

CHAPTER 8

Sandringham, Norfolk: Martin Woods (Head Gardener).

CHAPTER 9

St Fagans Castle, Cardiff, Wales: Andrew Dixey and Juliet Hodgkiss (Estate Managers); Christine Stevens (Curator of St Fagans Museum).

CHAPTER 10

Swiss Garden, Old Warden, Bedfordshire: Malcolm Amey; Frazer Chapman (Head Gardeners).

CHAPTER 11

Madresfield Court, Malvern, Worcestershire: Lady Morrison.

CHAPTER 12

Waddesdon Manor, Waddesdon, Buckinghamshire: Beth Rothschild; Sophieke Piebenga (Garden Historian); Paul Farnell (Head Gardener); Andy Flitney (Head Gardener of the Water Garden).

CHAPTER 13

Holly Hill Park, Fareham, Hampshire: David Redwood (Chairman of the 'Friends of Holly Hill Park'); John Waters, David's colleague; Dorothy Turner ('Friend of Holly Hill Park').

CHAPTER 14

Sheffield Park Garden, Uckfield, East Sussex: Steve Walker (Property Manager at Sheffield Park), Jo Hopkins, Andy Jesson (Head Gardener), Nigel Davis and Sue Medway.

CHAPTER 15

Worth Park / Milton Mount School, Crawley, Sussex: Joyce Lacy (an Old Miltonian); Margaret Clark, (Treasurer and Archivist of the Miltonian Guild); Nick Hagon (Head Gardener at Milton Mount); Claire Denman, (Crawley Borough Councillor).

CHAPTER 16

'The Dell', Englefield Green, Surrey: Steve and Sandra Randall; Col. John Prosser; Jean DaRe; Roland Granville-Smith; Graham Dennis, Blacklock's Bookshop, Englefield Green.

CHAPTER 17

Ross Hall Park, Glasgow, Scotland: Christopher Dingwall (Scottish Conservation of the Garden History Society); Ian Fraser (Project Officer, Land Services, Glasgow Council).

CHAPTER 18
Ewell Court House, Epsom, Surrey: Bob and Cathy Scott; Carol Hill (local historian); Members of the Ewell Court House Organisation.

CHAPTER 19
Bawdsey Manor, Bawdsey, Suffolk: Niels Teottcher.

CHAPTER 20
Belle Vue Park, Newport, Wales: David Morris (Grounds and Countryside Services Manager, Newport Council); Frances Hope, (Head Gardener for the Park); John Woods.

CHAPTER 21
Madeira Walk, Ramsgate, Kent: Terry Wheeler (Secretary of the Ramsgate Society, and author of its magazine, *About Ramsgate*).

CHAPTER 22
Dewstow House, Caerwent, Monmouthshire, Wales: Elwyn and John Harris.

CHAPTER 23
Blakesley Hall, Blakesley, Northamptonshire: Philip Burt, Bob Tebb.

CHAPTER 24
Friar Park, Henley-on-Thames, Oxfordshire: Mrs Olivia Harrison; Hugh Netley (Head Gardener), Peter Crook (local historian), Denise Theophilus, Michelle Cole.

CHAPTER 25
Merrow Grange, near Guildford, Surrey: John Royle; Pat and Mick Hibberd (residents of 'Fairlawns', who have done so much to restore the gardens at Merrow Grange, and provided a lot of the historical research); The late Dr Norman Gibbs (devoting so much of his time to restoration at 'Dellwood').

CHAPTER 26
Abbotswood, Stow-on-the-Wold, Gloucestershire: Bridget Fox (Gardener in the Stream Garden).

CHAPTER 27
Batsford Arboretum, Moreton-in-Marsh, Gloucestershire: Chris Pilling (Visitor Services Manager).

CHAPTER 28
Danesfield House, Medmenham, Buckinghamshire: Brian Miller, (General Manager); John Guildford (Landscapes Consultant).

CHAPTER 29
Heatherden Hall, Iver Heath, Buckinghamshire: Kevin Bowen (Property Manager), Steve Beeson (Head Gardener).

CHAPTER 30
Buckingham Palace, London: Mark Lane (Head of the Royal Gardens).

CHAPTER 31
Rayne Thatch, Bristol, Avon: Peter and Ann Fisher; Kyriakos Kyvelos.

CHAPTER 32
*Warren House, Kingston upon Thames, Surrey***:** Andrew Fuller (Head Gardener).

CHAPTER 33
'The Watergardens', Kingston upon Thames, Surrey: Jacqueline Tarrent, Nick Beeston (Head Gardener).

CHAPTER 34
'The Node', Welwyn, Hertfordshire: Mike Creasey (Codicote Local History Society); Frances Brooks.

CHAPTER 35
RHS Garden Wisley, Surrey: Alan Robinson (at that time Supervisor, Rocks Dept, Wisley); Paul Cumbleton (Senior Supervisor, RHS Garden Wisley).

CHAPTER 36
London Exhibitions: Michael Goodchild, grandson of James 4; Maggie Cammiss (Archive Assistant, History of Advertising Trust).

CHAPTER 37
Lytham St Annes, Lancashire: Brian Turner (Secretary of the Lytham St Annes Local History Society); Margaret Reynolds (Parks Development Officer at Lytham St Annes); Sharon Saunders, (Parks Community Liaison Officer, Wigan UDC); Arnold Sumner, 'Friends of Ashton Gardens', Lytham St Annes.

CHAPTER 38
Abbots Pool, Bristol, Avon: Diane Stewart (Committee Member of the Abbots Leigh Civic Society); Chris Richards (local historian from the North Somerset Museum Service); John Flannigan (Tree and Countryside Officer responsible for the management of Abbots Pool).

CHAPTER 39
Bracken Hill, Bristol, Avon: Nicholas Wray (horticulturalist responsible for the Bristol University Botanic Gardens).

CHAPTER 40
Folkestone, Kent: Chris McCreedy (Folkestone Coastal Park Manager); Dave Illsley (Regeneration Officer connected with the Coastal Park Renovation Project).

CHAPTER 41
Ramsgate, Kent: Terry Wheeler (Secretary of the Ramsgate Society, and author of *About Ramsgate*); Nick Dennot (Conservation Manager of Thanet District Council).

CHAPTER 42
Memorial Gardens, Stoke Poges, Buckinghamshire: Graham Pattison (Head Gardener).

CHAPTER 43
Hoddesdon and Broxbourne, Hertfordshire: David Dent (local historian and author of *Broxbourne and Wormley's Past in Pictures*).

CHAPTER 44
*Diary of a Rock Builder***:** Norma Milligan, daughter of Fred Rickett.

Class Gardens: Jack Sexton; Valerie Christman.

INDEX

Page numbers in **bold** refer to images and/or captions